# A WOMAN
# OF NO
# CONSEQUENCE

Memory,

Letters

and

Resistance

in Madras

Kalpana Karunakaran

# cntxt

Published by Context, an imprint of Westland Books, a division of Nasadiya Technologies Private Limited, in 2025

No. 269/2B, First Floor, 'Irai Arul', Vimalraj Street, Nethaji Nagar, Alapakkam Main Road, Maduravoyal, Chennai 600095

Westland, the Westland logo, Context and the Context logo are the trademarks of Nasadiya Technologies Private Limited, or its affiliates.

ISBN: 9789371971607

10 9 8 7 6 5 4 3 2 1

Typeset by Mukul

Printed at Thomson Press (India) Ltd

# A WOMAN OF NO CONSEQUENCE

**Kalpana Karunakaran** is Associate Professor in the Humanities and Social Sciences Department, IIT Madras. Her research and writings are in the intersecting fields of gender, poverty, microcredit, women's work in the informal sector, women's trade unions and collective action in solidarity-based movements. She is currently serving as President of the Indian Association for Women's Studies (IAWS) for a three-year term. Kalpana's interests include writing on women's lives with a focus on the intersections of the personal and the political. She is the author of *Women, Microfinance and the State in Neo-liberal India* (Routledge, 2017) and the Tamil memoir, *Comrade Amma: Magal Parvaiyil Mythily Sivaraman* (*Comrade Mother: A Daughter's Portrait of Mythily Sivaraman*), published in 2018. She is currently working on an English translation of the memoir of Lakshmi Amma, a social and political activist from a small peasant household in Tamil Nadu. A bilingual public speaker and writer in Tamil and English, Kalpana participates actively in campaigns and workshops for gender equality, labour rights and human rights in Tamil Nadu. She has worked extensively as an activist-organiser with People's Science Movements, Right to Health campaigns and women's Self-Help Group federations. Kalpana has been involved in Tamil feminist theatre and hopes to return to it someday.

*For Pankajam,*
*My beloved gran,*
*Who*
*Protected and mothered her mother, Subbalakshmi*
*Nurtured and set free her daughter, Mythily*
*And filled my head with stories*

# Contents

# Foreword

(Pankajam, 1949)

Only great and famous people write their autobiographies. They have something important to tell others. Their lives are so very interesting. Some like to write political thoughts; others about their own achievements. Great people must narrate their lives. Artists and great souls like Mahatma Gandhi must rip open their hearts and reveal God's truth to the world. An autobiography by one like me, an ordinary middleclass housewife, need not be written, so one would say. And yet there are reasons why I thought it should be written.

Also, usually someone other than the author writes the foreword. But here I am doing it myself, for I want the readers to understand clearly why this autobiography should be written at all. I'm not recounting in these pages the incidents of my life because they are big or great or mighty. There is nothing here that might interest others except for an insight into the vortex of a soul thrown entirely on itself. I cannot narrate a life of brave deeds and spectacular sacrifices such as we find in the lives of our leaders. You cannot expect to find in these pages the life of a politician, like any of the women of our time of national struggle. I'm not a poet, a writer, a great social worker or even a society lady.

My sphere is that of a humble housewife tied to mundane work, which always keeps the soul fettered down. But I write this so that I may show my dearest and nearest how my soul has been ever trying to soar up and break the bondage of the flesh. Heroes of mighty deeds and sacrifices are known and honoured, while humble souls struggle in obscure silence and make sacrifices as great as those of the known heroes. It is not for praise that I seek to put forth all that I can remember about myself. But I want this to be a torch to those who may, like me, be groping in the dark, seeking light and understanding of this world and who direly need help and an eye opener.

I'm anxious to write about my life because I consider this life of mine as the crisis of all my previous births. I firmly believe in the evolution of the soul through countless births, gathering experience on its travels and culling precious truths to feed itself with. Until finally, it breaks the fetters of its physical prison and exults in its own lustre and glory so that there is no need to ever go back to the school of life again. I consider this birth or *janma* of mine as being very different from the previous ones. I think I have left or am leaving the worldly ways and that I am ready for a new path. So, this is a turning point in my life, a turning point in the evolution of my soul. Is it not very important?

Many small incidents in our lives, small disappointments, the small rewards and joys have tremendous spiritual significance. It is not tremendous tragedies alone, but insignificant, petty occurrences that may suddenly change the whole course of our lives. Every individual's life is given daily problems which, in solving, we may come across the solution to the riddle of life itself. Hence this tale of what has been happening to me through seemingly worthless actions and incidents. Therefore, I ask my children's permission to put forth in all humility whatever has happened in my life through which the Lord has taught me lessons. Bear with me if it is tedious or dry, for I do it with the express desire of lighting the way for those who come behind me, those whom I love.

Another thing I would like to say is that I do not claim to lay bare everything that has happened, like Mahatma Gandhi does.

For one thing, I do not believe in washing dirty linen in public and, for another, in trying to be outspoken, I may have to involve others in this story, who may quite resent it. It is necessary therefore that I should avoid as much as possible complicating other people's lives and be fair to those concerned. I may like openness, but they may prefer secrecy. But this one thing I will swear, that not a word of lie shall be written. I will gladly leave so many things unsaid, rather than twist them. This autobiography is not to glorify me nor justify my actions, but it is to lay bare truth, the great merciless Truth which kept relentlessly pursuing me till very unwillingly I did learn what was required. Therefore, do depend on me to speak nothing but truth in these pages.

Lastly, there is one thing more to be said and that is I'm attempting a great thing when I write in a foreign tongue. A language, which is not my mother tongue and in which I do not think during the stress and strains of my life, is not at all the proper medium to convey subtle thoughts, nor the habits and customs of our everyday lives. And even if it is permissible to write in English, I feel I am not qualified to do it. I have never seen the portals of a college. I have not listened to lectures, nor written essays and compositions. Whatever education there has been in my life, it has been self-acquired. I have been self-educated. Hence there are bound to be many grammatical and idiomatic errors, all of which my more learned readers must forgive. I have chosen English and not my mother tongue because I want my friends and everyone I care about, to read this. There are some among my closest friends who do not know Tamil, for instance, my lifelong friend V.S. Lakshmi, who is eagerly expecting to read this.

Hence, please take whatever good you may find in this and leave out the bad like the proverbial swan and milk. I shall be immensely happy and consider myself as having achieved a great thing, if on reading this, someone finds some feeble light to brighten their life and lighten the loneliness of the way from the thought of a previous traveller on the same path. Then I shall not consider this labour of mine as wasted.

# Foreword

## (Kalpana, 2025)

In the summer of 2017, I stumbled upon a small, plain wooden box on which my grandmother Pankajam (1911–2007) had stuck a sheet of white paper with the words 'My writings for Kalpana'. I had always been aware of my grandmother's voracious reading and her literary interests. I had grown up on a steady stream of stories from the world classics (*Jane Eyre, Pride and Prejudice, Anna Karenina*) that she narrated with as much flair as the Ramayana or the Mahabharata. Although she had no more than six years of formal schooling, she had been a prolific writer of essays, poems and short stories in Tamil and English. I had my treasured copy of the spiral-bound volume of her writings, *All My Yesteryears*, that she had circulated among close friends and family in 1987. The school friends I invited home were usually taken aback when the diminutive, elderly woman they met would quiz them on the books they were reading, ask which of the classics they had read or, if it was science they preferred, urge them to watch the scientist Carl Sagan's *Cosmos* (telecast on Indian television in 1986-1987) that she herself anticipated with great excitement every week. They were awestruck when she would invite them to discuss Stephen Hawking's *A Brief History of Time* (1988) with her to help her understand his ideas better. My grandmother Pankajam had a fearsome reputation for showing up the textbook learning and domain-bound knowledge of her school- and college-going grandchildren.

I had always known that my book-reading, nature-loving, bird-watching, shell-collecting, story-writing, science buff grandmother was a woman driven by multiple passions and interests. And therefore, I was not particularly surprised when I found the box of her writings. When rummaging through its contents however, I was not expecting to find what I did— Pankajam's autobiographical writing (in English) and her thinly-veiled 'fictional' writing on her life narrated through four stories, two in English, two in Tamil. I was transfixed by Pankajam's autobiographical narratives (first-person and fictional), much of which I was reading closely for the first time. None of this had found place in *All My Yesteryears* which she had pressed her grandchildren to read. I realised that she had begun to write her autobiography in 1949 (when she was thirty-eight years old) and kept returning to this project sporadically over a fifty-year period. Her last piece of autobiographical writing was in 1995 when she was eighty-four years old, one year after she had suffered a stroke.

In this book, I reconstruct the life of my grandmother Pankajam through a biographical exercise that captures the distinctive singularity of an exceptional woman, even as it situates her in an unexceptional social universe shaped by the conventions of Tamil Brahmin orthodoxy. Pankajam was not involved in public life through the usual routes available to those from her background, should their families be open to them crossing traditional boundaries—of employment, education or participation in the anti-colonial movement of her times. Accounts of such lives are available to us today, as is evident from the rich autobiographies published by India's leading feminist presses. Pankajam's life though was unlike these other public lives that women chose for themselves. She was a wife, a mother of five children and, in the later years of her life, a nurse and caregiver to her ageing parents, especially her mother. In a retrospective piece on her life that she wrote on her eightieth birthday, Pankajam writes, 'five children, their children, cows in the shed, managing a household, nursing and looking after my old and ailing parents, kept my nose tied to everyday mundane things'.

Why did Pankajam write about her life? In her foreword, Pankajam insists that a 'humble housewife tied to mundane work' such as herself may have a story or two worth telling and she writes to show that her 'soul has ever been trying to soar up and break the bondage of the flesh'. She is acutely aware that women, consigned always to their bodies, are forbidden a life of the mind or a cultivation of the intellect. Her Hindu faith provides a template for her to envision a soul that will evolve towards complete liberation (*mukti*) from corporeal embodiment, the cycle of births and deaths, and in the case of women, the seemingly endless birthing of and caring for life. Yet, as Pankajam knows, it is only through the act of writing in the here and the now that she may realise a soul that will not be enslaved by the (female) body.

In an undated piece written in Tamil when she is older (possibly in the 1960s or the 1970s), Pankajam returns to the theme of why she writes an autobiography. She writes so that her 'very young' grandchildren, who might forget that a grandmother such as her lived and loved them well, may know her. However, Pankajam's concerns extend beyond the sentimental. Aware that the history books only record 'governments, kings, wars and conflicts' and not the 'people's everyday lives', Pankajam fears that her grandchildren will only have a partial account of her times should they rely on the published histories. Pankajam deftly makes us see why, therefore, she can and must write a life history whose sheer ordinariness warrants chronicling. For it is not only a story of the everyday, but also of the possibilities for transcendence that a spirited woman might discover in its unfolding.

———◆———

Pankajam's autobiographical narratives are animated by the self-assured voice of a woman who writes with unsparing honesty of girlhood, its joys and heartbreaks, the psychosocial effects of parental strife and domestic violence, the fragility of a melancholic mother, the loss of school life, an adolescent's dreams of romance, a young woman's yearning for companionship, a troubled marriage and conjugality, the delight and apprehensions of a mother discovering the distinct personas of her five teenaged children, a housewife's quest for intellectual growth and her efforts to nurture her mind, the exhaustion of ceaseless caregiving, a hunger for books and travel and the bond of camaraderie and friendships forged across cultures and continents. Despite reiterating that she is 'a woman of no consequence' whatsoever, Pankajam is nonetheless aware that she is a subject of history. And it is precisely this self-reflexive quality of Pankajam's writing that allows me to attempt a biographical exercise that is far more than the story of one woman's life.

Through Pankajam's writing on her childhood and girlhood, I narrate the story of the Madras Presidency in the early decades of the twentieth century. The monopoly that Tamil Brahmins enjoyed over education and employment in the British Raj had secured Pankajam's father a comfortable job in the department of salt and customs. Growing up amidst salt pans in small, godforsaken seaside towns along the Coromandel Coast of Madras Presidency in the 1910s and 1920s, we see little Pankajam forge surprisingly close friendships across the boundaries of caste, community, language and religion. Pankajam's account of her early years gives us a child's view of the world of adults, of women, men and domestic arrangements. Through her evocative prose and keen eye for adult–child relationships, Pankajam seamlessly interweaves landscapes, seasons and people. We note how unusual it was for the times that a free-spirited girl should be exploring her habitat with abandon—running wild, climbing trees, riding horses, seeking out adventures that included snakes and jackals and constructing imaginary universes.

Pankajam's story is also one of girls' education in colonial Madras, of school friendships among adolescent girls and of what schooling—as well as its abrupt, cruel end—could mean for young girls. The book gives us glimpses of girlhood from the 1920s as experienced by a classroom of high-spirited, ebullient teenage girls in the Lady Willingdon School and Training College of Madras. Using Pankajam's writing on the six precious years of school life (1921–1927) that she had in the city of Madras, I trace an adolescent's yearning for autonomous self-hood which I set against colonial-era debates about the worth and value of female education conceptualised as a training ground for women to become enlightened homemakers and dutiful mothers. In cultivating her sense of herself as a confident, talented and intelligent young woman, I show how Pankajam used her brush with formal education in ways that contrasted rather sharply with the visions of the educationists, writers and philanthropists of her times.

In this book, I present Pankajam's writing in ways that reveal the making of a young girl's subjectivity and her consciousness of (her) self in relation to society. Pankajam, as a child and adolescent, was raised on the English classics as well as tales from the world of Hindu mythology, the Puranas. George Eliot, Jane Austen, Charlotte Bronte and Louisa May Alcott shaped her notions of female personhood, as did Sita, Sati and Savitri. Pankajam shows us what it meant for a young girl to grow up imbibing such a diverse repertoire of ideals and ways of being in the early decades of the twentieth century.

I juxtapose images of Pankajam as a young girl of marriageable age in the late 1920s with the new models of womanhood that had begun to gain currency among the educated, urban middle classes from the last decades of the nineteenth century, as the histories of colonial India reveal. Men of the middle classes and upper castes were seeking wives who would be companionate partners. Women were therefore to be groomed and educated (in a prescribed, formulaic way) to be worthy, fit companions for young men. However, the case of Pankajam turns this gendered logic on its head. A woman shaped by the books she had read, Pankajam desired nothing less than a companionate partner for herself. Her fictionalised autobiographies show us a young woman courageously navigating the treacherous minefield of a profoundly unequal marriage and staking a claim to romantic and sexual fulfilment. Pankajam gives us a fine-grained account of caste conjugality—as it was lived out and fought over—in the early 1930s through the lens of a newly-married woman who sought to hold her husband accountable for his actions and seize her one chance of conjugal happiness.

The book maps Pankajam's life unfolding against the tumultuous events and epochal shifts that she witnessed and wrote about—the World Wars, the anti-colonial freedom movement, the city life of Madras (in the 1930s and 1940s), the bustling street life of its neighbourhoods, the bombing of Madras by the Japanese (in 1943), the evacuation of the city and the early years of post-Independence India. In the 1930s and 1940s, we see Pankajam building a home, raising her young children and fashioning herself as an enlightened and progressive mother, conscious that she was doing so amidst a 'great cry and shout for independence'. We see Pankajam's enthusiasm for her children's well-being tempered by her sense of herself as a patriot who must heed the call to arms of a nation-in-the-making. This book is therefore as much about the historical context and social milieu of an era as it is about an unusual woman and the many ways in which she stands out, commanding the readers' attention and interest.

Through the prism of Pankajam's life, this book tells a story of mothers and daughters (of upper-caste and middle-class households) in colonial and post-colonial India. During various moments in her writings, Pankajam reflects on her life in the light of her mother Subbalakshmi's (unfulfilled and unhappy) life and that of her own two daughters, the older one giving up a promising career in classical dance and settling for marriage and motherhood early in life, and the younger daughter studying and working in America, before choosing a life of public action with working class and women's movements in India. Unlike her reclusive mother who retreated from people and relationships in the face of her disappointments and suffering, Pankajam engaged with the world robustly. If Subbalakshmi's life underscores the structures that enclosed and confined a woman's life, Pankajam's life speaks to the redemptive power of human agency and makes us rethink the possibilities for self-making, within the limits of a life hemmed in by caste conjugality.

Despite their contrasting ways of being, the lives of Subbalakshmi and Pankajam alike are synecdochic in the ways they expose the fault lines of an emergent nation state and its approach to the 'women's question'. Pankajam's letters written to her younger daughter Mythily, who was working in the United Nations in New York during the 1960s, reflect her sense of bearing witness to the forces of history ever-remaking individual destinies and women's lives. By giving us glimpses of Mythily's life (as seen by Pankajam), this book dwells on another possibility of being and doing that opened up for women in the mid-to-late 1960s. In doing this, it allows us to see what enabled Pankajam's younger daughter to leap ahead of her time and chart out an extraordinary life for herself.

In the final reckoning, this is a book about the chequered trajectories of a newly-born nation as seen from the lens of its daughters—restless women forcing home and nation to reckon with their stubborn striving for self-actualisation. In equal measure, this book tells a universal story of the defiant striving of the human spirit to infuse life with meaning and purpose and explore to the fullest the potential for transcendence of one's circumstances.

———•———

The treasure trove of Pankajam's writing that I discovered in the wooden box made me see her for the extraordinary woman that she had always been. It made me also see more clearly the familial and household context that had produced a woman as unusual as my own mother (and Pankajam's daughter), Mythily.

Mythily Sivaraman (1939–2021) was a well-known left political activist, trade unionist, writer and leading figure in the women's movement in Tamil Nadu.[1] Mythily's four decades of public action began shortly after she returned from the US in mid-1968 as a committed Marxist and anti-imperialist. On 25 December 1968, forty-four Dalit landless agricultural workers, mostly women and children, were set afire in a little hut and burnt alive in the village of Keezhvenmani of Thanjavur district. Mythily's first visit to Keezhvenmani village within a week of the massacre led to her political journey as a leading Communist party activist and organiser.

In 2006, Zubaan, India's well-known feminist press, published Mythily Sivaraman's *Fragments of a Life: A Family Archive.* Mythily wrote the book as a reckoning of sorts with her highly intelligent, deeply unhappy maternal grandmother Subbalakshmi (1897–1978), Pankajam's mother. As a child, Mythily, like others in her household, had taken for granted the remoteness and eccentricities of her maternal grandmother, whom some had even considered 'mad'. But an adult Mythily, feminist and activist, was haunted by the memory of a socially distant and withdrawn grandmother—a fascinatingly unconventional woman who would not be contented with her assigned fate as a wife, mother and grandmother.

A well-known public figure in Tamil Nadu, Mythily was once asked by a Tamil magazine to name someone who had inspired her. To her great surprise, Mythily found herself saying, 'My grandmother Subbalakshmi'. As she writes in the preface to *Fragments of a Life*, 'Her name leaped out of my mouth without any conscious search for an icon'. And therefore, when Mythily chose to carve out time and step back from her everyday activism to write a book on her grandmother in the early 2000s, she must have seen this new project as no less political than anything else she was doing in her life. A woman who held herself to exacting standards and felt that every minute of her life must be

---

1    More information on Mythily Sivaraman is available in Agnihotri (2021); Ali (2021); Geetha (2021); Kalpana (2021) and Menon (2021).

devoted to fighting the good fight, Mythily would not have done it otherwise.

Drawing on a range of archival sources, Mythily's book re-created Subbalakshmi's historical period and located its protagonist in her social milieu. Married at eleven and mother at fourteen years of age, Subbalakshmi had never been to school. The demands of caste purity dictated early marriage and stringent control of women of the dominant castes, although opportunities were proliferating for the men of their families, their brothers, husbands and sons. Reading her older brother's textbooks and library books, Subbalakshmi was an auto-didact whose interests spanned philosophy, psychology, art, world history, politics and literature. Subbalakshmi had maintained a diary for two years of her life, with no mention of her emotional state or her everyday joys and frustrations. Creatively supplementing the diary with what she gleaned from elsewhere, Mythily parsed together disparate and fragile sources from a 'family archive' to make her reticent subject speak.

In her book, Mythily traces Subbalakshmi's dreams and ambitions for herself and her daughter, her lone surviving child, and shows how they were thwarted, each one of them. Subbalakshmi's heartbreaks were brought on by the early death of two sons, an unfulfilled marriage, the inability to throw herself into the anti-colonial movement as she had longed to do, the denial of permission (by her family) to leave for Shantiniketan (in 1924) in order to remake her life anew when she had a chance to do so, and her failure to secure her daughter's education and make her a doctor. Through the lens of Subbalakshmi's life, Mythily asks: What is insanity? What constitutes the 'normal'? And how are these linked to gender identity and social oppression?

In *Fragments of a Life*, Mythily dwells on her grandmother's unrealised desire to get involved in the anti-colonial struggle during the heady years of the Non-cooperation Movement (of the 1920s) and be like the nationalist heroes that she so revered. Mythily speculates that Subbalakshmi must have believed that life must have a mission, a meaning, a goal and was not worth living unless one could live for a larger ideal than the family. It is not surprising that Mythily, who had devoted her life to the public causes that she cherished, should have identified closely with her grandmother and her uncompromising rejection of a life other than the one she would choose for herself. Interestingly, Mythily saw her grandmother as a feminist icon, but not her mother Pankajam. Subbalakshmi was recognisably feminist in her rejection of the conventional trappings of domestic life. Pankajam was, on the face of it, a 'well-adjusted' woman who embraced motherhood and adhered to a normative middle-class life, thus seeming to live out her life like so many others.

In the preface to *Fragments of a Life*, Mythily writes that she always regretted not having a typical Indian grandmother. When Mythily was growing up, Subbalakshmi was an emotionally distant figure who did not feed her grandchildren, sing lullabies, tell them stories, cuddle them or display physical affection of the usual grandmotherly kind. On the other hand, Mythily was raised by Pankajam, shared a household with her mother through much of her adult life, and was perhaps too close to her mother to see Pankajam for the extraordinary person that she was. I also suspect that Pankajam's passion for life and the enormous joy she wrested from everyday life had made her a somewhat unlikely candidate as a feminist subject! But this points perhaps to our failure to recognise the multiple ways in which women may choose to live out their desires for freedom, autonomy, and agency, their feminisms.

The distance of generation and a shared longing to sublimate oneself within a collective that transcends the family and household drew Mythily to the enigmatic figure of Subbalakshmi. Reading Pankajam's writings closely over the four years that I have been working on this manuscript, I have found myself drawn to the way that Pankajam seeks to unravel the 'riddle' of life that confronts all of us, as she writes in the foreword to her autobiography. Pankajam expresses the hope that her story will be a torch and throw a 'feeble light' for those who love her and who may be 'groping in the dark, seeking light and understanding of this world' as she herself was doing. Pankajam writes because she is intuitively aware of the universal purpose of all stories— lightening the loneliness of the way for a weary traveller cheered by the thought of a wayfarer on the path before her.

Pankajam's pointed reference to Gandhi in her foreword makes us wonder whether a woman may ever 'rip open the heart' and expose personal, intimate matters of her life to public scrutiny and survive unscathed or even win acclaim for it, as Gandhi did. We know that Pankajam must have grappled with these questions, for it is through fiction that she dares to do this. Her undated stories (two in English, two in Tamil) narrate the lives of three young women—Meena, Kamala and Lakshmi. Meena is on the verge of marriage, while Kamala has just been married and embarked on conjugal life. Pankajam stays for the longest period with Lakshmi's story, developing it to the point where her protagonist has five teenage children. Pankajam's Tamil short story 'Amma's Birthday' features the eponymous 'Amma' or 'mother' on her birthday, a day like any other in her life.

While Pankajam may well have been seeking catharsis in writing these stories, it would be a mistake to view them in these limited terms, for she had undoubtedly enjoyed the literary endeavour. We see evidence of this in the careful elaboration of the plot, the setting of the scenes, the development of the characters and the building up of dramatic tension. The interior world of the protagonists is delicately explored, not through a heavy-handed authorial voice, but conversations and arguments among them. Pankajam's felicity with words engages her readers and holds us spellbound. Nonetheless, it is my editorial voice that will interweave the many sources that I draw upon in order to hold this book together. In writing this book, I am conscious that I am reconstructing a life through my interpretive frameworks and, therefore, I show my hand to the reader. I juxtapose the sources that I use in a way that will allow the readers to clearly perceive and challenge (should they choose to) the way I read and present Pankajam's life and the questions it raises for us.

I must confess that this book project of mine was nowhere as planned as Mythily's book on Subbalakshmi was. In fact, it was entirely unintended. I was looking for material to write a political biography of Mythily when I found Pankajam's wooden box. I had been long planning to expand an article I wrote ('My Mother, Comrade Mythily') into a book-length memoir and I was impatient to get a head start on this project by organising the material that I had at home. But I found Pankajam's writing instead. When I heard Pankajam's voice on why she will not be silenced even if she has accomplished nothing in the world, I knew right away that I had no choice. I had to write about the 'utterly ordinary' life of a 'woman of no consequence' who was yet far from ordinary.

———•———

In the afterword to Mythily Sivaraman's *Fragments of a Life*, the feminist historian and film-maker Uma Chakravarti writes that the book offers us valuable insights on how to re-construct a life lived largely in shadows and silences. Mythily's sources included the lists of library books borrowed by Subbalakshmi, the receipts of books she had bought, news clippings of writings and speeches from journals and the receipts of donations made to the Indian National Congress, among others. Subbalakshmi's diary entries were confined to quotations from Tagore or the Tamil poet Subramania Bharati and her observations of nature, luminous descriptions of the sea by moonlight, the darkening evening, the gathering rain clouds. Unlike her reticent mother Subbalakshmi, Pankajam speaks naturally from the heart and has a lot to say about herself, her richly imagined inner worlds, her emotional states, the web of social relationships that cocooned her and all that she aspired to be and to do. In her autobiography, she writes that her memory is uninterrupted from the sixth year of her life and that she aims to put down as 'concisely as possible' all that she has experienced.

Pankajam's autobiographical narratives and stories were written in different notebooks, often the old school books of her children and grandchildren. Some were typed up and photocopied with multiple copies, while others remained handwritten. Pankajam wrote her autobiographical narratives (all in English) on and off over a span of nearly five decades. By all indications, the first attempt she made to write about her life was in 1949 when she was thirty-eight years old. Her foreword and a section titled 'Infancy and Early Childhood' present themselves as a single and continuous piece of writing in the same notebook. Since her autobiographical writing is always undated, a clue regarding the date of the writing must be gleaned from the narrative. In this instance, Pankajam describes a tragic event that took place in 1919 when she was a little child and notes that she continues to suffer its effects thirty years later. Hence, we surmise that she began to write her autobiography in 1949 when the youngest of her five children was about nine years old.

Pankajam had a new baby every two years from February 1931 (when her first child was born) to December 1939 when the fifth was born. Her last child Mythily, regarded as a frail and sickly child, was homeschooled by her mother till the age of nine and admitted in school as late as 1948/49. It is not difficult, therefore, to see why Pankajam had to wait until her young child began to go to school before embarking on a venture of this kind. The last piece of autobiographical writing that Pankajam did was in 1995 when she was nearly eighty-four years old. The stroke that she suffered in August 1994 had markedly altered her handwriting and the quality of her writing, making it possible to identify when the last sections were written.

In re-constructing Pankajam's life for this book, I draw on multiple sources that include her autobiographical narratives (1949–1995); her (undated) 'fictional' writing (four short stories in Tamil and English); the retrospective essays that she wrote occasionally on her birthdays reflecting on her life and how she had lived it; her essay on the city of Madras in the 1930s and the 1940s; her school autograph notebook (1927–28); the travel diaries that she maintained when she had opportunities to see other parts of the world; the letters she wrote her children and the letters that her family wrote her. Between 1963 and 1968, Pankajam's youngest child Mythily was studying and working in America. During this period, Pankajam, a prolific correspondent, wrote her daughter about two to three letters a month. Mythily never threw away a scrap of paper in her life. My mother's habit of preserving nearly every letter she had ever received turned out to be a stroke of good fortune for me. Pankajam's letter-writing, no less than her autobiographical writing, reflects her deep interest in herself as a subject of history, making sense of life's vicissitudes, sleights of hand and unpredictable twists and turns.

Besides the letters that Pankajam wrote, I draw on others letters to her in order to trace the unusual friendships that she cultivated with an Anglo–Indian school girl (Catherine Brown), a British traveller and adventurer (Paxye Thornhill) and a Russian scholar of Tamil studies (Alexander Dubiansky). I draw also on interviews with family members, in particular my ninety-one-year-old uncle (and Pankajam's first child) Ramachandran and the recollections of his boyhood written by my (now deceased) uncle (and Pankajam's fourth child), Sundaram. I corroborate and supplement these sources with my own memories of time spent with Pankajam, my primary care-giver during my childhood and adolescent years. Pankajam was for me the story-telling grandmother that Mythily had once wished she had had. Through the years of her full-time involvement in the trade union and women's movements, Mythily shared a household with her mother in order to draw on Pankajam's assistance and care labour in raising her daughter. And therefore it is that I find myself walking the path that my mother did nearly two decades ago—writing a book, seeking my grandmother and dreaming of her.

# Cast of Characters

**Explanatory Note**: This is not an exhaustive list of all family members or friends of Pankajam. The list only contains the names of those who appear in the book.

| Cast of characters | Name |
|---|---|
| Key protagonist | Pankajam |
| Pankajam's siblings | Raja and an unnamed baby brother |
| Pankajam's mother | Subbalakshmi |
| Pankajam's father | PR Gopalakrishnan (PRG) |
| PRG's older brother | Seshan |
| PRG's young brother | Subramanian (Uncle Subbu) |
| Subbalakshmi's mother and father | Kamakshi and Sundaram Iyer |
| Subbalakshmi's older brother and his wife | Ananthakrishnan and Subamma |
| Subbalakshmi's younger sister | Kanagam (married to Pankajam's adored uncle) |
| Family friend of Subbalakshmi and Pankajam | Soundaram, married to Rangachari |

| | |
|---|---|
| Miss Barrie | Swiss headmistress of Lady Willingdon School and Training College (1920s) |
| Pankajam's school friend | V.S. Lakshmi |
| Pankajam's school friend | Lakshmi Sehgal (or 'Captain Lakshmi') |
| Pankajam's friend (late 1920s–1930s) | Catherine Brown |
| Pankajam's husband | Sivaraman |
| Pankajam's first child | Ramachandran (or 'Ram') |
| Second child | Lalitha |
| Third child | Srinivasan (or 'Srini') |
| Fourth child | Sundaram |
| Fifth child | Mythily (mother of author Kalpana) |
| Pankajam's daughter-in-law | Nirmala (Ram's wife) |
| Pankajam's daughter-in-law | Danielle (Sundaram's wife) |
| Pankajam's friend (1950s–early 1990s) | Paxye Thornhill |
| Pankajam's friend (1987–1990s) | Alexander Dubiansky |

## The key characters in Pankajam's stories

| Name of story | Key character | Other characters |
|---|---|---|
| *Vidhiyum Madhiyum* (Tamil, translated as *Fate and Intelligence*) | Kamala | Sundaresan (the husband), uncle and aunt ('chithi') of Kamala, their daughter Saro (Kamala's cousin), Saro's husband Sridharan |
| Untitled story #1 (English). Referred to as the Meena–Subbu or M–S story | Meena | Subramanian (or Subbu, the husband), Meena's grandfather, Sadasivam ('Thatha'), grandmother (unnamed), the cook Valamba |
| Untitled story #2 (English). Referred to as the Lakshmi–Ramanathan or L–R story | Lakshmi | Ramanathan (the husband), Lakshmi's grandfather, 'Thatha' (unnamed), the cook Chellammal |

# 1

# A curious Indian father (1890–1910)

A toddler sits in her aunt's lap, playing on the large wooden swing in her house. Outside, lightning flashes and the rain falls in torrents. Her aunt, barely nine or ten years older than her, carries her to the window to watch people wading knee-deep in the water. Suddenly, she places the child on the ground and runs towards a staircase, chasing after a big tomcat trying to escape with a newborn kitten in its mouth. Since everyone runs to retrieve the kitten, the toddler, eager to know what is happening, starts to climb the staircase in the open courtyard, crawling on all fours. The child hears her great-grandfather sitting by a pillar, shouting orders, telling her to stop. Paying no heed, she continues to climb and soon finds herself tumbling down, hitting her head on a tap at the bottom of the staircase and falling into a vessel of water beside it. She hollers out loud. His face close to hers, her great-grandfather, serious and stern, says, 'Now you know what will happen if you disobey your elders. Do not forget it!'

The year is 1914 and the Great War has just begun. The house with the open courtyard is in Sydoji Lane of Madras city, the administrative headquarters of the Southern Presidency and one of the three major cities in the Indian subcontinent. Years later, the memory of the tumble and her great-grandfather's face, his voice would remain with Pankajam, the curious toddler. She would wonder why this stray incident and its lesson of obedience had made such a deep and lasting impression on her, often flashing through her mind when she was discussing something of importance with someone. Sandwiched between a mother who would not conform to anything that was expected of her and a daughter who flouted social conventions with flamboyance, Pankajam would ask herself how it was that she had somewhat tamely (as she saw it) acquiesced with the life that was given to her to live. But this introspection was to come much later.

When this story begins, Pankajam is a toddler and Subbalakshmi, her mother, is a teenager, about sixteen years old. Subbalakshmi's life had turned out to be rather different from the one that her father had envisioned for her. Sundaram Iyer, who worked as a surveyor in the royal court of Travancore, a princely state in British India (now part of Kerala), had dreamt of educating his daughter at the Maharani's Arts College for Women, originally founded in Mysore as a girls' school in 1881. Born in 1897, Subbalakshmi was about five years old when the school in Mysore was upgraded to a women's college in 1902, motivating her father's desire to have her educated there. Sadly for the little girl, her father died the same year, effectively terminating the prospect of any kind of formal education for her, leaving behind his wife Kamakshi, five-year old Subbalakshmi, two sons and a fourth child, a daughter, born shortly after his passing.

Tamil Brahmin men like Sundaram Iyer, who constituted about three per cent of the population of Madras Presidency, held an inordinate number of official posts in the colonial bureaucracy by the turn of the century. From the mid-nineteenth century onwards, Brahmins of the Southern Presidency, leveraging the advantages of their privileged status in the traditional caste hierarchy and their monopoly over formal learning, had started to migrate to towns and cities from their villages to attend colleges and learn English, with Maratha Brahmins taking the lead and setting an example that was subsequently emulated by the Tamil Brahmins. By the early 1880s, Tamil and Telugu Brahmins had replaced Maratha Brahmins in the local bureaucracy, forming the bulk of a new administrative elite that had emerged in South India. With the opening of Madras University and its affiliated colleges, Tamil Brahmins overtook all other communities in education and employment. Nearly three-fourths of the graduates of the University of Madras between 1870 and 1918 were Brahmins. They were preponderant among the successful candidates who had passed the Provincial Civil Service exams between 1892 and 1904 and had a comfortable presence among the district munsifs (lower-level judges), sub-judges and deputy collectors in the early decades of the twentieth century (Fuller and Narasimhan, 2014).

Therefore, it was not surprising that Sundaram Iyer had found a job in the administrative hierarchy of the princely state of Travancore in the 1890s. However, what might have set him apart from many others of the upwardly mobile, urbanising social class and orthodox upper caste that he belonged to was his dream of education, higher education, at that, for his daughter. The agenda of school education for girls had begun to find promoters and advocates among the affluent citizens of Madras only about two decades before Subbalakshmi's birth, making what the historian Sita Anantha Raman describes as a 'tentative start' in the Presidency between 1870 and 1880 (Raman, 1996). The earliest schools drew mostly girls from Eurasian and Tamil Christian families, with the upper castes among the Tamil and Telugu population keeping their daughters at home in order to maintain caste purity by ensuring the pre-puberty marriage of their girls.

While some form of education for women was seen as inevitable by the anti-colonial nationalists and social reformers in the later decades of the nineteenth century, much thought and effort was invested in carefully calibrating educational systems, texts and curriculum in keeping with the (then) dominant ideas of what Indian women could and could not be exposed to. The sort of education that might cause women to reject indigenous (usually upper caste) culture and traditions, acquire 'anglicised' tastes or emulate too closely the ways of Western women was anathema and to be guarded against. Like elsewhere in the country, Tamil women were also required to provide the reassurance of cultural stability and continuity by guarding the 'timeless values' of the hearth and home in times of rapid social change. In the Madras Presidency, the prevailing consensus was that women neither required sound knowledge of the English language, nor were they suited for higher (college or professional) education. Most Tamil women who were educated even in the early twentieth century were likely exposed only to the English alphabet (Raman, 1996).

When viewed against this backdrop, Iyer, who wanted to send his daughter to college as soon as he heard that a women's college had been founded, does appear to have been a somewhat unusual man. In *Fragments of a Life*, Mythily writes that he must have been influenced by the pioneering efforts of the rulers of Travancore in promoting female education and the matrilineal system of inheritance that some of its castes followed. Iyer was known to have expressed admiration for the queens of Travancore, who wrote and spoke English fluently despite living in seclusion within the palace. Citing their example, he would often say to his wife, 'Why must our women be shielded from English education?'[2] In her writings, Pankajam wonders about her grandfather, whom she never had the opportunity to meet or get to know, but who seems to have piqued her curiosity nonetheless.

> This grandfather of mine was a unique man. In those days people learned just enough English to earn their bread under their foreign bosses. But their outlook on life was unchanged … I do not know what made my grandfather a man so eager for knowledge and keen to seek the good in another culture. He was very much interested in the English people and their way of living. He wrote to England to get playthings and picture books for his children and tried to bring up his children in English fashion. He was

---

2    My interview with Pankajam's cousin Chella Kailasam, also a granddaughter of Kamakshi and Sundaram Iyer.

so devoted to his children, says my grandmother, which is curious to me, for most of our Indian fathers are not the least interested in their children.

Sundaram Iyer and Kamakshi's home in Travancore exemplified the new form of households and conjugal life which, the scholar Mytheli Sreenivas notes, were beginning to gain currency from the 1890s among Tamils in the Madras Presidency. Tamil Brahmin men like Iyer, who were leaving their natal villages for cities, took their wives and children with them and set up households in which the conjugal couple was no longer embedded within a web of extended kith and kin consisting of familial and other dependents. Women could assume a greater role in the care and early education of their children in these newly-emergent households (Sreenivas, 2008). One might add that these households also appear to have freed up and enabled men like Iyer who were inclined to involve themselves in the upbringing and socialisation of their children.

After Iyer's early death, Kamakshi arrived with their four children to live with her father, a Brahmin landlord who owned agricultural land in Thiruvaiyaru, a town in the fertile belt of Thanjavur district, plentifully watered by the Kauvery. But the seeds of difference had been sown. The English storybooks remained with the family and Kamakshi would recall with nostalgic emotion what her husband had wanted for their daughter. Serendipitously, the child Subbalakshmi had to learn English in order to read out the daily newspapers to her maternal grandfather, who was losing his eyesight. When her family moved from Thiruvaiyaru to the township of Trichinopoly (Trichy) to further the education of her brothers, Subbalakshmi began to read the textbooks and library books that her older brother Ananthakrishnan brought home.

Intrigued to hear of a young girl who had never been to school, yet showed interest in her brother's college books, the librarian of St Joseph's College of Trichinopoly, a missionary father, visited their home (in 1908 or so) to see for himself this 'remarkable girl', as he described her. Stunned by her serious engagement with the books that she had been reading from his library, he urged her family to send the girl to school.[3] But while the family did not reprimand Subbalakshmi for reading her brother's books or confiscate them and order her to spend her time in the kitchen instead, they would not send her to school either. And a father's dream for his daughter remained unfulfilled.

3    Mythily Sivaraman, *Fragments of a Life: A Family Archive*, Zubaan, 2006.

# 2

# A child in a world of adults (early 1910s)

Subbalakshmi was married at age eleven to P.R. Gopalakrishnan (PRG), who had a secure job with the imperial government and was the second son of the Tahsildar of Trichinopoly, the chief officer in charge of assessment and collection of land revenue in British India. Eleven years older than his child bride, PRG had a promising career ahead of him in the Department of Salt and Customs in which he was assistant inspector when he acquired a wife. In keeping with the customary practices of orthodox Brahmin families, Subbalakshmi was married well before puberty and sent to live with her husband as soon as she came of age. With the marriage being consummated when Subbalakshmi was about thirteen years old, she had her first child, Pankajam, within a year.

> I was born in Thiruvaiyaru in my grandmother's ancestral home. Their house was in Sannidhi Street. Facing the street was the famous temple of Lord Panchanadeeswara. The night I was born was the Sivaratri [night of Shiva] of

the month.[4] Providence must have chosen the day perhaps because it knew that my heart would be drawn towards Lord Siva till the end of my life. The date according to the English calendar was 18 November 1911. My birth star is Swathi. They say it is an auspicious star. The astrologers gloat over it, but I find it has not brought me anything. But then the astrologers say the star brings good fortune to others—those linked to the person born under the star. Well, if it is not able to do me any good, let my star bring good to those I love, which is the next best thing, is it not?

My mother was only fourteen when I was born. My maternal grandmother, uncles and aunt made much fuss over me as I was the first child in the family after many years. My parents could not decide on a name for me. My father wanted to call me Abhirami, which was his mother's name. The others thought the name was very old-fashioned. My maternal grandmother gave me my present name as it was a rare name then, she said. For many years, my father called me by various names, Sita and Kutty [little one]. But the name my grandmother gave me has stayed.

Tasked with the responsibility of supervising the salt pans, PRG was posted in remote coastal villages, making it necessary for his young wife and their infant child to stay often with Subbalakshmi's mother, who was living in Madras with her oldest son at that time. As such, Pankajam's recollections of the earliest years of her life revolve around the household in Madras that consisted of her grandmother Kamakshi, her two sons and a daughter, Kanagam. When Kanagam was married to a young law student, her husband, whose professional training was financially supported by his wife's family, also became part of the Madras household. In

---

her autobiography, Pankajam describes a household that did not lack material comforts. Older women worked in the kitchen and cooked and fed the family and while they could hire other women as domestic helpers, the latter could not enter the kitchen if they were of a lower caste. The Madras neighbourhood in which Pankajam's family lived during the 1910s does not appear to have been caste-segregated, judging from her description of it. Their neighbours were shepherds by profession.

If there was not much social contact between Pankajam's family and the world outside, this was likely due as much to the persona and temperament of the adults as to anything else. Raised by a melancholic mother living out an unhappy married life and a 'moody and serious' grandmother who was widowed early in life, Pankajam reflects with tender thoughtfulness on how the unexpressed sorrows and disappointments of adults influence the psychosocial development of children. When her uncle arrives, bringing jokes, games, fun and laughter into her life, we see a child's instinctive adoration for an adult who takes her seriously, in contrast to the others who exhibit casual disregard for the worlds of children.

I clearly remember all that happened when we lived in Nagoji Rao Street (Triplicane, Madras). It was a narrow, congested lane. Our house was next to a milkman's. The milkmen were shepherds, families living together, about thirty members with two dozen children and several cows and buffaloes. Our place was a comfortable household. My grandmother cooked, served everyone, attended on the children of her daughters and did most of the work alone. There was only one woman to help sweep and clean the vessels. But we had good food and nice clothes as my grandmother had private means and my maternal uncle Ananthakrishnan was employed in a good position in the Secretariat.

I remember very well my mother's younger sister Kanagam's husband, whom I still call 'uncle' in English fashion. When I was three or four years old, I made my acquaintance with this uncle of mine, newly married to my aunt. I remember that I was always hugging to myself a doll, which my uncle used to make fun of. Uncle was the first person who opened out the outside world to me. Before he came to our family and even after, but for him in Madras, my life was secluded and cut off from the world. My grandmother and her son Ananthakrishnan, were people who did not care for friends or neighbours. They were each company enough for themselves and so was my mother. Therefore, I neither knew nor met anyone besides my family.

My grandmother, by nature, was moody and serious as the majority of her years were unhappily spent. She was a young widow who remained ever in wounded reserve. My young mother would have been happy had fate let her, but no, she was subject to miseries beyond what anyone could endure. Her disappointments in life and dejection could not help affecting me unconsciously in my childhood and even infancy. An infant and its mother are one and the same though apparently two bodies—their thoughts and feelings communicate telepathically. Therefore, the travail of her soul did not escape me, but left its impressions deep on my conscious as well as sub-conscious mind and emotions. Hence, from my birth, I began to be sad, chastened, afraid and insecure. This very fact led me to seek laughter, gaiety and happiness more strongly than any other child had occasion to.

Into this hushed and serious life of my babyhood came this uncle of mine. He was a gay student, when he married my aunt. He was inclined to music and had a pleasant voice. He sang, laughed, cracked jokes, told wonderful stories and would often play with my little brother and me like a child. Naturally, I adored this uncle who was unlike anybody I saw or knew. Through him I learnt that there was gaiety and songs in the world and one could have them if one wanted to. He even made my grandmother smile and my mother's brother, my maama, was agreeably moved by his gaiety and liked to converse with him. Uncle also tended to help people. He had a special knack for nursing and curing people's pains when illness visited the house. This character in anyone I simply love.

I remember playing hide-and-seek with my uncle. He used to hide my brother in unlikely, clever places and make me search. He told us stories, good ones. Some of them were apparently vulgar and yet worldly ones, which taught one a homily or the other, some wisdom or moral. The stories were all folk tales and he sang a lot of folk songs, all of which captured my childish heart and imagination. Uncle celebrated a Deepavali very grandly. I had by then a little brother, two and a half years younger than me. I must have been six years old that year. We were all given fine dresses. My brother got a yellow and green velvet combination suit. My uncle bought a lot of fireworks. I still remember how he tied the firecrackers over a clothes line—the whole length of it and set fire to it at one end and in what delighted fear I saw and heard it with my ears shut! That Deepavali was so grand and happy that we did not have the next one, nor any for some years after.

Uncle was a very shrewd observer and it was his praise of me that removed some of my inferiority complexes that the others in the house made me feel. I still remember his observations of me and the unfolding of my character as I grew up, that he would make to my aunt. Sometimes they would talk in English about me thinking that I did not understand. But I would have understood what they were saying of me perfectly well, had they spoken Urdu or Persian or Greek. In my childhood, I understood everything that people said or thought, whatever the language. It was a faculty given to me as a child.

This uncle talked to me as if to an equal, while the rest of the household considered me a silly, timid child and paid no heed except to feed and clothe me. He would appreciate my play and praised whatever I said or did, which was such a surprising thing that slowly my uncle became a hero to me. He was for me a fairy godfather and one who understood the minds of children for many, many years and even after I grew into a young woman. I still believe he is an extraordinary man, for he is truly great, who is able to win the approbation of an innocent child.

# 3

# A desolate, howling wilderness (mid–1910s)

Through writing, Pankajam sought to know herself better. In her autobiographical narratives, Pankajam reflects on the making of her consciousness from her earliest years and attempts to identify the formative experiences that had shaped her interior world of emotion and sensibilities. Turning away from the mood of solitary quiet that had reigned over her household, Pankajam saw herself, even when very young, as reaching out for all the 'laughter, joy and gaiety' that she could possibly grasp.

When writing of life in the salt pans where her father worked, Pankajam's description of the aching loneliness of its bleak and barren landscapes, occasionally punctuated by a sudden burst of rich vegetation and the happy cries of children at play, segues into a depiction of her mother's shifting moods. In an extract from her autobiography, Pankajam describes her family's stay in the coastal villages they lived in when she was a little girl, from 1916 to 1918.

*Pankajam as a child (likely 1917)*

Manal kudi or Manakkudi:[5] From the name of the place, you must know that the place was all *manal* or 'sand'. There was not even a village nearby. Three furlongs or so away from our bungalow was a dilapidated, abandoned temple very near the beach. The temple was abandoned because the sea was steadily encroaching upon the village and the waves beating on its walls. It was a great big temple. The gopuram had fallen down in huge pieces and trees and creepers climbed over the other portions. Huge

---

5   Manakkudi village is located in Mayailaduthurai Taluk of Nagapattinam (Nagai) district in Tamil Nadu.

rifts were seen all over. My mother frequented this temple that nobody took care of. She would often grind *dosa mavu* [dosa flour] in its big grinding stone. My brother and I played hide and seek among the fallen pieces of the temple. My mother would sit on the washing stone of the temple well and read till the light faded.

One evening, our mother called us to go back home. Engrossed as we were in our games, we did not heed her. When we started, it was already beginning to get dark. We had to cross a small dirty stream to reach our bungalow. When we came to the rickety wooden bridge across the stream, we saw a huge black snake (a cobra) lying coiled, right in the middle of the bridge. We had no light and though my mother was frightened, she took a long stick and made noises to frighten the snake away. But it did not stir. It must have dined sumptuously and was sound asleep. We children began to cry. By God's grace, we saw hurricane lanterns coming towards us. Seeing that we had not returned, the men in the village had come looking for us. At last, many men came and somehow coaxed and pushed the snake with sticks into the water, wherefrom it slowly crawled away.

Theethandathanam:[6] The name meant a place where Lord Siva danced with fire flying from his hair. A more desolate place you cannot imagine. The beach was very close to us, just behind the bungalow. The roar of the sea was ever so loud that on nights it would appear to beat on your head—so imposing the sound and so still the silence around! My brother Raja and I found ourselves always playing on the sand, collecting shells and a huge seed called *ravana muzhi* (that resembled the protruding eyeball of a person) until we were tired. The beach was criss-crossed by a creeper bearing convolvulus flowers. Our

---

6    Theethandathanam village is in Thiruvadanai block of Ramanathapuram (Ramnad) district.

thatched bungalow and the clerks' quarters three furlongs away were the only sights that marred the open landscape, except of course the salt heaps near the seashore.

My father was often away on long camps lasting about twenty days a month. Every evening my mother took us for a walk in the countryside. The country was rough with thorns and thistles and dead leaves for miles. On our walks, we ran and picked flowers and wild berries to play with, while our mother observed the scenery or read the book she had brought, sitting on a fallen tree. She would speak to us now and then pointing to a running fox or a snake. I remember one night when I awoke with a terrible stomach ache and how frightened my mother was. I do not know what it was that cured me.

My grandmother used to send us toys, picture books and clothes from Madras for our birthdays. How these things reached us is a wonder to me now, for there was no post office or railway for miles. On a day that such a parcel arrived, my mother found two or three new-born hawk fledglings forsaken by their mother. Maybe the mother hawk was dead. My mother put them inside the cardboard box, which brought us the presents and reared them for many days. My mother was a great naturalist—a lover of nature, birds, insects and flowers—she knew them all in their native and English names. It was in this desolate town that mother began teaching me the alphabets. Every evening we used to sit on the verandah. I would find it very difficult to focus my attention, for the garden with its myriad sounds and my playing brother would distract me. I'm sure I was vexing my poor mother with my wavering interest in it all.

On one such monotonous evening, we were suddenly surprised by two horses entering our stable without their riders. One of the horses was my father's. He had left for a camp eighty miles away the previous evening. Evidently our horse had escaped and returned to its stable, accompanied by its companion. I watched the horses fascinated—how they conversed putting their heads together. Another day I saw our horse suddenly falling to the ground, writhing in pain. The vet had to come from a far-off town. Meanwhile, a European officer came to my father and offered to shoot it. But my father would not hear of it. Why, he would not allow anyone to kill even a snake or scorpion! When the horse died after severe pain, I was witness to it and I wept bitterly for it.

In the compound where we lived, there was a huge pit where garbage was thrown. On the side of the pit, *kodukapuli* plants (Manila Tamarind) and foxgloves grew in abundance. Snakes were aplenty by my side and they slithered away at the sight of me. But I never feared them then as I might now. My brother Raja and I played under a huge tamarind tree. I was the king and he the servant. I would spread a cloth on the bough of the tree and sit on it with my father's walking stick in hand and Raja would kneel and bow taking the orders. And together we would slay imaginary dragons or enemies and thrust them into the big pit. The pit was an unfathomable hell to us. I can still hear Raja say, 'Sister, sister! There the fellow is trying to climb the pit but is falling in again and the snakes are eating him.' 'Let them eat—he was wicked, was he not? Such was our happy play.

I loved the nights the best, for our mother would light the *kuthu vilakku* (bronze lamp) with castor oil and we would gather around it and huddle near her. She would read us all the fairy tales and stories of great men and women. My brother would go to sleep soon, but I would lie awake thinking of the characters in the stories. I would hear my mother sobbing silently by my side and, though I pitied her, I dared not offer consolation ...

# 4

## Sea, sand, salty tears (1910s)

When sifting through the flotsam and jetsam of one's memories, stray incidents capture our attention and hold us to ransom, forcing us to weave them into the stories we tell ourselves about our lives. Pankajam perhaps sought likewise to make sense of a mishap that she believed had had a significant impact on her and, by extension, her mother too.

When I was five or so and my brother Raja two years and something, my mother developed some womb trouble. To explain the cause of this, I have to go back even further. My readers must forgive me for going back in time. When I was one and a half years old, it seems a girl, in whose charge I was left for a few minutes, dropped me down and fell over me. It seems I cried pointing to my leg, which swelled soon. From that day I did not walk for a year, I was told. They brought me to Madras and a doctor advised my mother to dig a pit by the seashore, make me stand in the sand pit for half an hour and then massage my legs with cod liver oil and hot water.

My mother attended to all these instructions devotedly, carrying water from a well without anyone's help, with the result that when I recovered slowly from the accident and began to walk about, she developed womb trouble. I believe that it was this accident, which has made me so short in life. My legs, though strong and sturdy, never grew in length. This has been one of the crosses in my life. Now I do not mind it, but when I was a young girl, I did feel so bad about it.

When my mother developed her womb trouble, she was in my father's house and he directly took her to the hospital in Conjeevaram (Kanchipuram), admitted her as an inpatient and left her there. He then left for a place called Thondi where he was transferred, taking my little brother Raja and me with him. He should have left us at our grandmother's house at Madras on his way as my mother thought he had done. But he did not and took us with him instead. This brought me some suffering. I remember but faintly those feelings of fear and depression. Well, my father took us to his place and left us in the care of the cook Natesan who, though a good man, could not be expected to be a good nurse. My father, who was a serious man and never free with his children, only inspired awe in me. He was a great deal out of the house. All I remember is that I missed my mother. I dared not ask my father about my mother for I knew instinctively that he would not like it. And I secretly thought that she must be dead.

One day my brother and I were playing in the compound, about two months after my mother went away, when to my great joy, a lady friend of my mother, a clerk's wife, walked in. She embraced us, took us to her house, gave us an oil bath and plaited my hair. I asked her where my mother was and I was told that she was not dead but, in the hospital, and would soon come and see us. This was news indeed to poor me. We were without our mother for six months. Sometimes, I would not eat and I remember how my father would have my plate brought before him, when the cook complained. I would have to swallow the food under my father's stern eye. Once he asked me why I did not eat and I replied, 'Natesan makes awful curries'. Henceforward my father ordered the cook to ask me what to make. I said 'Brinjal and potatoes'.

One day when walking back from the kitchen to the bungalow, I suddenly saw my mother enter the house. I ran towards her in all joy calling 'Amma, Amma'. I remember this instance clearly because of the fear and sorrow at having lost my mother's presence for several months and the great joy in finding her come again ...

Before I come to other intimate and sorrowful experiences, I must explain certain things regarding my parents. My father lost his mother when he was very young and my (paternal) grandfather married again. The two boys, my father and his older brother, were left a trifle neglected as they thought, during which time they became very close to each other, protecting each other. This elder brother [Seshan] always had an emotional hold over my father.

When I was young, I did not know all these details, but observed that whenever a letter arrived from Seshu Uncle, quarrels would spring up between my parents. One day, as usual, a quarrel ensued soon after a letter came. My father, though a good person, yet had a quick temper. When angry, he lost his control and often used to hit my mother. One such day, when my father hit my mother, my little brother Raja took a stick and rushed to hit my father. My father pushed the boy away. I ran and hid myself in the next room and when things flew out of the doors, I ran to the 'line' where the subordinate officers stayed. My mother had a friend there about her own age. I ran to her and pulled her sari saying 'Come and see my mother, come and see my mother.'

'What is the matter? Is she ill?' asked the lady. But I went on tugging at her sari. She came with me, but before we got back to the house, we saw my father riding away on his horse and leaving for the camp. Such emotional experiences occasionally marred our peaceful lives.

About four feet and nine inches or so, Pankajam would speak (to me) of how, as a child, she would stand before a looking glass mirror daily and will herself to grow a few inches taller. She would chant, 'I am growing every day, a better girl in every way' replacing the word 'better' with 'taller'! In *Fragments of a Life*, Mythily refers to Subbalakshmi's illness as a distended uterus, but does not speculate on what might have caused it. In a different context though, Mythily wonders how PRG's initiation of physical intercourse with his wife of thirteen years, leading to a pregnancy shortly thereafter, may qualify as anything other than rape of a child bride. But, as Pankajam chose to remember it and as she was told the story perhaps, it was her accident and her mother's physical exertions on her behalf that had brought on Subbalakshmi's 'womb trouble'.

In her autobiography, Pankajam is candid about the troubled relationship that her parents had and her father's role in precipitating the rift between them that never healed. Mythily writes that PRG and Subbalakshmi enjoyed a happy period together in the early months of their marriage when they shared mutual interests in English literature and poetry. Pankajam's contention was that this brief honeymoon was rudely interrupted when PRG's older brother Seshan allegedly turned him against the notion of a wife who was educated, read English literature and discussed books and ideas. In her book, Mythily is more forthright in her criticism of PRG's own inability to accept his wife as an intellectual companion, with his latent conservatism being fuelled by his brother's patriarchal worldviews. While Pankajam may have struggled with her sense of loyalty towards her father, she minces no words when she describes his assault of her mother that she witnessed as a child.

*Pankajam, in a white dress, is seated next to Aunt Kanagam. Her baby brother Raja is next to his mother Subbalakshmi (1914/15)*

In her later years, Subbalakshmi would recall with sadness and gratitude her little boy Raja's heroic defence of her against his father's brutality. Pankajam herself forever cherished the 'dog-like devotion' that her brother had shown her and his inability to bear the slightest separation from her, when she was sent for a few hours daily to the *thinnai pallikoodam*, a traditional school in the Tamil countryside in which teachers conducted classes in the outer courtyard of their homes.

1917-18: My father was next transferred to Sankaridurg, a small town in Salem district. I remember going there in a *jutka* (horse-drawn cart). The scenery on either side of the road was rocky—rocks of purple, blue and white were heaped up and thrown about and the heat was terrible. My father was reading and singing *thevarams*[7] inside the jutka and mother quietly observing the landscape. We crossed Bhavani River—I heard my mother say so. Well, Sankaridurg was a proper town—unlike the two godforsaken deserts we had lived in. We did not have a compound around our house, as we lived in a street house. In the backyard, the masons had left a pile of mortar heaped up like a hill with a deep depression on top, like a volcano. My brother and I took at once to this hardened mortar hill. Filling the pit with water, we endlessly played in and around it. This mound played a large part in our imaginations. From our doorstep at the end of the long street could be seen a huge hillock. That was Sankaridurg. They said that some small wild animals lived there.

One notable event took place in my life here. My mother, who found me very playful and inattentive about lessons, was worried about my schooling and sent me to what we call a *thinnai pallikoodam* quite close by. This *thinnai pallikoodam* did not even have a *thinnai* (pial). There was a huge tree under which were benches on which we children sat. I remember a man wielding a cane and beating the boys left and right. I was mortally afraid of the rough boys, who snatched my coloured picture book and painted wooden pencil box and were fighting each other for the possession of it. I was too frightened to even report it to the teacher. And when he asked me if the things were mine, I kept silent as I saw that the boys were making signs and threatening to beat me if I let the teacher know. The girls pinched me or left me alone to play and quarrel among themselves. I remember very little of that school now, for it did not impress me and I made no friends.

---

7   Part of the twelve-volume collection of devotional hymns that extol Lord Shiva, the *thevaram* hymns were composed by three prominent Tamil poets in the seventh and eight CE.

But there is a pathetic incident attached to my school-going which moved me so much that the memory of it lasted to the day when my children started going to school. You must have all understood by now that my brother and I were close friends and inseparable companions. Now that I think of it, I have never known such dog-like devotion as he had for me. Not understanding the depth of the boy's feelings, my mother insisted on sending me to school. Each morning when I left, Raja would accompany me to the door and stand there on the steps with a woeful face. He was there till I disappeared at the end of the street, and the first joyous sight of home that I had in the evening, when I turned the corner of the street, was his curly head. He would cling to the door and hang far out of the steps to get a first sight of me. My mother said that he would go to the door as early as three 'o'clock, in spite of her words. Poor darling! Raja used to hurl himself on me as soon as I reached the door and would demand to be told all that I did and saw and heard in school.

To this day the memory of those days, his eagerness, his enjoyment of my company and that simple love move me to tears and a sudden pain shoots across my heart. I remember those childhood years of mine made so rich by the rain of sweet love that he poured on me ...

# 5

# Saddest day of bitterest sorrow (1919)

Pankajam stayed with her mother and brother in Sankaridurg for a couple of months, or a year at the most, before Subbalakshmi found herself pregnant again and returned to her mother's home in Madras for the delivery.

In 1919, my grandmother brought us back to Madras. I was admitted to a small school. It was not a big or popular one. My mother had come to Madras for her confinement. So had her sister. Both of them gave birth to boys within fifteen minutes of each other. The whole street and our relatives congratulated my grandmother on this lucky event. Everything was festive and I began to admire my infant brother. The superstitious would say that it was the 'evil eye' cast by everyone that was responsible for the following events.

A fortnight or so after the birth of this baby brother, my darling brother Raja fell ill of some foul fever. They got hold of a doctor who made the greatest blunder in his diagnosis, which caused suffering that has stayed with us even now thirty years after the event. The doctor was a well-meaning but idiotic one. He thought it was chicken

pox or measles, although there were no marks of any kind
on the body. In those days there was no treatment for
measles and people prepared a cooling diet and waited for
the rashes to appear and subside on their own. But even
after the second week there were no rashes, the fever rose
higher and my brother became delirious. It proved to be
typhoid and the boy succumbed to it one fateful day.

The memory is so green and graven on my soul to this
day. The anguish is fresh and poignant. I knew he was ill as
he was put in a separate bed from me, in a separate room. I
was not allowed to see or talk to him. But I used to stand
near the door or window and snatch a few looks at his
fevered and flushed face. Whenever he caught sight of me,
he got excited and would try to get up and talk to me. I do
not know why my mother and grandmother were so stupid
as to keep me from him. I would not have caught the disease
if I were allowed to talk to him a few minutes every day. I
could see from afar how desperate Raja was about coming
to me and how miserable he was at the restraints. I felt
miserable too. But my people, they had little imagination
and could not understand children's hearts nor feelings.

One night, I was suddenly awakened from sleep by my
brother's shouts and cries. I listened—he was in delirium
they said, he was calling me at the top of his voice. He
shouted, 'Pankajam, Pankajam, come and play ball with
me. Bring the ball here.' This he was repeating many times.
Towards morning he was getting quieter. The next day I
went to school as usual. When I was returning for my midday meal, I saw a crowd in front of our house. On seeing
me they cried, 'Oh unlucky child, you have lost your
brother, your brother is dead.' I did not believe it. But when
I went in, my uncle kept me from entering the rooms. No
one came forward to give me lunch.

I heard my grandmother telling somebody that Raja
had called out to me continuously in his last hours. I can
only say that they were cruel in sending me off to school

that day and keeping me away from him. I am not to this day reconciled to his death. My sorrow would not have been so keen if we had both at least chatted and played at his bedside. A cruel and vengeful fate that took him away without satisfying his last childish desire was heart-rending. It rankles in my heart forever ...

Well, that evening I saw some men carrying him away wrapped in a white cloth. I saw his curly head through the cloth. In the melee of all the rushing and weeping, I escaped and ran out of the gate, following those who carried the little body, but many hands caught me and pushed me into the house. Then they shut the door and I could see no more. And even then, in the childish heart came the clear thought that I will never see him again and that was the last sight of him. I saw my uncle and aunt trying to pacify my mother. I saw her pull out all her jewels, her earrings, her nose ring and throw them away. But no matter what she cast away from her person, she could not cast away her life and follow her boy.

The very next morning after my brother's death, I woke up early. The first thought that rushed to my mind was 'Raja is no more'. It is one day since he died. Thus, I kept count for a full year and a little over. I clearly remember counting 40, 50, 100, 200 daily after his death. When it was that I gave up counting the day each morning, I cannot remember exactly. But it was over one year, for I did count up to 500 something. I do not remember weeping copiously. I only know that I was stunned for a few days and there came a big void in my life and a profound sorrow filled the heart of a child of seven, for I was only seven then. I wondered where he had gone and whether he could see me and hear me. When there was no one in the room, I would raise my voice and call out 'Raja, Raja, come and say just a word to me. Where are you?'

However, being a child, I slowly began to miss him less and the newness of the world and its happenings made me forget him as the days flowed into months and years. I never said a word to my mother about him after his death. Though we never referred to his name, he was constantly in both our minds and we both suffered in reserved silence. I feared that I would awaken her grief if I alluded to him and she maybe thought the same and wanted to spare me.

Pankajam's first experience of deep sadness and her lasting regret at being kept away from her brother's bedside during his last days speaks to the wrenching quality of grief and helpless anger that many might have known in the months of the pandemic, when the death of a loved one took place in punitive isolation, bereft of the comfort of physical presence and the human contact that might have eased their suffering. In 1930, eleven years after Raja's death, when Pankajam was probably pregnant with her first child, she wrote a poem in his memory.

*My Brother Raja (1930)*

Oh, my brother Raja, sweet
When and where shall we meet?
God did break my heart
When He, you from me did part
The saddest day of bitterest sorrow
My heart's darling, was the morrow
That dawned after the awful night
When your soul to heaven gave flight.

To others you are dead and gone
But oft I seem to hear thy prattle when alone
Once again, I see you in flesh in a gleam
But no—it is the shadow of my dream.

# 6

# Lost and found (1919–1920)

When Pankajam's family was rocked by grief and loss, the nation was going through no less tumultuous times. An important constituent of the British empire, India and her people were part of the Great War that exacted an enormous human and material toll. Between August 1914 and December 1919, the colonial government recruited a total of 1.4 million Indians for war purposes. About 1,096,013 combatants and non-combatants (labourers, porters, cooks, washermen) fought and served overseas in Flanders, France, Mesopotamia, East Africa, Gallipoli, Egypt, Palestine, Persia and Central Asia. Between 50,000 and 70,000 of them were killed. Although India was dragged into the war as a colony of Great Britain, the country witnessed an outpouring of support with all hues of nationalists and political parties publicly committing themselves to the Allied cause. Mahatma Gandhi, among others, hoped that Britain's reward to India for its war service would be the gift of self-government within the empire. Speaking at the Madras Provincial Conference in 1918, the nationalist poet Sarojini Naidu appealed to the 'flower of India's manhood' to join the standing army (Das, 2018).

During the years of World War I, Pankajam's father served the empire by executing his responsibilities in the salt pans and the family remained financially comfortable. After her brother's death, Pankajam's family moved to the town of Ellore or Eluru (now a district headquarters city in Andhra Pradesh) where her father had been transferred. Pankajam's writing during this period of her life evokes the wonder, curiosity and natural delight with which a free-spirited child explored her habitat—running wild, climbing trees, riding horses, seeking out adventures and constructing imaginary universes. This was unusual for a girl child raised in a traditional Tamil Brahmin family in the 1910s and 1920s. Living with a very young, withdrawn and melancholic mother who often retreated into her books and a father who travelled frequently on inspection tours and camps, Pankajam had few restraints on her movements and was free of close adult supervision when growing up. Further, Subbalakshmi, herself a woman who defied conventional stereotypes of a wife and mother, could hardly be expected to impose restrictions curbing her daughter's everyday freedoms. The glimpses we get of Subbalakshmi from Pankajam's writing show us a young woman spending hours outdoors and taking long evening walks in the countryside with only her little children and her books for company.

When my father was transferred to Ellore, he was promoted as inspector. We had a fine bungalow in Ellore with a big, well-tended garden. As soon as we entered the house, I ran into the garden. It had a well and a green-and-orange tortoise swimming in it. My mother was all tears when she saw it and turned to me saying, 'Wouldn't Raja have enjoyed seeing this?' That was the only reference she ever made to him.

In Ellore, I was alone and had no companion to play with, having lost my brother. I was not sent to school because school was far way and we lived in the outskirts of the town. Most evenings I spent playing in the garden and even ventured into a large, open ground (*maidan*) that lay beyond our gates and extended for miles up to the railway station. Many sports tournaments, military exercises, police, salt and customs department drills and kit inspections took place there. A zamindar, who was called the Raja of Bobbili used to play polo on horseback in the maidan. He was also called the Kukkalu Raja because he loved dogs (*kukkalu* in Telugu) and had about a hundred different breeds. He lived in a palace in the town.

The Raja, his friends and British officers who played polo, rode on horses of different hues. The horses were magnificent. So well-fed and well-groomed! Their skins were polished and shone like silk. There were pure white stallions, ebony black and grey ones, dappled ones and brown ones. I admired the black ones and the brown ones for their sheen. Watching the game itself was exciting for me. As our gate was locked, I had to watch it all from a huge guava tree in our garden, which had two large branches running parallel and close to each other, just a little above the gate. Some pillows were tied onto the branches with ropes. Perched on this comfortable forking point, I watched the beautiful and brilliant horses gallop and prance.

The Kukkalu Raja's dogs were often brought to the maidan. You would not believe how they filled the ground! There were dalmatians, greyhounds, borzois, golden retrievers, mastiffs, bulldogs, terriers and hosts of others. My father told me their breed names whenever I pestered him to do it. The trainers, attendants and dogs that overran the maidan would make a terrific noise. Although the fierce barking dogs frightened me, I loved to watch them and observe how they were trained and fed. My own father had a horse that he rode to work and he gave me a ride on it occasionally. And so, I came to love horses and dogs.

One day, a big army camped in the maidan. It must have been World War I, for hundreds of huge tents were pitched all over the open space making it look like a city in cloth. Battalions of soldiers and high rank officers were sojourning and camping in the tents. If one battalion left, another swiftly occupied the tents. But the fun for me came only at the end of their stay when the soldiers left and the tents were being slowly dismantled. Sometimes my father's peons would take me to the tents while they conversed with the tent men. I would open the flaps and see the rooms where they cooked and others where the soldiers slept.

One day soon after breakfast, as no one came to take me, I ran off alone to inspect the tents. I roamed by myself exploring the beautiful tents with satin and silk inside, beds, cushions, chairs and tables. The coloured satin, the lattice work windows and other luxuries fired my childish imagination. I gave full vent to my fancies imagining that I was the sultan or princess, freely borrowing from the *Arabian Nights* stories I had heard from my mother. I must have gone deep into the tents, for I began to feel hot and stuffy. As there were no windows, I felt suffocated. I sat down, tired and frightened. When I was thus sitting, I seemed to hear a voice say, 'Come sister, let us play'. At first, I could not believe it. Then it dawned on me that it was the voice of my brother, Raja. I felt equally happy and frightened and waited tensely without replying.

Nothing happened. After this, I tried to go back home, but could not as I had wandered very deep into the tent rooms. On realising that I had lost the way, I began to shout for help. No answer came and I began to cry. After a spell of crying, I got up and wandered in different directions to find the side that was near our gate, all the while shouting. If I had stayed inside the tent for some more time, I could have fainted. But by God's infinite mercy towards my parents perhaps, I heard my name called by my father's peons who were looking for me. As it was lunch time, my mother had sent them to find me. They took me home to receive a very good scolding. Never after this day, did I hear that beloved voice again.

I had another adventure, which was responsible for bringing my mother and me some good friends and good luck too. My father used to go to a club in town, an English club. Sometimes I accompanied him when there was a function. On one such occasion, I went with him on horseback as we had no carriage. There was a great crowd in town. I saw many English children playing with puppies and kittens, which attracted me. My father pointed to me an officer, a sub-inspector, and told me to go find him whenever I wanted to go home. I began to play with the children, who invited me to a room where they showed me a cage full of all sorts of birds and rabbits. Enjoying myself with the children, I lost count of time. When I became conscious that I must go home, I looked for the sub-inspector and my father but could not find either. Each thought I had left with the other.

When the crowd had dispersed, I was standing alone when some constables came and asked my name and whose child I was. Fortunately, I knew my father's name and position. They brought their boss, the police inspector Mr Rangachari, who took me to his house and called out to his wife, 'Soundaram, come and see what I have brought!' A young lady, hovering over the stove, looked up. 'Ah, a child!' She ran to me, picked me up, kissed me and fussed over me. She immediately fell for me and they both took me back home in their coach. From that day, Soundaram Mami[8] and my mother became great friends. I learnt afterwards that the couple had no children and the lady was yearning for a child. She often took me to her house and kept me there for a few days. I enjoyed my stay there because I was very lonely at home and the husband and wife made much of me and took me out in their coach. I also liked the freedom

---

8    'Mami' is a common term of address for older women among Tamil-speaking Brahmins.

from lessons and the disciplining by my mother whose love for me, though deep and pure, was not demonstrative at all.

It was Soundaram Mami who bought a violin for me and sent the then famous violinist Govindarajulu to teach me to play. When Deepavali approached, she purchased a sari and a pair of gold bangles for my mother and clothes for me. The couple sent the bills to my father who had no other go but to pay the money in instalments! And when a money order came from my grandmother in Madras, Soundaram Mami quickly took it and bought a simple gold belt for me like many girls in Andhra wore then. My own mother never asked my father for anything, having learnt the lesson early in life ...

# 7

## The little women of Eluru (1919–1920)

In her autobiographical narratives, Pankajam was writing of events that took place several decades ago. Yet, her prose resonates with dramatic tension and conveys a sense of immediacy and urgency. She makes us feel the mute sorrow of a five-year-old whose mother inexplicably disappears for several months and about whom she cannot speak to her father. We feel the helpless terror of a six-year-old who sees her father raining blows on her mother. We suffer with seven-year-old Pankajam when she recounts the events that led to her brother's death, even as she makes us see the subtly different ways grief and loss leave their imprint on adults and children. We rejoice with her when, as a lonely single child of eight years who has just lost her younger brother and devoted playmate, she embraces with passion a world of horses and dogs, birds and insects and, more occasionally, children when chance encounters bring her new friendships.

For all her zest and enthusiasm for life, Pankajam was conscious that she was growing up in a household riven by conflict. Her narrative suggests a child's unhappy awareness of being a pawn in her parents' competing visions of a life and future for her. When her mother and her orthodox father battled over whether she should learn English or Sanskrit, Pankajam was forced to learn three languages as part of an uneasy truce of sorts. An incipient spirit of independence probably drove the eight-year-old to take matters into her own hands by learning and making swift progress in a fourth instead! The Ellore period in Pankajam's life is one of self-discovery, a growing recognition of what moved her and what did not, a deep attachment to a new friend, the test of loyalty that it provoked and the start of what was to be a lifelong commitment to letter correspondence with those she loved.

I was eight when we moved to Ellore and I left it when I was nine and a half. This period of a year and a half was an important phase in my life as I was very young and at an impressionable age. I remember very well how every little detail and incident forged my character and influenced my thoughts and ideals.

Next to our house, there were three or four similar bungalows all in a row. They were occupied by a PWD engineer and a police official. The PWD engineer was an Iyengar and he had a daughter of my age with a younger brother. For a few months, this girl was my playmate. I am afraid I never liked her, for she and her gossiping mother were very different from my mother and me. To begin with, this girl had lots of fine clothes and jewels, which she displayed to me. I envied her these things for my mother always dressed me in simple frocks and I had no jewels. My father had no extra money with him as he had to support his older brother [Seshan] and his large family. Besides, he aided and assisted every holy man or anyone who came to us in the garb of one.

Though both my parents loved me much, their love for me only brought them into greater conflicts with each other. Mother wanted me to learn English and engaged a Christian lady tutor for me. But my father criticised it and tore up the coloured plate English primers bought from Spencer's [Madras]. He wanted me to learn Sanskrit instead. This was not his idea, but was suggested by his brother, and conveyed through his letters. So ultimately, my father taught me Sanskrit whenever he had leisure, my mother taught me Tamil and the tutor taught me English. But I showed no interest in any of the three languages, and preferred to learn Telugu. I asked our maid to get me a Telugu primer and learnt the characters from her and showed great improvement in it.

My mother, after she emerged from her intense stupor and misery following the death of my brother Raja, devoted herself entirely to me and my education. She read to me every night and told me stories of our ancient myths and Puranas. Of course, the Ramayana, the eternal story, gripped my heart with its beauty of thought and emotions. But the story that affected me much and even shaped my character was the *The Little Women* of L.M. Alcott. All children love it. But to me it was something dearer to the heart. I tried to live up to the ideals in the story. At different times I identified myself with one character in the story or the other and for weeks went about behaving strangely. My mother at once noticed the change and asked me about it. She was pleased to see that the story was changing me. Before I heard the story, I was wilful, not fond of doing lessons, obstinate, selfish and playful like most children. But the desire to be like the girls in *The Little Women* whom I greatly admired, and comparing my mother to Mrs March, I slowly learnt to master my waywardness and childishness and apply myself to my lessons.

Now I must dwell on the death of my second brother. This brother was two-and-half-years old when he died. He suffered from enlargement of the liver or cirrhosis—a malady of children common at the time. I must say that the death of this brother did not touch my heart as Raja's did. I was much older than him and we never were companions or playmates. I felt his loss more for my mother's sake than mine. However, I kept Lord Siva's picture in a corner and prayed every day for my brother's recovery. When he died, I stopped my prayers for months.

Before he died, I had contracted a friendship with a girl six years older than myself, which caused a great emotional upheaval in me. A Christian doctor used to call on my brother every alternate day for three months. He was accompanied by his daughter who took a fancy to me, as I did to her. Here I must say that I loved company and loved friends passionately. For that matter, whomever I loved, I loved with passion. This girl became my great friend. She was also a single child like me. She went to a convent school unlike me. And her talk enlightened me and pleased me. She was gentle and kind to me. We played and told stories to each other in spite of the age difference. This went on for three months when, despite the doctor's best efforts, my baby brother passed away one day quietly in my mother's lap. I could no longer see my friend when her father, the doctor, stopped visiting us.

I was dejected and lonely. One day, I met her at a friend of my father's, and she told me to write to her every day and send the letter through a servant whose house was near hers. Her suggestion made me happy and I started writing to her everyday with the servant's help. She did not write to me in English, perhaps because she knew I did not understand it enough. We had to correspond in Telugu. And as I did not read and write Telugu well as yet, I had to ask the peon's help. I dictated and he wrote the letters. Her replies were read out to me. One day, my mother found out and asked me why I did not seek her help with the letters. I was too sensitive to touch upon the death of my brother and the consequent resentment of my mother towards the doctor, which I sensed. I do not know if I was right or not in thus judging my mother. But she never chided me about the letters.

I'm afraid I was too frightened of my mother's sorrow to be of any solace to her. If I expressed any sympathy, it was silent. My second brother's death was her last straw and she lost her balance of mind. All mothers are not made the same way. There are some to whom things can never be the same again. My mother began to eat her heart out and bleed for the loss, until the body began to take revenge. But it came gradually, this sickness of the mind, and imperceptibly changed her.

One day. my mother was cooking and I was eating my lunch. She served me rasam rice and *keerai* [spinach]. Asking for curd and rice, I called out to my mother. But she did not come, nor was there any response. Wondering where she had gone, I went to look for her and, to my horror, found her lying in the garbage pit outside. Hearing me shout, everyone rushed and brought my mother to the hall and laid her on a mat. Meanwhile, I ran to our neighbour's house where the engineer's family had gathered for lunch. I went straight to his wife and tugged at her sari, demanding, 'Come, come, my mother has fallen down.' The engineer immediately sent for the doctor and telegraphed my father who arrived the next day. The whole night I sat by my mother and would not let the engineer's wife go home either. I thought my mother was dead.

This was the first manifestation of my mother's mental problems. Though she recovered from this, she would suddenly withdraw into herself and remain silent for a few minutes after which she came back to herself. This state occurred on and off. I was ordered by everyone to keep a watch on her lest she fell and hurt herself.

Pankajam's life is a testament to how early encounters with storytelling and books can enrich a child's inner world and her sense of self. Living with a mother who raised her children in the absence of a husband often touring the salt pans, it may not have been difficult for Pankajam to imagine Subbalakshmi as Mrs March, the matriarch who headed a household of four daughters when her husband was away serving in the American Civil War.

Pankajam may even have found the impoverished circumstances of the March family somewhat relatable since tensions in her own household also revolved around finances and what was due to a wife and a child from a man's earnings. Soundaram's swift purchase of a piece of gold jewellery with the money order from Madras was clearly aimed at creating an asset for Subbalakshmi before the money was spent on household expenses.

But above all, the classic that has travelled across time and space with tremendous success, appealed to Pankajam because, as writer Anne Boyd Rioux observes, it allowed girls and young women to understand themselves through Alcott's portrayal of four very different sisters, with each of whom one could choose to identify herself or not. In her book, *Meg, Jo, Beth, Amy,* Rioux (2018: 310) writes , 'What *Little Women* did so well was to show readers there was not one way to be a girl or to grow into womanhood, but many ways.' And therefore the *Little Women* had cast their spell on Pankajam who went about 'behaving strangely for weeks' identifying with one character or the other in the book. Listening to Subbalakshmi read the story of the four March sisters huddling protectively around their mother, reminding each other to warm her slippers by the fireside while awaiting her return in the evenings, Pankajam empathised with her own mother's troubles and heeded her home-schooling efforts with greater zeal than before. For Pankajam, the experience of *Little Women* dovetailed with a period of growing maturity and perhaps even enabled her to see more clearly her mother's unhappy marital situation and the household's troubled dynamics for what they were. When Pankajam's pre-school years draw to a close (in 1920/21), we see a precocious nine-year-old recognising that her fragile and grief-stricken 'mother (who) was not like other mothers' must be looked after and protected by those around her, including her little girl.

# 8

# A mother like no other (1920–21)

Pankajam was admitted in 1921 to the Lady Willingdon School and Training College of Madras by Subbalakshmi against her husband's wishes and without his knowledge. In *Fragments of a Life*, Mythily describes how Subbalakshmi upped and left with Pankajam for her older brother Ananthakrishnan's household in Madras, taking advantage of her husband's absence from home. In the chapter 'Flight to Madras', Mythily narrates Subbalakshmi's clandestine departure from Ellore when her husband and his older brother forbid schooling for Pankajam. However, Pankajam appears to recall the sequence of events slightly differently.

Some months after my brother's death, when I was just running wild, climbing trees and playing alone, my mother began to worry about my education again. She mustered courage enough to ask my father what he thought about sending me to my grandmother in Madras to be schooled. My father, of course, wrote to his brother asking for his permission. This was the reply he received from his brother: 'Why should you want to get your daughter to learn English? English educated girls do not make good wives. Teach her Sanskrit at home. Stop the violin teacher.

It is enough if she can sing lullabies. Do not send Pankajam to her grandmother.' My mother had preserved this letter for long.

Sharp quarrels broke out between my parents when my father refused to send me to Madras. Soon after he left for camp, my mother did a very bold thing for my sake and brought upon herself the censure and ridicule of the whole world for doing so. She sent for my grandmother and packed me off to Madras. When my father returned, he was terribly angry and told my mother to go away as well. She tarried for some time and feeling unhappy, lonely and unwell (suffering occasional seizures), she left for Madras. In Madras, she frequently wrote to my father, wanting to join him, but his brother was adamant that she should not, unless she brought me back to Ellore with her. And for once, my mother was strong and determined. She said, 'This is going to be my only surviving child and I do not want her life to be wasted. I want to educate her and make her a doctor'.

Thus ended my nine years of life without proper education. I joined school in Madras, the best and most popular one in the city. I found life completely different but very interesting. This was the best period of my life; it needs a separate chapter. The first part of this chronicle is over and a new dawn had blossomed not only for me but my mother too.

As Pankajam chooses to tell the story, Subbalakshmi sent her away to Madras, staying behind and leaving only after she failed to placate an angry husband. Pankajam also takes care to emphasise that, while living in Madras, her mother often wrote to her husband asking if she could return to him. One may surmise that it was Pankajam's guilt at causing this major estrangement between her parents, both of whom she dearly loved, and her deep gratitude towards her mother for having braved social censure to do the right thing by her daughter that motivated her to protect her mother by somewhat tempering Subbalakshmi's drastic 'flight to Madras'.[9] For who knows who might be reading Pankajam's autobiography and passing judgement on Subbalakshmi for her near-scandalous act of deceiving and abandoning her husband so recklessly? Pankajam underscores her mother's courage for she knew that Subbalakshmi was indeed putting her marriage on the line. There was no certainty that PRG would ever reconcile with his wife or take back his family.

But what in the early twentieth century, was this education that Subbalakshmi wanted for her daughter that led her to risk so much? Since its origin in the later decades of the nineteenth century, the agenda of female education in colonial India was shaped by the instrumental objective of making women intelligent companions for the young men (of the middle classes and upper castes) who were exposed to western education and sometimes also found jobs in the colonial bureaucracy. As Malavika Karlekar (1986) writes of colonial Bengal of the 1880s, even enlightened social reformers, who advocated female education, held the view that there was something special about a woman's nature, which could be ruined by excessive exposure to education. A basic knowledge of reading and writing in the vernacular language (and sometimes English), arithmetic, hygiene and needlework were deemed suitable for girls, who must not be exposed to science or mathematics.

In the Madras Presidency, too, the curricular needs of girls were seen as inherently different from those of boys. In her book on schooling for girls in Colonial Madras, the historian Sita Anantha Raman describes how training in craft and handiwork was welcomed as a refined leisurely pursuit for girls of the upper classes and an occupational activity for poorer girls. School syllabi were designed with a view to nurture and promote the moral

---

9   When writing this book, I discussed this episode with Pankajam's oldest son, my uncle Ram. He confirmed Mythily's version of Subbalakshmi's flight to Madras, planned and executed with the help of her mother Kamakshi.

and religious instruction of girls, who, it was believed, required neither higher education nor employment-oriented training. In the early decades of the twentieth century, the editorials of Tamil journals expressed the fear that educated women would grow vain and neglect family commitments since 'academic pride' may impede a girl's future life as a daughter-in-law. Tamil poets, eminent writers and social reformers exhorted young women to study so that they might better carry out their 'maternal duties' towards their children and society at large.

The theosophist and educationist Annie Besant, whose views were widely shared by the Tamil and Telugu philanthropists who started private schools in the Madras Presidency, was an influential advocate of female education. Besant valourised Indian women for their 'selflessness' and their greater commitment to their homes than 'fickle' Western women. She envisioned a national movement for girls' education that would see a woman as 'a wife, a mother and a learned ascetic', not the rival of man in the outer world or public employment. The 'modern Sitas and Savitris' were urged to groom themselves to become 'lights of the home' and devote their energies to teaching their children 'timeless' Indian values (Anantha Raman, 1996). It is in this cultural milieu that we must situate the radical nature of Subbalakshmi's aspiration for her daughter to pursue higher education and be trained for a career as a doctor. But what of Pankajam herself? How was her notion of selfhood shaped by school life? Does this correspond to colonial-era debates about female education and why girls must be given a formal education? Or does it diverge from it in interesting ways?

# 9

# A schoolgirl in the 1920s

Homeschooled by her mother until the age of ten in solitary coastal towns, Pankajam's sense of herself, reinforced by her family's judgement of her, was of being a 'dull, unwilling scholar', a 'day dreamer', a 'disobedient good-for-nothing' growing up in a 'household of geniuses'. It was formal schooling that built her sense of herself as a person of some worth. Pankajam movingly writes, 'I discovered myself only at school and my people also began to have faith in me'. School life gave Pankajam a fondness for sports that she enjoyed with such fervour that she organised tournaments in the coastal town where she lived after schooling ended. School was where Pankajam acquired the confidence to successfully contest a 'black mark' unfairly awarded by a teacher. Taking up her case with the school's European headmistress, Pankajam's courage, fuelled by her righteous indignation, astonished her schoolmates and her family. It was in school that Pankajam had her first experience of leadership as a class monitor. As Pankajam makes us see, there was no school activity without her, be it theatre, sport, music orchestra or group dances. Interestingly, needlework, drawing and gardening—the practical arts subjects that were conventionally seen as the cornerstone of female education (especially the fine arts and ornamental needlework), were the only activities that Pankajam did not enjoy.

I joined a school in Thulasinghaperumal Koil Street in Triplicane, which was then the best school for girls. It was called 'Lady Willingdon Training College' (it trained teachers also). It was a huge residence, a palace of Zamindars where pupils up to fifth standard were housed. Meanwhile, a new, modern building was being constructed near the beach facing the sea, next to the icehouse. The school had mostly English teachers, one or two Europeans and Anglo-Indians and very few Indian Christians. My first day in school was anything but pleasant. All the teachers, though very kind, spoke to me in English. The girls also spoke in English. I understood the teacher, but could not reply, perhaps because of timidity. Though I could read English, I was not taught to speak in English. Being shy and silent, I did not make any impression on the head mistress. However, she admitted me to class one. As there were only three months in the last term, she said she would promote me if I did well. To my mother's rapture, I was promoted to class three (a double promotion) in three months!

I studied in the school for six years. And I must say that those six years were the only happy and successful years in my life. I discovered myself only at school and my people also began to have faith in me and in my abilities only after I went to school. My mother being a genius, her brother and my grandmother also being very intelligent, they all thought very poorly of me before I was put to school. I seemed to them a dull, unwilling scholar and given to daydreaming. Besides they never liked my disobedience or independent spirit. I was far too fond of playing in their estimate and a good-for-nothing. So, these ideas being expressed openly and some of them pitying me, I had acquired an inferiority complex. The first few months in school gradually removed my own fears. When I was promoted to class three very soon after joining school and stood first in class, I remember how my mother laughed and cried and ran to her brother and mother with my progress report, which was full of praise for me. This card is still in my mother's box.

Soon after I joined school, a great change took place in our school. A Swiss lady named Miss Barrie was appointed as headmistress. She was a very fine lady, vivacious, fond of children and genuinely interested in teaching. Miss Barrie liked to experiment with teaching methods. She was not one who believed in herding many girls in a class irrespective of their capacities. She chose intelligent girls who answered her and did good work and promoted them to higher classes. In the same year Miss Barrie had promoted some girls to two higher classes, while some remained in the same class and yet others were demoted. The whole school, including the parents, was in a state of agitation. But I benefitted from this change. I was promoted from class one to class three, then to class five and on to class six. In two years' time, brilliant Miss Barrie was sent packing to Switzerland by the English government since her system was unpopular with the parents.

I had by now shifted to the new school building by the beach. The building was imposing, with a huge garden, tiffin rooms where the girls ate their lunch, space for sports and conducting tournaments and space for gardening, which was a subject too. The headmistress and the principal, a British woman, Miss James talked to us and conducted the morning prayers (from the Gita as also the hymns) in the spacious assembly hall where all the classes gathered. Our headmistress was Sister Subhalakshmi Ammal, a keen educationist. A child widow herself, she started taking widows from the villages desirous of education into our school. Suddenly there was a flood of widows among us, in our classes. Some of the regular scholars and young students made fun of them. Children are cruel ...

I liked the vast gardens, the playground and the large library of my school. The library was my refuge. There was a very good library system in which the students were required to review the reading material comprehensively and expected to understand each book sufficiently well to be able to grasp the author's intention in writing that particular book. We were required to read two books every week—I read three. Reading was a passion with me. I would read mother's books, the ones she brought from the university library—Jane Austen, the Bronte sisters, Charles Dickens and many others. Reading these novels made me proficient in English and I topped my class. My teachers and fellow students, unaware of my voracious reading habit, thought highly of me. I stood first in all the subjects in the six years I was at school. Some of the girls were naturally jealous of me and happy when I left school. I had, however, many friends and usually Telugu girls were my best friends.

Our school boasted of many sports activities; chief amongst them was a cricket-like game called rounders. I loved to play rounders. Although I never excelled in any particular sport, I played them all—badminton, volleyball, three-legged race, lemon and spoon, skipping etc. Needlework, drawing and gardening didn't interest me much. What I really loved was the piano march-past every day. From the assembly hall, we all had to march to our respective classes, keeping steps to the strains of the piano. I felt so proud as I marched to class to the rhythm of the piano music. Although forbidden to play the piano by my family, I loved to go to the music room in the evening and listen to other children as they took their music lessons. I was known in school by the name 'Drama Pankajam'. This was because I actively took part in every school play, be it English or Tamil, in orchestras and kummi kolattam[10]

---

10  A popular folk dance performed by groups of women in Tamil Nadu, the kummi kolattam involves a rhythmic clapping of hands and dancing in a circle.

dances. There was not one school activity without me. And that is how I earned that name. Many years later, I was once accosted by that name to everyone's surprise.

There was one tragedy in my school life. It had to do with a newly appointed teacher. She was disliked since she did not teach well and would get angry at nothing at all. One day, some mischievous girls drew a caricature of this teacher and wrote her name beside it. This provoked laughter from my friends and me. Suddenly we were asked to stand up and bring her the book in question. The teacher was furious at what she saw and gave us black marks. Now, black marks were usually given to girls who stole, lied or cheated. We remonstrated but she would not listen. That day, the whole school was astounded when the word got round, since everyone knew the injustice of it. My friends were all crying, but I did not shed a tear.

I waited till evening and refused to return home. I sought an audience with Miss Barry our headmistress. I waited till she emerged from a teachers' meeting and when I had her ear, recounted the morning's incident to her, not forgetting to make a point of the injustice meted out to us. The next day, the headmistress's peon summoned the three of us, who had been involved, to the office. The class predicted that we would surely be expelled. On entering the office, we were surprised to see the teacher in question sitting there. Miss Barry asked her to apologise to us and she did! We thanked Miss Barry and left. We were overjoyed. The whole school was astonished by the sudden turn of events. I was admired by one and all. My family at home was also taken by surprise.

I was made class monitor and responsible for the meals, the tiffin room and class room keys and was required to be in school very early. This presented problems for me. I lived in a joint family and was expected to obey implicitly both my grandmother and Aunt Kanagam, with whom I lived. Each morning before I went to my own school, I was required to escort all my little cousins to theirs first, even though their school was located at quite a distance from our home. Though my school was so near home, I was the last to reach school. I was always dreadfully afraid of being late. The bell would invariably ring as I crossed the bridge and I would be late. I would always be upset, in tears, angry and frustrated. This became so deep-seated that even today I dream of being late to school and feel all the unpleasant emotions connected with this incident in my life.

While Indian nationalists, social reformers and educators had their views on female education and the appropriate curriculum for young girls, Pankajam's autobiographical writing gives us a bottom-up view of a young girl's experience of schooling in the 1920s in a prominent girls' school in Madras. If colonial-era debates about why girls deserved an education foregrounded women's selfless service to the family and community as the overriding rationale, here was Pankajam, who used her precious years of schooling to cultivate her sense of self as a confident, intelligent young woman.

In later years, Pankajam would recall with nostalgia an incident that involved Captain Lakshmi Sehgal, freedom fighter and revolutionary, who headed the women's regiment of the Indian National Army (Azad Hind Fauj), founded by the nationalist leader from Bengal, Subhas Chandra Bose. Captain Lakshmi had been Pankajam's classmate in the Lady Willingdon School. Several years after Independence, Pankajam found herself standing amidst a large crowd on a street corner when Captain Lakshmi visited Madras and toured the city, receiving a rousing public reception everywhere. Hardly expecting to be recognised, Pankajam was delighted when Captain Lakshmi, catching sight of her, vaulted over a barricade and rushed to embrace her, shouting 'Drama Pankajam'!

# 10

# Tiger dancers, acrobats and agitators: Madras in the 1920s

In 1921, Subbalakshmi and Pankajam became part of a large household in Triplicane (Madras). Subbalakshmi's older brother Ananthakrishnan's job in the secretariat financed the household, while his mother Kamakshi managed and presided over its affairs. Subbalakshmi's younger sister, Kanagam, was also staying with her brother and mother in order to educate her three young children, since her husband was working as a lawyer in the town of Dharmapuri. The newest entrant to the family was Ananthakrishnan's young bride from Madurai, also named Subbalakshmi (and addressed as Subamma), who was only about six years or so older than Pankajam. Subamma was relegated to the responsibility of cooking the family's meals.

Interestingly, Subamma's position was rather different from that of her mother-in-law Kamakshi's in the Travancore household of the mid-to-late 1890s. As Mythily notes in *Fragments of a Life*, the young Kamakshi had probably gained freedom and respite from her own overbearing mother-in-law and her two widowed sisters-in-law when she went to live with her husband in Travancore. However, Subamma was not as fortunate as her mother-in-law had once been. Subamma's husband lived with his widowed mother, besides extending his hospitality to his married sisters, who were keen to educate their children in the schools of Madras city. But female friendships could blossom among affinal kin, and Subamma forged a close relationship with Subbalakshmi, who disapproved of the disparaging remarks her mother, Kamakshi, was prone to make about her new daughter-in-law. Subbalakshmi's sympathy for the situation of her young sister-in-law, the household's drudge, was to be consequential for Pankajam much later. But we must turn now to Pankajam for a child's view of the joint family she was suddenly thrust into and the neighbourhood of Triplicane, teeming with the performance of street entertainers and multi-religious festivities in the 1920s.

> Near the Nawab of Arcot's palace was a mosque in Triplicane around which Muslims plied their trade. From the turret of the mosque came the voice of the muezzin calling the faithful to prayer. Certain sections of Triplicane—Pycrofts Road, Tramcar Road and Sydoji Lane—were predominantly Muslim. The Muslim quarters were never completely separate. Hindus and other communities lived side by side quite peacefully. When Muslims celebrated Ramzan, the Hindus of the area joined the festivities, painting themselves yellow with black stripes [*puli vesham* or tiger dance] and danced and rejoiced. When the Muslims mourned in public the death of their saints by beating their breasts and marching on the streets, some Hindu neighbours also took part in the *maradi* [chest-beating].
>
> There were many street entertainments performed in the broad streets of Triplicane after eleven o'clock when the women of the house had finished cooking and eating. Chief among the entertainers were the Dhoma performers. Researchers say that the Dhoma or Dhom are an ancient tribe related to the Dravidian people. They were acrobats more skilled than the circus performers of those days. I remember an infant being thrown into the sky and caught

on its back and balanced for a few seconds with a bamboo pole held by a man even as onlookers shouted, 'Don't do it! Don't throw the baby!' It seemed very cruel to me but I could not help admire the man's perfect sense of balance.

We stayed in a huge rented house in Sunkuvar Street. In most big houses in those days, the front of the house began in one street and the end was in another street—a parallel street. The main door was made of thick teakwood and profusely carved like temple doors. The door led into a corridor that opened out to a courtyard, a *mitham* ... There was a huge hall upstairs with windows on all sides. The eastern windows opened to the sea—giving a wonderful view of the sea, which changed colour hourly. From the western window, I could see a narrow lane cutting across our street ... All the biers carrying corpses had to go through this lane to the burning ghat. I used to count the biers that passed every few minutes as I did my homework.

My grandmother ruled the roost in my uncle's house. The children in a joint family learnt valuable lessons about sharing work and responsibilities. Children had definite duties. Implicit obedience to elders was accepted by children and others without question. The rewards were appreciation and being petted and made much of by uncles and aunts. In summer, carts brought fresh tamarinds for sale at very cheap prices. My grandmother would buy enough to last a year and store them in huge pots. The children were put to the task of removing the seeds from their pods before storing the tamarinds. We loved it for we needed the seeds to play *pallanguzhi* [mancala] and other indoor games. We used to eat the tamarinds too!

We also liked the other tasks set for us in summer. Our grandmother used to make *karu vadams* [savoury rice fryums] and *appalams* [pappads] at home. The children were asked to watch the wet *karu vadams* being dried on mats in the open terrace to prevent crows and squirrels from eating them. I am afraid the children helped themselves freely even before the crows could get them. So, grandmother would set one mat of fresh *vadams* for the children as a price for watching them. In spite of it, the other mats were found encroached upon too!!

When a child, I had unique habits. Whenever anything either happy or unhappy occurred, I would run to the Parthasarathy Temple which was close by to give thanks or complain to the Lord and Sri Ambal.[11] I would talk to them as though they were real people. I thought this to be perfectly natural and ordinary. Apart from learning the violin with my music master, I loved to sing. I had a powerful voice and would often go to the kitchen, asking my aunt [Subamma] to teach me new songs. Soon after music class was over, the children would run down to the beach. Thinking back, I must have been a strong and healthy child. I am surprised now that I, who was so young myself, was asked to carry two little children and escort the other three, all much younger than me, to the rough but inviting waves. We were each given half an anna with which we would eat our fill of *sundal* [chickpeas] and *vadai* [fritters]. We were so happy and content with this treat of savouries, the thrill of playing in the wet sand and wading amongst the rough waves.

My uncle [Ananthakrishnan] took me often to Fort St George where I roamed around the museum with its many guns, cannon, swords and shields. He would take me to see the big steamers like the Queen Mary and other warships, which visited our harbour. And I have seen the manmade pleasures inside the huge steamers—swimming pools, tennis and ballrooms to distract and amuse the travellers! There were circuses too, big and small and grand ones. The most famous were the Russian and European ones.

---

11  A Vaishnavite temple built by the Pallava kings in the sixth century CE, the Parthasarathy temple of Triplicane is one of the oldest temple structures in Madras.

There was a portly woman in an Indian circus [the Tarabai Circus] who had a boulder tied to a strand of her hair, which she then lifted, hair, boulder and all without snapping!

In the early 1920s, the streets of Madras reverberated with impassioned responses to Gandhi's call for a nationwide 'non-cooperation' with the colonial government that had reneged on its promise of self-rule despite India's enormous sacrifices during World War I. Public anger at the Rowlatt Act of 1919 that extended repressive measures introduced during the war years and the brutal massacre at Amritsar (the Jallianwala Bagh tragedy) galvanised millions to public action, Subbalakshmi among them. Always accompanying her mother, Pankajam saw, from close quarters, renowned nationalist leaders address meetings in the Marina, among them Gandhi who 'squatted on the sand in his usual fashion' in the absence of a raised stage in 1924 or so, the Tamil poet Subramania Bharathi whose stirring, 'emotional singing' she enjoyed while 'sitting almost at his feet', and leading Congress members Bulusu Sambamoorthy and S. Satyamoorthy whose 'fiery speeches' she heard but understood little of, being too young. During six eventful years (1921–27) together in Madras, the young girl and her mother (only fourteen years apart in age) experienced an expansion of their social worlds, as they made their way through school life, the library of Madras University, art exhibitions in the Theosophical Society, Adyar and public sessions of the All-India Congress Committee.

In those days, the cry 'Swadeshi, Swadeshi' rent the air. 'Down with foreign cloth!' was the slogan. When Gandhiji asked people to embrace khadi, it became hot for the merchants who dealt in foreign cloth. These included renowned British shops on Mount Road like Wrenn Bennet and Whiteaway Laidlaw that sold fine quality cloth from Lancashire. Time came when they could not sell a yard of cloth as Congress volunteers picketed at the doorsteps of shops, preventing customers from getting in and pleading with them to not buy foreign cloth. Not knowing what to do with the bales and bales of cloth which they had already stocked in their warehouses, the shop owners loaded the cloth onto hand-pulled carts and sent them to the streets to be sold at very cheap rates. Carts came into every street and some people were tempted to buy them. But the volunteers too came door-to-door dissuading them from buying. At the sight of the Congress volunteers, the cart men abandoned the carts and hid themselves or pushed piles of cloth into houses saying, 'Take them, give any money you like.' Sometimes one found oneself left with bales of cloth without even the cart men who ran away at the beseeching of the Congress volunteers. This happened when the Swadeshi campaign was at its height.

It was at this time that mother joined the Congress Party and took part in picketing action. She would return from demonstrations splashed with soap water ... When I was in school, mother would often take me to painting exhibitions by Tagore, Nandalal Bose, Asit Kumar Haldar and others belonging to the Bengal School. Mother also loved to show me Chinese and Japanese paintings. She would take me to the university library with her. As is evident, mother introduced me to a wide variety of subjects, which have contributed to enriching my life over the years. All this was suddenly stopped by fate.

A turning point came in our lives when my father was transferred on promotion from Tuticorin to a place very near Madras called Marakkanam. When my father moved so near Madras, he came to see us and invited us to live with him.[12]

Refusing to leave school, I stayed with my grandmother in Madras, while my mother went to live with my father in

---

12   The demise of Uncle Seshan also made possible the reconciliation of Pankajam's parents.

Marakkanam. I was just past fifteen and turning sixteen and had written my half-yearly exams of class nine when father stopped my schooling and took me away to Marakkanam. I did not leave school without a struggle with my family.

My father, grandmother and Aunt Kanagam were the chief persons who pointed out that I had to leave school and be of some help to my already ailing mother. My poor mother took my side, for she had always wanted me to become a doctor. Finally, it was decided that I leave school. I informed my teachers and the principal, Miss James, who was sore about my leaving. She even wrote a letter to my father urging that since I was a brilliant student, I be allowed to study up to the S.S.L.C at least. The most fateful day in my life was the day I left my school once and for all.

Even as the demand for self-rule gained momentum in the hearts of Indians, male family heads like PRG continued to exercise their sovereign right to reign over the internal affairs of their families and decide just how much education and independent living would be acceptable for their daughters and wives. For Pankajam, the world of school friends, sports and games ended in 1927 when her father withdrew her from school, despite her protests and entreaties that she be allowed to call herself 'Pankajam, S.S.L.C' by staying in school for 'just two more years' as she pleaded with him. The Secondary School Leaving Certificate (SSLC) would have marked the successful completion of school life at the end of class eleven during Pankajam's school years.

# 11

# Home and the world

The earliest 'fictional' story that Pankajam appears to have written is in Tamil and titled *Vidhiyum Madhiyum* (or *Fate and Intelligence*). In the story, Pankajam identifies closely with the central character Kamala, an orphan growing up in the household of her *chithappa* (father's younger brother) in Madras. Besides Kamala and her uncle, the family consists of the *chithi* (uncle's wife) and her three children—an older girl Saro and two young boys. In the story, there is no love lost between Kamala and her chithi who resents the girl for being a contender for her uncle's affection, when she has three of her own children. There is no obvious or glaring discrimination such as a paucity of clothes or food that Kamala suffers but only 'the absence of love'. Kamala's chithappa is wary of displaying his affection towards his niece, sensing that it irks his wife.

It is not unlikely that Pankajam drew on some of her experiences of life in the joint household in Madras in this story. In the Triplicane household, Aunt Kanagam (Subbalakshmi's younger sister, chithi to Pankajam) had three children—a girl closer in age to Pankajam and two young boys. I am not suggesting that Pankajam felt unloved by her aunt and she certainly did not express this sentiment anywhere in her writing. The unfeeling chithi (usually a stepmother), who neglects a stepchild or any child that is not her own, is a widely-used trope in popular Tamil culture, as elsewhere. And Pankajam could have been drawing on this image to construct the characters of her story. Yet the story is interesting because of the way in which Pankajam weaves into the plot some of the tensions of co-habitation in joint families that she briefly alludes to in her autobiographical writing.

In the story, when Saro (Kamala's cousin) breaks a costly *thailam* (massage oil) bottle of a neighbour, the chithi deliberately misinforms the neighbour that it is Kamala who has broken it. The neighbour leaves town and Kamala's chance to establish her innocence is lost forever. When playing games, Kamala is scolded by her chithi for declaring the younger Saro 'out' and making her cry. Kamala is aggrieved as she was only playing by the rules of the game and says to herself, 'If I had my own brothers and sisters, I would have played with them freely.' Kamala's sense of justice and fair play is hurt by what she sees as her chithi's partisanship towards her own children in the distribution of gifts before festivals. Kamala's participation in a school-organised excursion with classmates one evening is disrupted by her chithi who wants her to 'look after the house' while she goes out with her children to Mylapore. Kamala is reasonably close to her cousin Saro, who feels that her mother is sometimes unfair to Kamala, but is too young to stand up for her.

While children were expected to implicitly obey the rules made by adults in a joint family, as Pankajam writes in her autobiography, a child's injured feelings and sense of being unfairly treated by adults who wield power over her and apportion rewards and punishments may yet remain, as Kamala's story suggests. In her autobiography, Pankajam writes of her frustration at having to first escort her younger cousins to school, even after she was made class monitor and expected to show up early. We must bear in mind that Pankajam was a child who could not have taken her grievances to her parents as other children may have done. Her father was in a distant place and unhappy with his wife's decision to send their daughter to school in Madras. From what we know of Subbalakshmi (from Mythily's book *Fragments of a Life*), it seems highly unlikely that she would have intervened in family quarrels to take her daughter's side or anyone else's. Astute as she was, Pankajam would have known that her mother's reserve, her disinterest in family affairs and absorption in a world of books and political happenings would make her an unlikely mediator on her behalf. It is not surprising that Pankajam took her woes and her joys primarily to the deities in the Parthasarathy temple close to her home and 'talked to them as if they were real people'.

By using the identity of an orphan for her lead character in the story (as she did in all her fictionalised autobiographies), Pankajam may have been expressing a sense of abandonment in ways that she did not (could not?) directly write about in her autobiography. Be that as it may, what is of particular interest in this story is the way Pankajam juxtaposes the world of home (the inside, *aham*) and the world of school (the outside, *puram*) and their different meanings for her protagonist Kamala, the unloved orphan. Here is an extract (in English translation) from *Vidhiyum Madhiyum*:

> Kamala's heart was full of compassion and love. Since there was no other outlet for the love that overflowed in her heart, she showered it on her teachers and classmates. School life was a source of great comfort and joy to her and she felt for it all the emotional attachment one would feel for a mother.
>
> Time spent in school was starkly different from time at home. She felt sorry whenever the evening bell rang and she had to head home. This was because the teachers, the headmistress and the students praised her and feted her at school. They say that some adults have two lives. One life at home, another outside. In similar fashion, Kamala's life proceeded along two divergent paths. The English classics say that the most humorous books are written by authors whose lives and minds are filled with sadness. Kamala's life too was marked by sadness and humiliation at home and

joy and good cheer at school. In school, she would laugh all the time. The very sight of her would make everyone happy.

When the teacher came into the class to announce the marks in tests and exams, the girls would cry, 'Kamala first mark!' in chorus. The teacher too would laughingly concur with them. The girls would say to each other, 'Why must we study at all? No matter how much we study, she bags the first mark'. Not only in exams, but in drama, elocution and ball games too, Kamala led the show. Her friends would teasingly call her 'Sita, Maharaja, Budha and Rani'—all the roles she had donned in school plays. When talking to each other, the teachers would speak of her as a girl who had come to honour their school.

When Kamala turns sixteen, her uncle and aunt quickly find marriage alliances for Kamala and her cousin Saro and both girls are summarily informed that they must leave school. In the following passage, Kamala describes her last day in school ...

The day of parting from school arrived. As soon as she opened her eyes in the morning, she said to herself, 'I am going to school for the last time today.' Rivers of tears flowed from her eyes. '*Ayyo*, Nirmala, Lalitha, how will I live without you all?' she thought as she put her autograph book in her school bag. On that day, nobody paid attention to the lessons. Kamala's class was full of tear-filled eyes and running noses. The teachers kept casting affectionate and sympathetic glances at Kamala. 'This is the last time I will sit at this desk. Tomorrow, someone else will sit here. Everyone will forget me. But I will not forget a single one of them so long as there is breath in my body!' she thought.

A fear clutched her heart. 'If I leave school, how will I ever gain knowledge? Will I also become like other uneducated village girls confined to the house? No, even if I do not study here anymore, I will somehow study from home and become equal to the educated.' Kamala tried to comfort herself with these thoughts. The evening bell rang at 4.00 p.m. The teachers, having written words of love and blessings in her autograph book, turned their faces away from their darling Kamala and took leave of her. Her friends surrounded her and would not leave crying. Finally, Kamala extricated herself from them and left the school. She cast a last look at the imposing school building. 'Even you seem to have life today. I feel that you too are weeping for me. My love, I am separated from you in this *janma* today. Will I ever be as happy as I was here?' she kept repeating to herself like one possessed long after the school building vanished from her sight.

We see in these passages the enormous debt of love and gratitude that Pankajam owed and the tribute she paid the Lady Willingdon Training School for shaping her sense of self during the formative years of her adolescence. The reference to Kamala's autograph book in the story was the cue I needed to look for Pankajam's autograph book. To my great delight, I found it. A dark blue, rectangle-shaped autograph book, carefully preserved among Pankajam's books and papers, bore poignant testimony to the social experience of schooling for girls that often ended prematurely.

In the first page, Pankajam has written:

G. Pankajam's book
Containing treasures of love
More in measures than gold and silver
Can ever weigh

Some of the entries in Pankajam's autograph book are reproduced here:

Dear friend, your sweet smile
Was joyful to me

Lo, you leave us, thus
Make our class dull
Alas! When shall again
I enjoy your happy company;
Farewell! Oh my dear
Ever loving friend
R. Kanakam (Form IV A, classmate)
9.1.28

Smiles the earth, smiles the water
Smiles the cloudless sky above us
But I lose the way of smiling
When thou art not with me my friend
I love thee always
As nature is wanted by all
You, my favourite, are wanted by me
Remember, remember your favourite friend,
Alamelu (9.1.28)

Make your life a poem
By sweetness and noble ideals
L. Philipsy (12.1.28)
Lady Willingdon Training College, Triplicane

There is sacredness in tears,
They are not the mark of weakness,
But of Power, they speak more
Eloquently than ten thousand tongues
They are the messengers of overwhelming grief,
Of deep contrition and of unspeakable love,
Yours with love, Visalam T.S
10.1.28, Ice House

To my dear Pankajam
Face unto face, then, say
Eyes mine own meeting

Is your heart far away?
Or with mine beating?
R. Mangalam, 12.1.1928

As the star never forgets to illuminate the cloudy canopy
You should never forget to brighten the heart of your dear
    friend
Never, never forget that once you had a very dear friend
    Lalitha
And think that you still have her with you in your heart
(9.1.28)

Come to me, O Pankajam!
And whisper in my ear
What the birds and the wind are singing
In your sunny atmosphere
For what are all our contrivings,
And the wisdom of our books,
When compared with your caresses,
And the gladness of your looks.
Your loving friend,
A. Ranganayaki (1.2.28)

Rule by Love, Oh Pankajam!
C.B. Jaya (10.2.28)

Therefore, though few may praise, or help, or heed us,
Let us work on with head, or heart, or hand,
For that we know the future ages need us,
And we must help our time to take its stand
Merlin Dias, Vepery (20.1.28)

The following entry is by Pankajam's cousin Padma (called
'Baby' by the family) who was about twelve years old at this
time. Pankajam was also taking leave of her five cousins in the
Triplicane household.

*My Sweet*

Only a simple line
Tender and true
Sent from this heart of mine
Straight unto you
Oh sister darling, have a little
Corner in thy heart
For your own heart's dearest
K. Padma (1.3.28)

Sprinkled among the farewell messages of teachers and students
in the autograph book are quotes from the poets Wordsworth
and Tennyson, the hymn-writer Dorothy Gurney, W. Garrett[13]
and the diplomat and author Sir John Bowring among others.
Pankajam's autograph notebook underscores the significance (for
all of us) of belonging to self-affirming collectives and convivial
spaces larger than the family and household where we may see
our dreams, hopes and visions reflected back to us. They help
us understand Pankajam/Kamala's emotionally-charged leave-
taking from school and remind us of what was at stake for
Pankajam when she lost school life forever.

---

13  This may have been the American diplomat John W. Garrett (1872–
1942).

# 12

## A kingdom of the mind

Having been taken out of school, Pankajam spent about two months in the Triplicane household before leaving for Marakkanam with her father. Since half a page of Pankajam's autobiographical writing is missing in this section, the context is not very clear. However, it is possible that Pankajam's domestic responsibilities increased (as described below) as she no longer had school-related schedules or work. It is equally possible that Pankajam was being trained by the family to manage the kitchen and run the house so that she could take over supervision of her father's home in Marakkanam. On account of her frequent and unpredictable epileptic seizures and fainting fits, Subbalakshmi had withdrawn from participation in household chores for some years by then.

My uncle Ananthakrishnan taught me how to make coffee and light the kitchen fire using firewood. I have seen how the mud oven was cleaned after removing the ashes with cow-dung. So, I did it every day and cleaned the kitchen. The maid washed the clothes as it was too much for me to wash all the clothes, but I had to fold the washed clothes and bathe my little cousins. I was kept on my feet all day, running after the children. The last two of them (three and one-and-a-half years old), I had to spoon-feed and coax and cajole to make them eat. They would want me to tell them endless stories. I put them to sleep by rocking them on the huge swings. I had also to look after my older cousin Padma alias Baby, comb and plait her hair and restrain her from running away to her friends even when she refused to cooperate. She was twelve and I, sixteen. Whenever guests came, I would make coffee for them. Slowly, I became an expert in all this and the news spread through visitors to our neighbours, who were astonished at my resourcefulness.

My uncle, on whose shoulders all business affairs fell, would call me often to help him write private letters and type other letters too. I did not know how to type then, but he insisted that I help him. So, I typed with one finger when he dictated from his easy chair. He called me his secretary. Though my school friends called on me, I could not find time to go to my school and see my teachers. I was a temporary housewife for that two-month period by which time we had packed and were ready to vacate the house in which I had spent so many happy days. On the day I left, the whole neighbourhood and the mothers of my friends turned up saying, 'How is it that you never came to bid us goodbye? We heard you were running the house. May God bless you and may you be happily married.' Thus ended the happiest period of my life.

Pankajam was, no doubt, being groomed for marriage and motherhood by her family in Madras. But what were Pankajam's dreams of a future for herself during these crucial years of adolescence? We turn to her Tamil story, *Vidhiyum Madhiyum*, for a clue. While the story is undated, it narrates events that correspond very closely to those that took place in Pankajam's life after her marriage, indicating that it was written years after Pankajam's life in the Triplicane household. Pankajam appears to

have been using the literary form of a short story to recall and
explore the desires and dreams that her younger self may have
harboured during her teenage years in Madras. For instance, the
evening that Kamala misses the after-school excursion with her
classmates and is assigned the responsibility of 'looking after the
house', she is deeply dejected and says to herself,

> '*Chee*, what a life this is! It seems nothing I want will
> ever come to pass. When will I ever go out like everyone
> else and experience everything? I will study well, pass my
> exams, take up a job and go anywhere freely. Then if I
> should one day get married, I will travel to Europe. I will
> see the world and write a diary. If I have children, I will
> show them my diary.' Thus, she built castles and fortresses
> in her mind. Can the rejects of society enjoy anything
> other than a kingdom of the mind? It is only in this
> kingdom that they may gallivant with freedom and
> autonomy. The minds of those who do not inhabit this
> kingdom are but a dry desert. It is this kingdom that
> stimulates and enthuses the mind. Without it, a mind full
> of ideals and ambitions will shrink, lose faith in itself and
> lose its way in this barren world. The tender sapling of
> confidence can be rescued from the desert's scorching heat
> only if it is watered and nourished by the kingdom of the
> mind.

Interestingly, Pankajam invokes the idea of a 'kingdom of the
mind' through her usage of an old Tamil word '*mano rajiyam*'
rather than the more straightforward '*karpanai ulagam*' or world
of imagination. It seems to me that what Pankajam intended to
convey was the idea of an alternate universe where the 'unfree'
including housewives like her (that she had become when she
wrote the story) may exist and act in complete 'freedom and
autonomy'. Travelling, exploring new continents, writing about
her experiences, sharing her writing with those she cared about
and belonging to a loving family that would nurture her dreams
appear to have been the substance of Pankajam's dreams and

visions of the future. To an older Pankajam, possibly a young mother, when the story was written, it may have seemed necessary to envision a new state of being, a kingdom of new possibilities that would allow her 'soul to soar free' (as she writes in her foreword in 1949), unencumbered by the daily grind of work and responsibilities.

# 13

# Back to the Coromandel Coast (1928)

How did Pankajam adapt to life in the sleepy seaside village of Marakkanam after six eventful years in the hustle and bustle of Madras? With her characteristic candour, Pankajam writes of the heartbreak she endured that was somewhat eased as she came to realise that a life without routine or lessons was not without its charms or comforts either. For Pankajam was one who could and did find joy in the quiet pleasures of the everyday and even, on occasion, enchantment in 'a dirty malarial pool'. Pankajam's autobiographical writing on this phase of her life pulsates with a vivid, atmospheric quality and re-creates a luscious garden, the life of its trees, tailorbirds, honeyed jackfruit, eerie screech owls and a young girl seeking to recover the pleasures of school life in the salt pans of the Coromandel Coast.

Marakkanam is a small village by the side of the seashore. Our salt bungalow, the officer's quarters was two miles away from even the village. Our bungalow stood, or I should say was buried, under great spreading trees. A little further away, beyond the salt pans was the beach. If I had the ability to describe this beach as Thomas Hardy described 'the Egdon Heath' in *The Return of the Native*, people would admire the vast stretches of silver sands of our unending Coromandel coast too. For miles and miles, no man's feet had trod upon the beach. Crow's feet and crab's feet were the only imprints upon this sand ... Occasionally a clump of coconut trees and [a] casuarina grove made one surmise that there was a colony of fisher folk there.

The one year I spent in Marakkanam, I associate with great freedom and being made much of. Both my parents were so solicitous that every word of mine was carried out. Though I was treated like a queen, yet my mind was far from happy. I was depressed and moody for three months after I left school. Every night I cried myself to sleep in bed. During the day, my mind was filled with thoughts of lessons, teachers, friends and the charm of school life so dear to every schoolgirl. Whenever I attempted to laugh, there was a constriction in the heart and I could not laugh. But cunning fate has many tricks and snares to lay over our minds and distract us from our sorrows and frustrations. Slowly, slowly, I began to get used to my freedom from lessons and to being pampered. I had no particular schedule or work or duties then. The leisure and pursuit of what one likes is indeed a privilege that only a few enjoy in life...

Ours was a typical colonial bungalow, with broad, long verandas on both sides. Rose plants, oleanders and crotons were planted around the veranda. On the northern side of this veranda, my father had his table and chair where he dispensed with his files, which arrived after office hours. A few feet away stood a huge jackfruit tree that bore big, delicious fruit. Near this tree my father and I used to play cards, chess, *pagadai* [similar to chess], *pallanguzhi* [mancala] and *sozhi aatam* or unravel riddles, roaring with laughter. My mother used to come there often to peep into a tailorbird's nest which was hanging from a branch so close to the veranda that even while playing cards, I could see the mother bird making trips to its chicks with food in its beak.

Sometimes, father and I would lie on cots in the open veranda from morning to evening, discussing many things, a book in one hand and jackfruit immersed in honey in the other. The sweetness of the fruit and the games would keep me there long hours, in spite of mother calling us for lunch.

A little distance from the jackfruit tree stood a tall and stately rose apple tree. Some Englishman had thoughtfully arranged benches around the tree to sit and read. On this bench I read, while the rose apples fell, filled my lap and were strewn all around me. When the clerks' wives visited us and found me under the trees, they would laugh and say 'Why Pankajam, the *Naga* tree is anointing you with its fruit!'. In the southern veranda of the house stood a very huge tree with thick foliage and branches. It produced giant mangoes of a size I have never seen before or after. My mother knew all the birds that came to pick at the mangoes and nested there.

Beyond the garden, there was a small pond (or a water-logged pit maybe) over which a natural arch had formed. The arch was over grown with thorny creepers and wild flowers. The pond was too small and shallow for lilies, but it was full of all sorts of insects and frogs, and blue and red dragonflies swarmed over it. I liked that quiet shady place as it was idyllic. I would sit on the sand and watch the insects in the pond. There were frogs' eggs floating on fallen leaves and tadpoles swimming with some small blackfish. Water scorpions and water spiders rested on the surface of the water. The droning of bumblebees and the whizzing of dragonflies made a hushed sound … I was so fascinated with this natural bower and pond that I named it 'Fairy Bower'. My father called it a dirty malarial pool.

In one of the big trees in our compound close to the garage, owls of all sorts were living. I heard the screech owls every evening but occasionally I heard a strange, weird cry in the dead of the night, which woke both my mother and me. I huddled near her and she would whisper, 'It is the *oomai*

*kottan,'* (a 'horned owl with a weird hoot' in the bird books).
Now, the kottans were pronounced by everyone to be
inauspicious birds. It was said that the bird's hoot announced
death. The cry of the owl in the night precisely matched the
three words—*kuth-thi-chudu.*[14] The sound was loud and eerie
and we shivered in our beds. The wives of the officers told my
mother to have the bird driven away. You know that my
mother was a lover of birds and we both emphatically refused
to drive it away saying, 'How superstitious these people are!
Why should a bird know or care about people's affairs?'
Suddenly one day, we received a telegram from Madras that
my uncle Ananthakrishnan was in the general hospital,
seriously ill and his condition hopeless …

My mother's rapturous description and animated
interest in birds did not interest me much in those days.
My thoughts were elsewhere. Boredom or a letter from a
school friend would plunge me into a depression. One day
I received a friend's letter describing the annual sports day,
which lit my imagination. I wanted to get up a tournament
too. As my father was away on camp, I sent word to the
petty officer and the peons and explained to them my idea.
I made out lists on what to get and what to do. I recruited
the peon's children from their lines (the lines are where
their quarters were built) and the clerks' children, both
boys and girls. Unfortunately, almost all were boys. I set a
date and practice began. I taught the children high jump,
long jump, lemon-and-spoon, three-legged race, sack race,
skipping, rounders, obstacle race, etcetera, which I had
learnt in school.

After two weeks I told my mother that I intended the
tournament to take place on the day of my father's arrival,
as I wanted it to be a surprise for him. I asked for prizes to
be given away to the children. This worried my mother,
who did not know anything about such things. My father's

---

14  This can be loosely translated as 'stab-shoot'.

head-clerk came to my assistance and bought everything in my list from Tindivanam town (twenty miles away). My father arrived home, found the arrangements being done and was pleased for he was a great sportsman and a lover of sports. Needless to say, the sports day went off very well. All the peons took it seriously and prepared the ground. Three older peons took part in the events of their own accord. One did the pole-vault and the other two were boxers who loved exhibiting their skills. Our garden looked beautiful, full of festoons and children. There were more than fifty people altogether. It was a proud and happy day for me. Afterwards, I wrote a long report of the day to my best friend at Madras, who showed it to the teachers it seems.

In February 1928, Ananthakrishnan suddenly died of cerebral malaria (initially misdiagnosed as the plague) shortly after he returned with high fever from a work-related assignment in Bellary. The household in Triplicane financed by Ananthakrishnan's income was disbanded thereafter. His young widow Subamma returned to her natal home in Madurai with her two little girls, while his mother Kamakshi left to live with her younger daughter Kanagam in Dharmapuri. As Pankajam's firstborn child Ram recalls, Pankajam would later say that it was fortuitous indeed that she and her mother had left Madras shortly before her uncle's death rather than after this tragic event. Pankajam had said on more than one occasion to Ram, 'We were fortunate to leave Madras with our self-respect intact. If we had left after my uncle's death, many tongues would have wagged that Subbalakshmi was returning shamefaced to the husband she left so many years ago now that she has no place else to go.' The Tamil phrase '*pokkidam illai*' that Pankajam used to describe what might have been the case if Subbalakshmi had gone back to her husband after her brother's death connotes a sense of shame and disgrace associated with the absence of refuge.

# 14

## The secret life of girls

Pankajam's life offers us rare and precious glimpses of girlhood from the 1920s. Letters from V.S. Lakshmi, a former classmate and dear friend of Pankajam, and from Catherine Brown, a schoolgirl studying in Bangalore, evoke tender images of friendship among adolescent girls. The following extract from V.S. Lakshmi's letter written in 1928 describes the classroom and its familiar rituals rendered hollow by the absence of Pankajam, who has just left school.

… We all are missing you very much in the class. Whenever we get a free period, we feel very dull because of your absence. All these days nobody sat in your place. Only yesterday a girl joined in our class and she has occupied your place. I can never forget your laughing, or doing all sorts of mischiefs and writing on the board all sorts of things … I saw your booklet and chart. There were marks put down. For booklet you got 15 out of 20. As far as we know, you got the highest mark in booklet. Every morning and in the afternoon when teacher takes the attendance, she calls G. Pankajam. Then we feel sad because you are not there to answer. One day Tamil teacher called me

Pankajam. We told her that you had gone. Then we all talked about your good qualities for 15 minutes and by the time we began our lessons, the bell rung ... Please don't feel sad and be reading as many books as you can and take great pleasure by reading storybooks.

When living in Marakkanam, Pankajam would occasionally accompany her father on his inspection camps if they were held close by. On one such visit to Chrompet, he asked her if she would like to meet an Anglo-Indian girl about her age, whose father was under his service there. Eager always to make new friends, Pankajam was escorted by the girl's father to their house where she struck up a friendship with Catherine Brown and her mother. Pankajam describes her as 'a very intelligent girl in school in Bangalore'. Among Pankajam's papers, I found two frayed and yellowing letters from Catherine, sent from Baird Barracks, Bangalore.

*Extract from Catherine's letter, 23 February 1928*

... I am very sorry we could not have another chat before we left Kilambakkam. I hope we will meet each other many more times ... I've started school again. This year I've joined the Intermediate Class at college. It is a pity you can't be here, we have such great fun. Can't you persuade your father to let you come here for a year or two? I'm sure you would enjoy it and we could have a fine time together ... I suppose Merkanam is like Kilambakkam and you cannot purchase books there, so I am taking the liberty of sending you a few pictorial papers. Please do not trouble to return them to me as I have finished with them and you might like to give them to some of your friends, after you have finished with them ...

*Extract from Catherine's letter, 9 April 1928*

... I am glad you liked the pictorial papers I sent you. The ones I am sending with this letter are all magazines, but

there are some very interesting pictures and articles in
them, which I hope you will like ... I am not very good at
skipping with a rope ... I used to be very fond of it a year
or so ago, but I had nearly forgotten all about it till your
letter reminded me how pleasant it is. I am not very keen
on games. I prefer to sit and chat to my friends. Last year
at school most of my classmates were great chatterboxes
... The teachers used to get very angry with us, and more
than once we were given impositions for talking when we
should have been silent. How used your teachers to punish,
with impositions or otherwise?

Not all the insights into the lives and hearts of young girls
that we glean from Pankajam's life and friendships are about
the expression of delicate emotion or an exchange of ideas and
intellectual interests. We also get a sense of how boisterous and
high-spirited teenage girls in the Lady Willingdon School could
be when Pankajam writes in her autobiography,

I must say that some months after I left school, I wrote a
long, long letter addressing all my classmates and joking
about the teachers in the way we used to. They say that
the teachers were laughing and crying over the letter and
the letter was still going around. Many months later when
I went back to my school as an old girl, all the teachers
mentioned my letter and accepted the hilarious remarks I
had made in good humour.

The visions of girlhood that Pankajam's life gives us are variegated.
We see Pankajam being groomed for adult womanhood and its
accompanying domestic responsibilities such as feeding and
bathing her young cousins, cleaning the kitchen and learning to
cook under the supervision of her aunt and grandmother in the
joint household in Madras. Shortly thereafter, we see Pankajam
gloriously escaping the rigid confines of a traditional household
when she returns to her father's home in the coast. Here, sixteen-

year-old Pankajam 'dances like a savage' and leads a troupe of children on assorted adventures in the wilderness of Marakkanam, with her presence of mind saving the day on one occasion. Yet again, we get a sense of Pankajam's delight in physical exercises, games and the freedom with which she explored her environment.

Once, I mentioned to my father the tents pitched in the maidan when recalling my younger days at Elore and my experiences there. What luck! I found a few men pitching an old, one-room tent in the garden near the veranda. Immediately, I carried a table and chair to the tent and spent most of the day in it, in spite of the stifling heat. I did not know what seized me for I suddenly began to dance wildly, whirling and jumping ecstatically. Our cook and my mother were watching through the slit window of the tent. Nobody knew anything about dance then. So, my whirling about must have been because of my robust health and spirits and the body reacting to it in joy. That is how all savages must have danced with the pure joy of life.

Four furlongs away from our compound in Marakkanam was a small scrub forest. It was full of bushes of berries, which were edible after pickling. I used to go for walks often there and the cook would always commission me to pick the berries. I enjoyed plucking them as well as gathering the small round red and black seeds [kundumani or rosary pea] in the long pods that hung amidst the shrubs. My companions and I played a game, 'pallanguzhi', using [a] wooden board with hollow pits and these seeds. One day, I went to the jungle with lots of young children, boys and girls. I was the oldest, but there was a bright boy who was very spirited and adventurous. After we had all gathered enough berries, one of the boys cried 'Akka, akka, look at that tree, it is full of kundumani. Let us shake the tree to collect the seeds.' I agreed, but we could not shake the tree because it was surrounded by cactus at the base and the branches were out of our reach. The bright boy Murugan suggested that he would climb the tree. I said

'No, you cannot, you are too short and your legs will not reach—I will climb the tree'.

The boys made a wall for me to climb the tree, using sticks to push away the cactus. In my enthusiasm, I quickly clambered up. When I was about to reach the pods, I heard the rustling of leaves behind me and without turning, admonished the boy, 'Muruga, did I not tell you not to come after me?'. Hearing the noise again, I turned and, to my utter astonishment, I saw a lean green snake with a red tongue climbing alongside of me. Instinctively, I jumped, landing in the thick cactus bush below. We all ran home, though I had to limp after the rest. My sari and skirt were full of cactus thorns and the sari was torn. It took an hour for my mother and the cook to remove the thorns from my clothes. I could not stand or lie down. Blood was oozing from my feet. For a fortnight I could not walk, [with] everyone ministering to me. My feet were so swollen that mother feared they would be infected and develop gangrene. By God's grace, my father always happened to be on camp whenever I got into a scrape.

One day, all of us, the whole family, went to the beach. The elders left early and my young cousins (visiting from Madras) and I stayed behind. My cousin Baby was twelve, Mani seven and the youngest just three years old. The elders shouted, 'Come back soon.' But we were playing on the beach, getting wet in the waves and enjoying ourselves so thoroughly that we completely forgot the time. Suddenly, the sunset reminded me that we should have been home by then. I was worried about this lapse of mine and we all ran fast to reach the road. Unfortunately, there was not a soul on the road, as there were no huts or fields—only the high bunds on either side hiding the salt pans. The poor children were scared and huddled close to me. They shuddered when they heard the familiar jackal howls. I reassured the younger ones by saying that we were near the house. They suggested running but I forbade them sternly as I began to see shining eyes all around us in the dark.

Soon, to my horror, about ten to fifteen jackals appeared. Some followed us and some came alongside. Suddenly they all began to howl as the moon was coming up. While I was glad of the moon and moonlight, I knew that home was far away, and the jackals were increasing in number. The jackals were big, as big as well-grown calves. Suddenly an idea occurred to me. I told the children to climb the bunds and get inside the pans, where I knew the peons or watchman would be stationed. So, we all somehow climbed over the mud walls overgrown with thorny bushes, got through the fence and were inside the salt pans—a vast expanse with no bush or tree. But goodness me, the jackals were there too, and coming after us!! Now they numbered about fifty. From everywhere, they sprang up, howling at the moon. Again, the poor children asked 'Why not run?'

'No,' I said, 'if we run, they will know that we are afraid, and they will race us and kill us.'

By now, I was carrying my youngest cousin, while Mani was clinging to my skirt. Poor Baby was terrified and was just praying. So, we all started saying, 'Rama, Rama' loudly, when the sound seemed to attract the animals and they raised a chorus too. I lost all hope and could not even pray mentally. Suddenly, I saw a light in a hut about a furlong away. Hope rose at once. I suggested that we once again climb over a barbed wire fence and walk to the hut. We all stood near the barbed wire wondering how to get over it. Courageous and ready to act, Mani, my cousin of seven, climbed the fence first and landed on the other side, even though his shirt was torn. The jackals now came on the other side too. However, I thought that the light was moving towards us. So, we became bold and all of us, one by one got over the fence, with me carrying the little fellow who had buried his head in my shoulder. We began to call loudly to the jawans [soldiers] who were running towards us, even as the jackals raised their howls. The jackals, seeing the men and lights, ran away. We went home and got a good scolding.

# 15

# Knowledge savoured and forbidden (1928)

In the Tamil story *Vidhiyum Madhiyum*, the legacy of school life leaves its mark on the protagonist Kamala who vows to herself that she will 'somehow study from home and become equal to the educated' even after the doors of formal education are permanently closed to her. In 1928, sixteen-year-old Pankajam, Kamala's creator, living in Marakkanam with her parents, complained to her father that she was going to be an 'ignorant village girl' since he had forced her out of school. He retorted that it was enough if she knew as much as her entirely self-taught mother, who had never been to school, did. The teenager immediately pointed out that her mother did not know subjects like physics or chemistry, but that she, Pankajam, wished to learn science. The remarkable young woman that she already was, Pankajam did not see why the universe of the sciences must remain alien to her, even if many prominent educationists and writers of her times did not quite see the value of a science education for girls.

Some weeks after his daughter confronted him, PRG surprised his daughter with a complete set of the *Book of Knowledge*, a junior encyclopaedia first published in 1912 by the Grollier Society. The 'twelve fat volumes' of the *Book of Knowledge* and six volumes of the *World's Best Books* that her father procured from the Christian

Literature Society (CLS) of Calcutta were hugely formative influences in Pankajam's life.

> ... One month later, I found that huge parcels had arrived and at first thought they were office files as they were so large. My father called me and said, 'Come and open this.' To my utter joy, they were huge books, twelve volumes of the *Book of Knowledge* and six volumes of the *World's Best Books*. I danced and whirled like a child of four and hugged and kissed my father and my mother, whose tears of joy reflected her happiness in my joy. From that day I never uttered the word 'bored'. School friends, parents and walks were all forgotten. I immersed myself in these books that contained everything—history, geography, geology, music, literature, biology, astronomy, physics, chemistry and mathematics. In short, the world with all its mysteries was in the books ... Nowadays we see many modern books better made up, with coloured plates. Yet no other series has been compiled so scientifically, so methodically and so comprehensively.
>
> I must tell you what the books, those twelve fat volumes, did to me. They were my school, my college and the very world for me. But for those books, I would be an ordinary ninth class school girl always. After I began reading them, I felt that the world was opened to me. These books instilled in me the desire to pursue knowledge and love the world of animals and creatures too. I read them again and again and knowledge made me a woman. I knew what to seek and what to appreciate in life. Years and years later, my children and grandchildren, friends and others continue to ask me, 'How do you know so much and how are you still interested in everything and curious and enthusiastic about the world?' I point to these books of knowledge and say, 'These are my guru and they made me what I am.'

In her autobiographical writing, Pankajam identifies the opportunity to cultivate her mind as the rite-of-passage moment that marks her transition to womanhood ('Knowledge made me a woman') and not, as might be conventionally expected, the maturing of the body with the onset of menstruation. Raised in a Tamil Brahmin household, Pankajam's menarche must have been celebrated with prescribed ritual form. Yet Pankajam makes no reference to it in an otherwise open and candid account of her adolescent years. Pankajam's early tryst, as an intellectually curious and lively sixteen-year-old, with the *Book of Knowledge* had helped her decide, as she writes, 'what to seek and what to appreciate in life'. For Pankajam, what was worth pursuing was the life of the mind that was denied to women, forever consigned to their bodies and bodily labour.

Though Pankajam writes that 'school friends, parents, walks were all forgotten' when she discovered the *Book of Knowledge*, a visitor from Madras re-ignited her passion to learn and experience all that she could from the outside world as well. And much of this learning takes place despite the disapproval of Pankajam's father who is unhappy that his daughter, waiting to be married, should throw herself into such unfeminine pursuits.

During the summer, my uncle Subramanian came to Marakkanam to spend a few weeks of the vacation. He was my father's stepbrother through the second wife of my (paternal) grandfather, my father's mother having died very early. Uncle Subramanian was a jolly fellow who was then studying in the Presidency College in Madras. His visit was a welcome diversion. He tried to teach me ever so many things because he saw how lonely and listless I was in that semi-forest life after my school days in the company of my cousins. He had brought a rifle with him, being in the U.O.T.C.[15] He offered to teach me to shoot. I learnt to hold the gun and take aim at the target, which was a huge

15  The University Officers' Training Corps (UOTC) created in 1917 was the precursor to the National Cadet Corps (NCC) that was set up post-Independence.

mango at the top of the big mango tree near the veranda. Soon I was putting iron pellets into the fleshy fruit. After two months, we found more than a hundred pellets inside the mango. I told my mother that I had learnt shooting.

One day seeing the book *The Count of Monte Cristo* on my table, my uncle said, 'Do not read the English version. Read it in French. I will teach you French.' I complied even though I had misgivings about ever learning French well since I knew my uncle would go away to his college once the holidays were over. But he was firm and began to teach me. I did learn and did not forget what little I learnt. I remember him asking me to repeat in French—'The sea is the cemetery of the chateau' ('*La mer est le cimetiere du chateau d'If*').[16] But I think he must have seen that I was not very eager to learn French, but more interested in learning to drive my father's car. And so, when uncle offered to teach me to drive, I was very happy.

One fine morning, when father was away on camp, my uncle and I went to the garage, which was a few yards away from the gate. He took the car out and I sprang into the seat. He went again to the garage, perhaps to shut the gate and before going, he said, 'Do not do anything. Wait till I come.' As I had been in the car the previous evening, I thought I knew how to start the car (after one lesson!) and was anxious to try. I think I must have started and pressed the accelerator, so the car began to move. My uncle shouted, 'Stop, stop!' I tried to, but did not know how to. The car was gaining in speed and moving straight ahead! My poor uncle was rushing after the car with raised arms and shouting. But the car would not obey and I sat in the seat stunned. Nobody could do anything. The car ran on and hit the gate and the mud wall of the compound which was

16  This is the last sentence of the twentieth chapter (*The Cemetery of the Chateau d'If*) in Alexandre Dumas' celebrated novel, *The Count of Monte Cristo.*

soaked due to recent heavy rains. Whatever the cause, the wall cracked and fell into pieces. At last, the car stopped upon this impact. We could not hide the fact from my father because the fallen wall was witness to all that had happened. Thus ended my ambition of learning to drive.

Every salt bungalow in the districts had a tennis court. Our compound too in Marakkanam had a tennis court in a clearing between the *Naga* tree and the mango tree. One day I asked my father, 'Appa, why don't you teach me tennis?'. He agreed and our lessons began. When he had to leave for camp, he would ask the marker to teach me. Once when the markers were playing with me, my father's junior officer, a young man and Anglo-Indian, who lived in the adjacent bungalow came over and offered to play and teach me. I was happy that I could learn the game sooner by playing more of it. But when my father came back, he forbade me from playing with any person other than himself. My mother was very broad-minded and intervened saying 'How can she learn if she plays with you once a month?' However, I never was allowed to play and thus my tennis lessons came to a halt. While both my parents doted on me, I had greater freedom with my mother. My father, though no less devoted, did not want me to learn to drive his car. Nor would he allow me to go to school or college or live in a hostel. Marriage was all the idea he had about my future.

But before this marriage could take place, Pankajam was to love intensely and suffer another heartbreak. When Pankajam writes of the losses she suffered (her brother Raja, school life or her many school friends), she does so without a trace of bitterness. If there is any, it is transmuted to stoic sorrow in the plaintive quality of her writing.

# 16

## For the love of Caesar

Uncle Subramanian found out about my love for dogs, which I had inherited from my father. He sent me a three-month-old puppy from Bangalore. A fox terrier, he was a handsome fellow. He was tall and lithe with a long furry tail and large ears hanging flat. His whole body was silky soft. No one would believe that he was only a puppy, for he was as tall as a newly born calf. He was dappled in colour, black and white. The most wonderful thing about him was his eyes. Oh, who can describe them! Those beautiful large shining eyes, gentle in expression and full of love! If ever love can be called a substance, that substance shone out of my Caesar's eyes!! Yes, I called him Caesar. I will not profane him by calling him a 'dog'. I could write pages about Caesar. But I will be brief, for writing reminds me of him. I still feel the loss and the memories hurt.

From the beginning, he would not eat unless I stood by. Every night, my father let him loose in the garden. As soon as the doors were opened early in the morning, Caesar rushed to my bed and licked my cheeks while I was still sleeping. As I was very sleepy, I would push him away roughly saying, 'Do not wake me, go.' Seeing that I did not want my face licked, he would sit at my feet by the side of the cot and eagerly wait for me to open my eyes. Immediately, he would run around the cot and show in every way that he was happy I had noticed him. After he had his milk, I would wander around with him in the garden. Realising that my attention was on birds and insects, Caesar would bark whenever he spied big lizards, birds, nests and so on. He had a booming bark which could be heard half a mile way. In the evening, Caesar frolicked around me and followed me to the beach or the woods, wherever I went. He was at my heels all day long. He would wait for me outside the bathroom and the kitchen. I was basking in the sunshine of his mute love.

But alas, cruel fate snatched away the most beloved of all creatures—my priceless treasure, my darling Caesar. It happened thus. As usual, my father was in camp when Caesar took ill. He refused to eat and was hot and had fever. We tried to cure him, but did not know how. The head-clerk said he must be taken to a veterinary doctor who was in Tindivanam town. So, my mother arranged for Caesar to be carried by a trusted man. Even when he was taken inside the bus, he made a feeble attempt to jump and come to me. That was the last I saw him—his beseeching look. In the evening, people were whispering to each other and I heard Caesar's name mentioned. At last came the terrible news that, as the bus was returning, the man who had Caesar on his lap was sleeping, and the poor creature slipped when the bus took a turn, fell out and was run over by the wheels!!

This was a second major tragedy in my life. I was grief-stricken and could not touch food for three days. My father, having returned, also fasted with me in sympathy. Oh, my Caesar, I wonder what he thought when he died. Where has his spirit gone? Perhaps God thought I was not worthy of his loyalty and love, and that is why I lost him.

# 17

# 'Are you the man, my girlhood's ideal?' (1929)

In early 1929, Pankajam's father PRG was transferred from Marakkanam and posted to the Madras office. The family stayed in a house amidst the salt pans in Vayalur village, a few miles away from Ennore (North Madras). They would travel during the night by barge along a shallow canal to reach Madras from Vayalur village. Pankajam and her parents also stayed part of the time in a 'French-modelled' bungalow in Ennore. It was in this bungalow with 'lovely French windows with flowers' that Pankajam's husband came to 'see' her for the first time. When fifteen or sixteen years of age, Pankajam turned to poetry as a mode of self-expression and began to keep a record of the poems that she would write through her life.

The First Meeting (1929)

On a hot summer day,
Beside a deep still lake lay
A stretch of green land
The other side a waste land

The sun shone clear and bright
Over a mansion of good height
A maiden by the window watched the lake
Suddenly she heard the thunders shake

Over the sky spread a mass of cloud
It covered the sun like a shroud
Sighed the girl, from the window of the house
Dreaming deep about her would be spouse
She was startled from her reveries by a car
That brought the groom from afar
She was called before the future bridegroom
Small, dainty, she came noiselessly into the room

A pair of eyes settled on him at last
It was a maiden's wondering gaze she cast
'Are you the man, my girlhood's ideal?'
His face said nothing, denied nothing
Her fingers listlessly plied the violin
Her very heart-strings joined in
She left the room, but the shadow of her future lingered
Would it be love and harmony in life,
Or discord, agony and strife?

Pankajam married Sivaraman in July 1929, when she was seventeen-and-a-half years old. She went to live with him after spending the first six months in her parents' house in Vayalur, as was then the custom. 'The First Meeting' must have been written soon after Sivaraman and his parents met her in the French bungalow in Ennore as part of the customary 'bride-seeing' ritual. Although a romantic idealist, Pankajam was not entirely without misgivings, as the poem indicates. She had, after all, grown up in the shadow of her parents' troubled marriage and witnessed marital 'discord, agony and strife' as a very young child.

*Pankajam and Sivaraman on their wedding day, seated in the centre, with
their parents on either side of them (1929)*

Intriguingly enough, Pankajam chooses to speak of conjugal life
and intimacy in the form of fictional narratives, which allowed her
to express a seventeen-year-old's sense of romance as well as its
gradual thwarting as conjugal life gathered apace. The following
extract is from Pankajam's story, written in English, that sheds
light on her wedding and the preceding weeks and months. The
story is untitled, and the year it was written is not recorded. In
the story, Meena, an orphan, lives with her grandfather who is
anxious to find her a suitable groom. The characters in the story
are thinly disguised. The young girl Meena, the protagonist,
takes long walks in the countryside with her dog, writes poetry
and reads voraciously. Dr Subramaniam, a medical doctor and the
man Meena marries, is an alias for Sivaraman, the engineer that
Pankajam married.

The story reveals how Pankajam's romantic sensibilities,
honed by the classics and novels she was raised on, had shaped
her expectations and dreams of an ideal partner ('a Darcy or a Sri
Rama'). It captures some of the ambivalent feelings that a teenaged

Pankajam possibly had about the institution of marriage and her sense of injustice at the social norms that dictated very different destinies and 'natural' characteristics for men and women. Meena's arguments with her grandfather, who is anxious that her 'modern ideas' and 'western notions' might keep her from being a 'good, respected housewife', may well have resembled the differences of opinion between Pankajam and her father PRG. It is not too far-fetched to imagine that these discussions were likely to have taken place in Marakkanam in 1928 when sixteen-year-old Pankajam enjoyed rambling, leisurely conversations with her father after years of living away from him in Madras, as she writes in her autobiography.

The conversations between Meena and Subbu in the story are likely those that Pankajam had with Sivaraman during the marriage and the post-marriage 'courtship' period in Vayalur before they began to live together in Madras. Even while capturing a sense of defiance and foreboding that Pankajam perhaps experienced during this period, her descriptions of the wedding, of nature and the evening sunsets remind us that Pankajam, the writer, remained keenly interested in the everydayness of the world around her. The extract begins with Meena's description of the stories she had heard as a child and young girl from her mother (before her early death), her grandmother and the family's cook. As Meena/Pankajam tells us the story of her life, we see that she was indeed a woman made by books and reading.

Meena's mother told her stories too when she lay beside her on the bed. These stories were about little girls and boys of her age or so, whose games and lives were much like her own. Only they belonged to a different nation. They were American and British children, who had the same feelings of love and hate and underwent the same experiences, as she and other little girls and boys of her neighbourhood. Since the stories of these foreign children were very like her own, she began to think of them as real people and learn to love them and imitate them. Her mother noticed the changes in her girl's life and was glad of the influence that books such as *Little Women, Good Wives, What Katy Did, Mill on the Floss* and the *Heir of Redclyffe* had on her daughter. It was the influence of these literary masterpieces that moulded and fortified, albeit subconsciously, Meena's character. She became a unique girl and later on a unique woman. The stories her mother told her were the ones she liked the most.

Her grandmother was another storyteller. Her stories were from the Puranas—Ramayana, Mahabharatha and Bhagavatham. Meena loved the Ramayana and wept for Rama when he was banished to the forest. But along with pity and admiration for Rama and Lakshmana, indignation rose in her breast. 'But why did Dasaratha listen to Kaikeyi? And why did he prepare to crown Rama if he had previously made some promise to Kaikeyi? Why did he not consult his ministers before he told Rama? He ought to have made it public?' questioned Meena. 'And why did Rama ask Sita to jump into the fire?'

'He was convinced of her purity child, but he had to prove it to the world,' countered her grandmother.

'No, I do not like it. And why did Rama send Sita away to the forest? And why did he kill Vali hiding behind a tree?' With tears running down her cheeks, Meena said defiantly, 'Poor Sita, she put up with everything. If I were her, I would have run away and never subject myself to all these indignities.' Her *paati* [grandmother] would gently admonish her and say, 'All these things have reasons child and you will understand them when you grow up.'

'No, paati, I will never accept injustice for any silly reason when I grow up. I will be like Jo[17] and always fight injustice.'

There was yet another person who told her stories. That was old Valamba, a distant cousin of her grandfather

17  In Alcott's *Little Women*, Josephine or Jo is the second of the four sisters of the March family.

and a child widow. Living with Meena's family, Valamba managed the household. Whenever Meena was left in the charge of Valamba, she seized the opportunity to narrate frightful tales to the child. She enjoyed the fright-filled eyes of the child and the way she clung to her sari, casting frightened glances around. Valamba's stories were always about ghosts, *pisasus*, dead persons, spirits and *vedalams*, which gave Meena vivid nightmares. Valamba was sure that there was a *pisasu* [ghost] in the tamarind tree in their compound and that whenever she went to the well to bathe, the spirit of the daughter-in-law of somebody's family, having jumped into the well to kill herself, would appear and laugh and cry.

In spite of her fears, Meena asked the older woman, 'But why did the daughter-in-law commit suicide?'

'Oh, because her mother-in-law was a nasty woman and her husband a worthless man,' came the reply. Little Meena was angry. 'Why did she jump into the well? She should have pushed the husband or the mother-in-law into it, as they were cruel and wicked,' she said in childish innocence. 'Oh dear, oh dear, do not say such things child. It is not done that way. Women should put up with hardship and neglect in life patiently and never complain.'

'No, Valamba, that is stupid. Why should a woman suffer injustice? If I were that woman, I would have run away,' said Meena emphatically. For a long time, Meena would not accept what Valamba or her grandmother said about how women should put up with things. Meena's heart throbbed with pain for all these injustices undergone without remedy. Somehow, she thought that she would set right these things when she grew up.

Yet another person told her stories too, but that was when she had grown up to be a maiden. That was her grandfather, who told her stories to impress certain things upon her. Meena was growing up and in the eyes of her grandfather and the world, old enough to be married. Her grandpa told her stories from the Upanishads. Meena and *thatha* [grandfather] often had arguments like the following: He would say, 'It is most becoming of a woman to be self-effacing and gentle, child. Remember how Savithri and Sita were.'

'But one need not necessarily be self-effacing, thatha. Why can't a husband also be self-effacing and gentle? Why is a man not asked to be dutiful to his wife?' retorted Meena.

'Yes child, I told you how Rama was a perfect husband ...' when she cut him short, 'No, no, thatha. Rama mistrusted Sita and asked her to jump into the fire to prove her chastity. Sita could also have done the same to Rama. It is natural, thatha.'

'Meena, you have an abominable tongue and perverse thoughts. Stop joking and go and read the scriptures where I have marked. Read the Gita as well. The Gita's injunctions are about the performance of one's duty, every kind of work being sacred. It is the duty of a woman to obey her husband and in-laws and perform her domestic obligations which to a woman is, like *yagna* etc, etc.' But Meena was not convinced. She would retort by saying, 'Thatha, it is shameful that Nalayini was praised for carrying her leprous husband to the prostitute on her head in a basket. It is cruel and stupid. Of what good is it? Men will become more selfish and women more miserable. If I were Nalayini, I would throw my husband and the basket into a ditch and let the prostitute take care of him. I would run away and lead a peaceful and honourable life.' Though the spirit of sacrifice and submission in the stories evoked some noble instinct in her, yet her common sense could not stomach such different rules for the different sexes. Her thatha was naturally horrified and dismissed Meena by waving his hand in speechless horror.

One day, Meena was sitting under the *mahisha* tree, stringing flowers, softly singing to herself the new song the music teacher had taught her that day. Now and then she looked up at the setting sun and the play of colours in the horizon. The sky was soon a burnished copper and the small pond nearby reflected the brilliant red and looked like a plate of *arti* to her. She often felt strange sensations stirring within her at the sight of sunsets and a gathering of massive rain clouds in the rainy season; the squall which scattered the leaves and twigs and made them spin round and round; the sound of birds calling to each other; the dazzling stars in the dark night like a diamond necklace set in black velvet. All this moved her and seemed to speak to her of some message, which only her heart could respond to and the brain could not comprehend.

Hearing Valamba call her, she gathered the flowers and ran in. In the hall, she met her grandfather waving a paper. 'Meena, come here. I received a letter a week ago and this telegram now from the groom's party saying that they will be here to view you tomorrow.'

'View me? Am I a strange animal in the zoo? Why don't you say that they are coming to visit us?' Meena replied.

'Well, well, have it so. But it is our custom to view the bride.'

'Arranged marriages are a gamble, thatha,' said Meena.

'Any marriage is a gamble, child.'

'But is marriage necessary?' asked Meena.

'It is a necessary evil,' he replied.

'But evil cannot be necessary, thatha. Evil cannot be desired. Only good things are desired.' But when she saw her thatha stir with impatience, she changed her line of questioning. 'Who are they, thatha? Where are they coming from?'

'They belong to Kumbakonam, they have migrated to Madras. The boy is a doctor, but the family is not well-to-do. But I agreed because ...'

'Because what, thatha?' eagerly asked Meena.

'Because the other chaps, the I.C.S fellows asked huge amounts as dowry. And also ...' he mumbled.

'And also what?'

'Some want a girl with a degree.'

'Why did you not send me to college then, thatha?'

'You ask the reason. You know why. I have no one in Madras to whom I could send you. But no one can deny that I have given you a very good education …' As he said all this, thatha looked apologetic. Perhaps his inability to send his granddaughter to college had been working on his mind. His look melted Meena's heart. 'And the astrologer says this boy will earn a lot in life.' She said nothing and acquiesced. She trusted thatha and thatha trusted the astrologer.

Meena lay awake long in the night thinking of this great change coming upon her and wondering what sort of person that man would be. She thought to herself, 'Will he be like the man I have been dreaming about since childhood, the kind I have encountered in novels? Let me see who I like very much … of course, Sri Rama first. No, no there cannot be another Rama in the world or in heaven. Perhaps a man like Darcy.[18] But this is too dream-like. Why can't he just be an affectionate, understanding and caring fellow? That is enough. I am no Sita. I am an ordinary human girl and let my husband be a noble person and loving. I will on my part try to be a Sita to whomever I marry. I will love him and his people and serve him till the end.'

The fateful day that was to decide the future course of her life dawned. Dr Subramaniam (hereafter Subbu) and his aged parents arrived. The cook, who had watched from the keyhole, said to herself, 'People of lower middle class. The boy looks elderly.' When they were seated in the hall, Meena was called. She came with a plate full of sweet and savoury and placed it on the table and was on the point of leaving. She was shy and a bit nervous. But the voice of the

---

18  Fitzwilliam Darcy is the love interest of Elizabeth Bennet, the central character of Jane Austen's novel, *Pride and Prejudice* (1813).

boy's mother made her turn. 'We were told you sing. Can we hear you?'

'Do you play any instrument?' asked the boy.

'Child, go and fetch your instruments and give us some songs,' ordered her grandfather. After she played, and while answering his mother's questions, she cast furtive glances at the man who was to change her life. She thought to herself, he would be better looking if his expression was less stern and if he dressed better. Soon she left the room, but the shadow of her future lingered. Fate was scheming to bring together two entirely different, but equally strong personalities.

Meena's grandfather was satisfied because they did not ask for money, though vague and inexplicable feelings assailed his heart. 'She is too beautiful, my doe, for him. But beauty is not everything. If he earns money and keeps her in comfort, that is what is important. And Meena will be in the city and enjoy life as she wants to.' The visitors were also well-pleased. The parents of the boy were struck by the house, the garden and the furniture and the mother was jubilant that they had, by luck, secured a rich girl, which they had not expected. Subbu was very satisfied with the girl's looks. 'She is fair with large eyes, isn't it, mother?' he said. 'The girl has lots of hair and her plait is so long,' said the boy's mother. 'But she is rather short,' said the boy's father. The mother kept repeating, 'Why Subbu, you will be marrying an heiress. You are lucky.'

The *muhurtham* [wedding ceremony] was fixed after a month. Relatives began to arrive a month before the wedding. They not only enjoyed the hospitality of the hosts but also lent a hand for the preparations. Those were times when everything required for the wedding had to be made at home. There were no shops to buy ready-made savouries and snacks, *murukkus*, *vadams*, *appalams* and *appams*, packed in plastic bags. People spent days, weeks and months preparing these basic necessities in large quantities for the wedding. The evenings and nights were gala occasions. Some talented children got up plays, acted and sang. The men, while playing cards and betting, raised a tremendous uproar. The women were either making food or eating, while older women supervised as they gossiped freely. The bangle seller never left the porch. Young maidens eligible for marriage learnt *nalangu* songs from the older women and decorated their feet and palms with *henna*. As Meena was very talented, she joined her cousins in conducting plays. She could also mime. The men stopped their card playing to watch Meena imitate the various calls and noises on the railway platform—'*Masal vadai, paal paal, beedi cigarette, kaapi kaapi, chai, packet sadham, vimto, spencer soda,*' and of course the long whistle of the train and the rhythmic noise it made as it proceeded on the rails. Meena's performance had everyone in splits.

Well, the day dawned—her wedding day. Her right eyelid had been twitching all morning and stopped only after the *thali* [*mangala sutra*] had been tied. Meena had been saying to herself defiantly, 'No, I will not take it as a foreboding. Even if it is, I will prove the twitching is nothing but some defect in the eyelid and is not going to affect my life. I am becoming very superstitious. I will defeat the foreboding and conquer the omen and change its effect by being perfect, clever and good. If my conduct is perfect, nothing will affect me.' By nature optimistic and happy, she forgot the nasty omen soon.

Meena's marriage was conducted over four days in a relative's house in Madras. On the day of the big procession, a coach with two pairs of horses was hired for the procession. The band and *nadaswaram*[19] groups played, competing with each other. There were fireworks in the midst. Some children from both sides of the family were

---

19  A double reed wind instrument, the *nadaswaram* is a traditional classical instrument in South India.

crammed into the coach with the bride and the groom. 'Look there, Meena, my mother is so happy. She likes all this pomp. To tell the truth, I never thought I would be married this way. I have come from very ordinary circumstances. I have never even seen what luxury is. But you are different. You were born with a silver spoon in your mouth. We were struggling for a meal a day. You will have to adjust a lot when you come to our house,' said Subbu.

'Certainly, I will adjust. I like our old ways,' said Meena hastily.

'Much you know about orthodoxy or the old ways. For all his spirituality, your grandfather lives and talks like a modern gentleman. He is westernised and so are you.'

'No, no, we are not westernised as you think! And I can learn from your mother your ways and customs and act and live as you all do in your house,' said Meena.

'Anyway, I like your willingness and enthusiasm. First thing is to adjust to life in a joint family.' he said.

'Oh yes, I like joint families, for I was an only child. I was happy when I heard you had brothers and sisters. How nice it would have been when you were young,' said Meena in all earnestness.

'Nothing is nice when you are very poor. You have to learn a lot,' he said.

'But you and your brother are earning now.'

'My brother has left his job and just floated a company. It will be very long before he can give the family some comforts ...' These were the conversations that passed between the newlywed couple, repeated verbatim by some of the children in the coach.

It was some months before Meena went to live with Subbu's family in Madras. The custom then was for the boy's family to extract as much as possible by way of festival gifts (*seer*) from the girl's parents. The boy and girl were allowed to frequently visit each other's house during this period to get them acquainted—a sort of courting and wooing after marriage. Meanwhile, Meena was expecting a letter from Subbu in romantic fashion. But after two months came a letter in which there was nothing but reproaches about her for not writing and about her grandfather saying that he had not yet bought the car he had said he would present Subbu. This came as a surprise to her grandfather as the car was not mentioned in the agreements. However, he sent a cheque at once to Subbu. Meena was very disappointed by the letter—the first letter she had been expecting so eagerly. This matter-of-fact letter with rebukes and reproaches she threw on the table for thatha to read. After glancing at the letter, her grandfather got up and walked away to hide his feelings. 'Some are not made to think sentimentally and some are matter-of-fact with few words,' he said. But soon Meena's young tender heart secured a pardon for him. She thought, 'I must try to understand his nature before I come to conclusions.'

At last came the day that Meena had to leave her home and beloved thatha. As Meena packed, tears were falling fast from her eyes. Valamba chided her, 'Child, you should not weep. It is inauspicious. Did I not tell you that a woman should control her emotions? Besides you must be happy that you are going to your husband's place finally.' Meena looked up at the wrinkled face she loved, thinking to herself, 'This woman has had no husband or home to go to except ours. What a world and what a society ours is.'

When Subbu saw Meena's packed boxes, he said, 'Oh my, such luggage! Where is the place in our small house in Madras? Do you want all of them?'

'Yes, they are my sarees, violin, silver vessels, delicacies/eatables and books.' At the mention of the eatables, he smiled and looked askance at the books.

She said, 'Come into the library.'

'I have seen it.'

'Yes, but come in. You have never seen my collection of books,' and she dragged him in and pointed out to him three huge bookshelves. 'These are my treasures and they have made me what I am.'

'How can books be called treasures? They are not money or jewels! I have never seen a safe in your house. Where does your thatha keep his money? He must have an iron safe or thieves will rob him,' suggested Subbu.

'These books made me. You will understand many things, valuable things about life if you read them. I will make you read books and you too will love books someday. They are good company,' she continued.

'Where is the time in a doctor's life to read books? Let me first enjoy your company when you come there,' he laughed. Meena laughed too, thinking to herself that this was the first time he had said something nice to her. 'Yes, I will learn cooking from my mother-in-law and prepare nice dishes that he likes to make him happy. He likes good food,' she thought to herself.

Meena's grandfather and Subbu were seeing to the baggage being tied. Thatha went in to get some rope when Meena seized him, hugged him and kissed him. He stood perfectly calm stroking her head while he murmured some slokas. 'Now Meena, control yourself. You must be happy. Obey and serve your husband and your in-laws and earn a good name. I must be proud of you. Remember what I have taught you. Forget your modern ideas and western notions and be a good respected housewife.' As the car was ready, Meena ran to get into the car. The first phase of Meena's life—her girlhood was over and she went to meet womanhood and face family life with hope and pride.

# 18

# The shadow of her future (1929-1930)

Besides the Meena–Subbu story written in English, Pankajam's Tamil story *Vidhiyum Madhiyu* follows the character Kamala, the orphan raised by her aunt and uncle, through the period just before her marriage as well as the first year of her married life. In the weeks before the marriage, Kamala suffers much nervousness and trepidation wondering about the unknown man she is betrothed to, someone she has not even laid eyes on. Kamala's family plans to conduct the weddings of both Kamala and her younger cousin Saro on the same day. Pankajam's portrayal of the earnest, principled Kamala and the more superficial Saro appears to have shades of the two lead female characters and step-sisters (Molly Gibson and Cynthia Kirkpatrick) of a novel that she admired much—*Wives and Daughters* by Elizabeth Gaskell (1866).

In *Vidhiyum Madhiyum*, the two cousins display starkly different responses to the impending event. Saro is eager to inspect the sarees and silver vessels that her mother has bought for the wedding. Kamala says to herself, 'The wedding is all sarees, jewels, pomp and festivity for Saro. She does not share my fears, as she has no ideals to speak of.' Kamala, on the other hand, keeps agonising over whether her husband-to-be (Sundaresan) will be the sort of man who will help her realise her dreams.

'Will he be a like-minded soul and our thoughts flow in harmony
with each other?' she asks herself with growing anxiety. She has
heard of men who drink and visit other women. Yet she resolves,
'However he may be, I will use my intelligence and shrewdness to
bring my husband to line. Do I not have education, intelligence
and character? Even fate can be overturned through intelligence.'

On the wedding day, she wakes with a start to the sound of the
wedding drums with mixed feelings of joy and fear. She says to
herself, 'From this day, he is to be my husband. Whatever he may
be like, my mind has accepted him fully.' Extracts from the Tamil
story (in translation) follow:

> She saw him for the first time when she garlanded him.
> He stared hard at her and she dropped her eyes, blushing
> profusely. The moment she laid eyes on him, she forgot
> her ideals and her dreams. That very second, she lost her
> heart to this strange new being in the garb of a renunciate
> (*paradesi*).[20] It seemed to Kamala that he was paying more
> attention to others than to her. But in the rush of the
> bodies and the din of the marriage hall, she could hear
> only his voice, his words. She felt as if the two of them
> were alone amidst the crowd. She forgot everyone else. She
> forgot everything else. She was conscious only of his hand
> interlocked with hers. Losing herself to this sensation, she
> spent four happy days in the wedding ceremony.
>
> On the first night, Sundaresan asked Kamala to bring
> him betel nuts and said to her, 'We are beginning married
> life today. There is something important I want to tell you.
> When I was a child, we were very poor. I struggled to

---

20   In the wedding rituals of Tamil Brahmins, the groom temporarily
     dons the attire of a renunciate, threatening to eschew marriage and
     the life of a householder and take off to Kashi (Benares) instead to
     live as a sanyasi. As the ritual unfolds, he is pacified by the bride's
     father who brings him back to the wedding hall and his life as a
     householder.

come up in the world. I was not born into money like you. When I suffered without food and money as a child, there was no one to help me. So, I want to keep my house open and generously help and support anyone who needs it. What do you say to this?'

'Yes, we must keep our house open to all. And we must practice charity as well. We must do something for our country, mustn't we?' she replied earnestly.

'You have good thoughts, Kamala. The two of us must lead a life that will win everyone's praise. First, I must save money and buy a house. Only if I have some money can we help others.' He continued, 'I have saved some money so far. I must give a little bit to mother. Do you need anything?'

'I need nothing at all. When you return from office tomorrow, do buy me some strings for the fiddle if you can.' In this manner they talked late into the night, visualising and making plans for the future they would have together ...

Kamala thinks to herself one day that it has been three months since she came to live in Sundaresan's house and yet not once had they gone out anywhere. When he returns from office, she asks him, 'Shall we go out to the beach today for some fresh air?' He is reluctant and resists initially but concedes, seeing that she is determined.

Both were sitting on the beach. As the sky darkened, the moon turned the sea into molten silver. The sight greatly appealed to Kamala's aesthetic sensibilities. 'Look at the moon and the ocean. How beautiful they are! Don't you want to be aboard a ship in the sea?' she asked him.

'Why should we be sailing anywhere in a ship?' he countered.

'To experience the beauty of the sea and the many shades of the blue sky.'

'Kamala, you are a strange girl. What on earth do you see in the sky and the sea?' he wondered.

Looking around her, Kamala remarked, 'There is no one here.'

'Why?' asked Sundaresan.

'I feel like singing now. When you hear the ocean roar, don't you want to express your emotions?' she said.

'Singing? Not here. Someone may hear you. You can sing after we go home. I have also not heard you sing,' he replied.

'You heard me sing during the wedding,' Kamala reminded him in a soft voice. 'Do you not like music then?' she asked him.

'I do. But should a fellow therefore keep asking his wife to sing for him?' he said, getting up from the sand.

'And why should he not?' she thought to herself. But her wounded pride would not allow her to say what was on her mind.

Within a short period of time, Kamala realises that she is pregnant and suffers severe morning sickness.

About six months after the wedding, Kamala noticed that Sundaresan's behaviour was changing. Although she had known from the beginning that he was not easy-going or natural in his speech and manners like other men, she observed that he was changing more than ever. Earlier when he got back home from the office, he would talk to his mother and to her when having his tiffin. He would pass the time chatting. But these days, he quickly pushed some food into his mouth and went out at once. Accompanying him to the door to bid him farewell, Kamala's eyes would ask, 'Won't you take me with you?' Whether he understood her beseeching eyes or not, he would leave the house. Earlier, he would read the papers and discuss with her the news from the papers. But now, he went out somewhere even before she rose in the morning. Then he would have his coffee and sit on the easy chair staring at the ceiling alone with his thoughts. Once, Kamala said to him, 'Today you have not read the paper. What have you been thinking about this half an hour?'

'I don't want the paper. I was thinking of something or the other. Must I even recite my thoughts to you?' he said in a harsh voice. From that day, she observed him keenly but did not try to strike up a conversation on her own.

Whatever work she was doing in the house, her mind would seek him out. If he were in the room, she would follow him with her eyes. If he were in the next room, her ears would prick up at the sound of his voice or his movements. If he left for the office, she would lose all interest in the housework. Such was the intensity of her feelings for him. All the affection she had bottled up for fifteen years flowed out of her and towards her husband like an undammed flood. Even her dreams were full of him. But in her dreams, it would seem that he was always loving and tender towards her. It filled her with unspeakable grief that he did not long for her presence or her love as she did for his. 'It appears that some people's natural state is like this,' she would think to herself.

Kamala's confinement period drew near. In this one year, Kamala was forced to change all her old ideas and expectations about conjugal life. The enthusiasm she had for married life had greatly diminished. The main reason for this was Sundaresan. He remained inscrutable to her. She saw that he did not have interest or involvement in anything in particular. She did not know how he worked in his office. But he took no interest in the home at all. Kamala decorated the house in many different ways and changed things ever so often. He would not even notice it. Why, he did not even notice her. Whenever she thought of it, a sad wry smile would appear on her face. 'He does not even look at me. Even if I appear in disguise before him, he will not know the difference. He will take the coffee and tiffin from me as usual and leave the house. Maybe all this is the result of the way he was brought up. Or the poverty in which he grew up has moulded him in this strange way,' she would think. Or, she would reason to herself, 'He has not had any acquaintance with books. That is why perhaps he has no lofty ideals or high-minded thoughts. I must change him. It will seem difficult now. Let the child be born. Then I will slowly give him a taste of good books and I will open the world to him with all its countless wonders and its truths.' She comforted herself with these thoughts.

# 19

# What of honour and love?

Pankajam's auto-fiction gives us valuable glimpses into the formation of her consciousness and subjectivity during her childhood and adolescence. Reading and listening to stories about boys and girls of her own age from other cultures and countries 'who had the same feelings of love and hate' and underwent the same experiences as the children around her made little Meena/Pankajam think of them as 'real people'. Why then must she alone be subject to a very different fate and be expected to be so radically different? In their arguments, Meena and her grandfather invoke starkly contrasting notions of womanly honour. When he tries to impress on her the idealised virtues of the Puranic heroine Nalayini, who devoutly carried her diseased husband in a basket so that he might keep his tryst with a prostitute, Meena is repelled by the model that she is being urged to emulate. To Meena, the celebrated ideal of Nalayini amounts to a 'shameful', 'cruel' and 'stupid' treatment of women that can only increase their misery and men's irresponsibility. While her thatha exhorts her to act honourably as a woman should by observing wifely duty, honour, to young Meena, lay in escaping as fast as she could from a situation detrimental to her dignity. Sri Rama himself whom Meena (and Pankajam) adored was not above reproach—given the fire-test of chastity he submitted his wife to, when it was but 'natural' for Sita to have likewise suspected him.

It was just as natural that Meena should invoke Josephine ('Jo') March of Alcott's *Little Women* to counter the images of passive, self-sacrificing femininity that she was also raised on. Jo, the most independent and free-spirited of the four March sisters, loved reading and writing, invented escapades and adventures, wrote and staged plays with her sisters and always spoke her mind. Young Pankajam, who was exposed to so many competing versions of female personhood drawn from the Puranas, Upanishads and the English classics, appears to have wrestled with these inside her head and decided that some of them served her dignity better than others. The voracious reading and literary influences that made Meena a 'unique girl' and a 'unique woman' (as Pankajam notes with acuity about herself) had likely shaped her critique of marriage as a social institution that legitimised the subordination of one partner to another. At the same time, Meena's interactions with the old cook Valamba (a child widow in the story) indicate that she was well aware of the fate of a woman without a husband, money or education—she could only be a domestic drudge and dependent in somebody else's house. In creating the figure of Valamba, Pankajam not only renders visible the structures that strip a Brahmin widow's life of meaning or worth but also hints, albeit subtly, at how they coerce all women to fall in line.

The novels that Meena/Pankajam had read since childhood had shaped her notions of love, romance, conjugal bliss and an ideal partner through whom she could realise them. Meena wistfully wonders about the strange man who came to 'view' her in the Ennore house: 'Will he be like the man I have been dreaming about since childhood, the kind I have encountered in novels?' In the stories she told me when I was growing up, a grandchild who would not eat a morsel without a story, the instances of charged banter and courtship that thrilled her most were those of Rochester and Jane Eyre, Darcy and Elizabeth Bennet, Bingley and Jane Bennet and Doctor Bhaer and

Josephine. It is not hard to believe therefore that Pankajam (as Kamala in *Vidhiyum Madhiyum*) experienced passionate love for her husband and longing for his company in the first few months of married life. As Pankajam says about herself, when describing her friendship with the daughter of a Christian doctor as a nine-year-old in Ellore, whomever she loved, she loved with passion. A deeply sensitive young woman, a lover of nature who wrote poetry, read avidly and had a great desire to know the world better, seventeen-year-old Pankajam was quite ready to accept the man she was to marry and experience romantic love with him 'however he may be', as she writes more than once in her *Vidhiyum Madhiyum*. For how could it be otherwise when she was a young woman brimming with the capacity to love and eagerness to savour all that the world had to offer?

# 20

## What he wanted, what She wanted

Like the characters Subbu and Sundaresan, Pankajam's husband Sivaraman came from a family of straitened circumstances. Born in 1901, Sivaraman was one of five children who survived to adulthood—two boys and three girls. His father worked as an *ameena* (lower-level clerk) in the Tahsildar office in Vizhupuram Municipality where Sivaraman was born. Living with their paternal uncle for about ten years (1908–1918) in the town of Kumbakonam, Sivaraman and his older brother attended the town school. Sivaraman's family moved to Madras for the higher education of the two boys. His older brother, who was working in an insurance company, financed Sivaraman's professional education in mechanical engineering in Guindy Engineering College, the only institution then offering engineering education in Madras. After securing college admission in 1923 and acting on the advice of a friend, Sivaraman sent a postcard to the national leader and theosophist Annie Besant, introducing himself as a poor student seeking assistance to purchase text books and providing a list of the books he required. In a week or so, a post arrived bringing the books and 'the best compliments of Annie Besant' to the Guindy Engineering College hostel where Sivaraman was staying.

A workshop superintendent in the municipal corporation of Madras when he married Pankajam, Sivaraman rose in the ranks of the corporation to the post of mechanical engineer. The money that was paid by Pankajam's father to Sivaraman to buy himself a car, as part of his daughter's dowry, was used to settle Sivaraman's debt to his older brother for having financed his college education. Both brothers regarded themselves as self-made men who had struggled with determination to rise above the poverty of their childhood years. While Sivaraman was not given to writing self-revelatory stories or poetry like his wife, he did attempt to write an autobiography, tracing the key milestones in his life from birth to his sixtieth year. Soon after finding a job, he writes of advertising in *The Hindu* and other newspapers for a bride in order to 'get the best girl possible' and eventually making contact with Pankajam's family through a Purohit (priest/astrologer). In his first meeting with Pankajam in June 1929 in the French-modelled bungalow in Vayalur (North Madras), he appears to have been more impressed by the place than by the girl herself.

> I was struck by the beauty of the blue backwaters, the bridge and the bright flowers in the garden. I was practically mesmerised by the bewitching surroundings. I had a great love for natural sceneries. Seeing Pankajam was merely a small detail in the great picture set for me. I did see her, but then I failed to note, at any rate her stature, of which I felt a few days during marriage.

During the post-marriage 'courtship' period of six months when Pankajam continued to live with her parents, Sivaraman writes of wanting to visit Vayalur every weekend (to enjoy the 'great picture', the 'small detail' or a combination of the two?)

> I used to feel like going to Vayalur every weekend. I did not have the courage to do so. I was under the impression that the parents of my wife may not like my going over there uninvited. I had rather a grouse against my father-in-law

that he did not invite me frequently. I did not thrust myself as, by nature, I was reserved.

Pankajam's stories reveal that Sivaraman's family was conscious and happy that they had somewhat unexpectedly secured an alliance with a family that was financially better off than their own. Sivaraman himself may have felt somewhat ambivalent about this stroke of good fortune and the social commentary it evoked.

> Some people used to say I was lucky in getting the only daughter of a big officer—I did not relish being told so. I would have liked my wife to have brothers and sisters, rather than see her lonely. This gives some strength to the mind.

In the stories, the husband is keen that the new bride is made aware of his very different childhood experiences (of deprivation and hardship) and his domestic circumstances so that she may adjust to life in his household. Sivaraman was probably concerned that Pankajam's relative affluence might make her unsuited or unwilling to do what was expected of her as a wife. 'What do you know of the old ways? There is much for you to learn,' says Subbu to Meena. But what of Pankajam's expectations? And how does Pankajam's sense of herself as a young girl of marriageable age in the late 1920s compare with the models of womanhood that prevailed among the educated, urban middle classes from the last decades of the nineteenth century?

Histories of colonial India reveal that educated men of the middle classes and upper castes were seeking wives who would be companionate partners. We see this, for instance, in the historian Uma Chakravarti's (1998) account of the relationship between the social reformer MG Ranade (1842–1901) of Maharashtra and his child wife Ramabai (1862–1924), whom he zealously sought to educate and make a worthy companion. If the men were government employees, teachers or other professionals, an educated wife could serve as a career asset too. In its essence a male fantasy, the companionate marriage, far from being a democratic ideal, could serve as a source of new power that husbands wielded over their wives, as feminist historians (like Chakravarti) have argued. Women were being 'recast' to fit the moulds of the new, emergent patriarchies in the making.

Interestingly, the case of Pankajam reverses this deeply gendered logic. If women were to be groomed and educated (in a prescribed, formulaic way) to be worthy, fit companions for men, here was Pankajam whom 'knowledge had made a woman' and who sought nothing less than a companion for herself. Pankajam yearned for a partner who would share her love of books and reading, nature and poetry. Kamala (of *Vidhiyum Madhiyum*) dreams of a like-minded soul, a man who will help her realise the 'castles and fortresses' she has built in her head. Sivaraman, who was shaped by very different circumstances, was evidently not the man for this. In the story of Meena, Subbu's genuine puzzlement very early in their relationship at 'how books may be considered treasures' presages the gulf between them that was never to be bridged.

Sensing perhaps that he may have landed himself a somewhat unusual wife who might see fit to make demands of him, Subbu, seated in the horse-drawn coach during the wedding procession, hurls the epithet 'westernised' at Meena, an accusation that she is quick to refute for fear that she will seem unsuited to be a good wife. The grandfather in the story insists that Meena must forget her 'western notions' in order to adapt and adjust to life in her in-laws' home. Sivaraman and PRG were not the only men whose anxieties were provoked by the spectre of the 'westernised' Indian woman. As envisioned by the anti-colonial nationalist imagination of the times, the educated Indian woman was required to inhabit a 'precarious position' and a 'self-conscious middle ground' between an unreformed orthodoxy and a 'western' modernity. She was expected to embody a 'modernity' that must scrupulously avoid being either western or westernised (Sinha, 2006). But where did these restrictive formulations leave Pankajam? And what did she make of life in her new household post-marriage? Did she 'adjust' well enough?

# 21

# Neither pride nor prejudice (1929–1932)

About six months or so after her wedding that took place in July 1929, Pankajam joined Sivaraman, who lived with his extended family in Gopalapuram (Madras), consisting of his mother, his older married brother and his family and his three married sisters, who visited frequently with their families. Of his three sisters, two had eight and seven children each, while the third had one child. Sivaraman's older brother had four children. In her autobiography, Pankajam reflects on what it meant for her to be married into a household shaped by rather different social and economic circumstances and, most upsettingly for the young bride, to live in a house with no books at all. Even girlhood could be differently experienced under these circumstances, Pankajam realises. Like an anthropologist engaged in immersive field work, Pankajam provides a 'thick description' of the joint family that she was married into. Her account of her marital home and its social relationships allows us to see the subtly different ways in which Brahmanical orthodoxy was mediated by exposure (or not) to English education and employment in the upper tiers of the colonial bureaucracy.

My husband was ten years older than me. For the first few years, naturally, I was a bit afraid of him. From the beginning, we could not behave with each other in a friendly and natural way. It was because I think of the age difference and the very different ways we were brought up—our ways of life, views and habits were very different. My husband had had his training in early childhood at Kumbakonam. Until he came to study in the engineering college at Madras, he had lived in Kumbakonam. His people were from the village, very orthodox and clinging to many superstitious ways. On the other hand, my people were just the opposite. They were westernised in their way of living, habits and thoughts. Even our speech differed. But I liked the orthodox ways when I came in contact with my husband's people. Firstly, it was new and secondly, and instinctively, in the patriotism of those days, when I felt that our culture was giving way to the west, I wanted to learn those viewpoints, habits, etc. And so, with gusto I began to copy their speech, phrases, the frequent way of using proverbs in everyday speech and so on. When I returned to my parents' house, they were astonished to see that I had changed so much, adopting and admiring the old ways.

My husband was a hardened man of the world when we married and I was an innocent schoolgirlish creature with romantic ideas mixed with great ideals (a legacy from my parents, who suffered in consequence of their idealism). I was innocent, timid and shy. My husband's people began to call me a 'child' or an 'innocent girl'. At first, I felt very strange in that joint family. No one was like me, frank, free or gay—not even the sister-in-law of my age. Their values and views, as I said before, were entirely different from what I knew at home. But I adjusted and adapted to their ways and became friendly with the younger relatives soon. I was eager to do housework and learnt the work quickly. Though they laughed at my innocence, they began to admire my helpfulness, my humility, my generosity and my affection for all of them.

I liked the joint family. I liked my mother-in-law, sisters-in-law and their children. It amused me to watch their conversations and quarrels too. I admired my mother-in-law for her beautiful voice and singing. She would sing away throughout the day while she cooked and went about the other chores. I admired her cooking too. My father-in-law I never knew, for soon after my marriage, he died. My brother-in-law was a stern man, of whom everyone, including his mother, stood in awe. He was not easily approachable. His main aim was to make money. He worked hard and was very industrious. He started an insurance company of his own which grew very big and proved a great success. He dabbled, always successfully, at many things. He ran a school for some years and even bought a farm and made it yield much, working away as if he was a farmer. He never resisted manual labour as he was brought up the hard way. His parents were not rich and he had had sisters to marry off. He took on the responsibility of the family when quite young. He was a man of action and had abundant faith in himself. One could not help admiring him for his tenacity, purpose and energy. Even though he appeared to be rough and formidable outwardly, he had a tender heart inside, which never showed. In that family, he was the only one who would fetch my violin to me and ask me to play.

I have nothing to complain about my husband's relatives. They were good to me because I did whatever they required of me and behaved with respect and affection to one and all. I must say a word about the children there. They were many and of all ages. I began to take care of them and they took to me also. They had none to love them and be friendly with them. I loved children and even now, at the age of seventy-five, I love them as much as ever. So, they took to me and began to follow me about. It was a vast relief to the elders to leave the children in my care. It amused them to watch me bathe the children, dress and feed them and play with them. There was a girl of eight years named Rajam, my brother-in-law's daughter, who became very attached to me. I used to dress her up as Lord Krishna, taught her songs, told her stories and played with her. She stuck to me throughout her girlhood till she married. Later in life, she would often run away to our house from her father's place and refuse to go home.

I had a few private problems at first in that house. One was my hair. It was a problem, for it was very thick and long, resembling the long hair of women advertised on the bottles of hair oil. Until I came to live with my husband's people, my mother or my grandmother attended to my hair. So, I never knew then how to plait my hair or how to take an oil bath by myself. For a few days, I just smoothed the hair on my forehead, never daring to untie the plait. Soon my sister-in-law found out to the amusement of everyone. My second problem was the lack of privacy. No one seemed to care about it or want privacy. The bathroom did not even have a door. However, I never complained about this to anyone and adjusted by copying what the others did.

Another problem was the lack of anything to read. My husband's relatives could not understand my passion for reading. I read whatever I could snatch, even the textbooks of the children in that house. My brother-in-law had no time to read and my husband was no lover of books, so there was no book there at all. Out of sheer necessity, I began to read my brother-in-law's insurance company law books and knew by heart the premium tables. And I began to read my husband's old engineering books, about how to mix concrete and about machinery, engines and cars, to the amusement of my in-laws whenever they caught me at it.

Before I could read my husband or understand him fully and the meaning of our lives, I found myself a mother. I became so absorbed in my infant boy and thought that the world had only waited for his arrival. This event completely changed my life. All disappointments in my married life receded for the time being, leaving the babyish face and coos and caws my only rewards and the baby's work, my only goal in life. But it did not entirely make me forget other things. Instead of the child drawing us together, my husband and I were drifting away from each other. He was engrossed in his bodily needs and introverted. Slowly, it began to dawn on me that my husband's needs and his ways were different and that he was a man who did not need a companion. He had no friends and would not visit anyone, nor did anyone come to our house. He kept to himself even when we were in a joint family.

I tried to attend on him more and more and to show love and understanding but strangely, he spurned my attitude. He never seemed to want anything from me. He was increasingly absorbed in his own self. Indeed, he was to be tyrannised by his body—the thralldom from which he could never escape, never become free till the end. To him, earning money and eating well were the only things that mattered. Well, there was nothing wrong with it and I began to accept his meagre allowance and run the household within it. Before I became a mother of two, I knew we could not keep a nice drawing room in the modern way with curtains and good furniture. Our house, in spite of all my efforts, was only better than the Kumbakonam house, as my husband used to proudly say. Soon I too came to see it with indifference. My children were my only solace. They kept me from worrying about other things. They preserved my sanity. But for them, I would have gone nuts. They tied me down to hard realities, gave me no time for anything else. Made me endure things.

While seventy-five-year-old Pankajam,[21] writing of the first year of her married life, describes her marital household as 'superstitious' and 'orthodox' in its quotidian habits and customs, eighteen-year-old Pankajam thought it her patriotic duty to identify with a more provincial way of life associated with Brahmin families that had only recently migrated from the village and small towns. We may therefore see Pankajam's embrace of the 'old ways' that were

---

21  By writing 'Even now in my seventy-fifth year …' Pankajam lets us know when this piece was written.

giving way to the new as an incipient form of resistance against the 'West', then closely aligned with the colonial power that was being fought on the streets and in the minds of its subjects. Pankajam's writing also hints at how her sense of the relationship between family and nation, in this case a nation-in-movement that was in the throes of struggle and birth, shaped the way she saw her marital family (as rooted in the village and more authentic perhaps than her own city-bred family) and her place within it. If Pankajam admired the 'old ways' that her husband's family embodied, her years of school education and her ability to speak and read English greatly impressed her husband's older brother and won her his respect. After the death of his first wife who bore him four children, he re-married and sent his second wife and his youngest daughter to college together.

Pankajam's two 'fictional' stories as well as her first-person account of the early days of her marriage help us glimpse the fissures that marked her marriage. Fortunately, for Pankajam, as her autobiographical account indicates, she was the sort of person who did not crave the comfort of the familiar, but thrived in an alien environment, enjoying challenges and opportunities for new experiences and learning. Pankajam has told my cousin Padmavati that she would wear multiple rings on her fingers as a young bride. In her enthusiasm, she would beg her sisters-in-law to let her have a turn at grinding the chutney on the grinding stone. They would point out that she would have to remove her many rings before she could do so! Pankajam's autobiographical account paints for us a picture of a young bride whose affectionate nature, enthusiasm for housework and physical labour, devotion to children and joyful embrace of new challenges, endear her to her husband's family. More ominously, she hints at what lies in store for an 'innocent schoolgirlish creature with romantic ideas' who weds 'a hardened man of the world'. While Pankajam alludes to her disappointments, she does not quite explain the worries that beset her or why she was in danger of losing her sanity, as she writes. For that, we must turn to another story that Pankajam wrote which fills the silences in the autobiography.

# 22

## How to live without love? (1929–1932)

This story, written in English, is untitled, undated and begins like the Meena–Subbu story. Lakshmi, the key protagonist, a mother and grandmother, looks back on her life on the occasion of her golden wedding anniversary. A mother of five children, she is married to Ramanathan, an engineer. Early in the story, it is made clear to the reader that the marriage was a rocky one. On the day of the anniversary, Lakshmi's children comment with sarcasm that 'Mother and father seem to have pulled on together for fifty years willy-nilly in spite of their rows.' The older daughter adds, 'How much mother has sacrificed and suffered! It is only because of her forbearance this marriage has survived.' Lakshmi remembers the day she came to that very house as a newly-wed bride. Pankajam writes, 'Lakshmi thought of the first night and its dissolutions and mortifications, but without a beating heart and in a quiet survey of the tragedy that was her life. Tragedy or comedy, she wondered without emotion.'

Like the Meena–Subbu story, Lakshmi, an orphan, lives with her grandfather who is anxious to quickly arrange a marriage for her, given his advancing age. The household consists of Lakshmi, her doting grandfather and the cook Chellamal who loves the girl deeply too. The young Lakshmi spends her evenings on the beach with her dog, a fox terrier named Caesar that 'Lakshmi loved only next to her thatha, even as the dog loved Lakshmi first and placed her even above himself for dogs have superb hearts full of love the like of which you cannot find in a human breast'. Lakshmi is described as an ardent lover of nature, who can identify birds from their call and their chirping. She asks her grandfather to subscribe to science magazines as she has read all the (outdated) books in his library and is eager to learn about quasars and the latest theories about stars and the origin of the universe. While her thatha agrees to get them for her, he urges her to go into the kitchen and take cooking lessons as her marriage may take place any day and she must be a 'good housewife'. When thatha tells Lakshmi about the prospective groom Ramanathan, Lakshmi wishes he were not an engineer, but a 'literary man'. There is little doubt that Lakshmi is, indeed, Pankajam.

Once the marriage is fixed, Lakshmi begins to dream about life in the 'great city' of Madras where she will be happy, reigning as a queen in her own house, loved by her husband and her children. The extract from the story begins on the wedding day:

> She forgot all her fears and forebodings as the day approached. And she was supremely happy on her wedding day. She went to the altar very happy—even the sheep feel uneasy when they go for slaughter, but Lakshmi did not feel any fear or portent. She went about so innocently. Were the gods laughing? Was fate tricking her? But none of these thoughts entered her head as she went to her husband's house after the wedding, with so much love in her heart for her husband and his mother. She thought to herself, 'I must be an exemplary daughter-in-law. People make fun of my mother-in-law as a country woman, but I am going to make her happy by loving her and then she will love me also. It is not necessary that mothers-in-law should hate their daughters-in-law. See what I am going to make of my mother-in-law and husband!' With this determination, she began her married life.

When Lakshmi entered the bedroom on the first night of her wedding, she really melted in love for her husband. Even Ramanathan's coarse nature dimly felt something great and unusual. He said, 'Oh, do not love me like that and do not make me a hero! I am not. I am an ordinary person.'

'You may think that, but to me, you are Sri Rama himself. I shall make you happy as long as I live. You need looking after. You go around the city's pumping stations and you must take more milk and fruits. I shall see to your food from tomorrow.'

'Oh, do not make me a baby. I am alright. There are no cows here like at your grandfather's. And my mother will expect you to help her.'

'Why I am going to cook and make your mother rest completely. I will look after the house and her too. She is my mother too now.' Lakshmi said this with such pride and intention that Ramanathan could not help remarking, 'You are really a very good girl. Amma said you would be and it is true.'

Then suddenly Ramanathan said, 'Come Lakshmi, let us pray for a noble son—like the Buddha.' This struck her as very strange. 'Why do you desire our first child to be a *sanyasi* [renunciate]? I want grandchildren too.'

'I did not mean a sanyasi, but let us pray for a boy who is chaste and I am sure you will see to it that he is a true *brahmachari* [celibate] until his marriage. You are an innocent, pure, unworldly girl. I trust you to bring up our child in a proper and protected way.' Why he said all this did not trouble her much then, but later on when she discussed everything with her grandfather, this became clear to her.

Lakshmi was an innocent prude and all her knowledge of love and sex were from books, classics and also some sex books that her grandfather had hidden, unsuspecting that she had ever looked at them (they were all scientific treatises). Yet she felt that in love-making, Ramanathan lacked gentleness, consideration and refinement. He was coarse and impatient in this too, as in all other things. But to Lakshmi, love overflowed and she always, then as in daily life, showed solicitude and gentleness. She began to observe and take an interest in all that he did. Two nights after her wedding day, she suddenly woke up from sleep around 4.00 a.m. She looked around and found her husband's bed empty. Suddenly she saw her husband enter, not from the bathroom, but from the main entrance. Half-sleepily, she asked him, 'Where have you been so early?'

'I heard something from the garden and went to see. It is nothing, go to sleep.'

The next night too she awoke to a distinct noise. Noticing her husband's bed empty, she looked out of the window. The sight she saw stunned her. She could see their maid Raji and her husband standing close. Instinct made her duck her head and watch from a corner of the window. She saw them both disappear into the tool shed in the garden. She waited with her heart beating against her brow as if it would burst and she stood there for how long and why she did not know. The power to think deserted her. Dully she saw them emerge from the hut and her husband climb the steps upstairs. 'Why are you lying there and staring at the roof? Look at me—I went for a long, refreshing walk. Go down and bring me coffee. I am thirsty.' And he went into the bathroom. The whole day Lakshmi went about her work in a sort of stupor that made her mother-in-law ask what was the matter with her. When she tried to think of it, her mind thrust back the terrible possibility of her husband's infidelity and her heart refused to accept it, though reason told her it was a fact.

Ramanathan noticed a change in his wife, the silent, sorrowful face was different from her usual frolicking nature. She never sang as she used to while working and did not come often to his room asking whether he wanted this and that. He did not so much as suspect that she had seen anything but her getting up at 4.00 a.m. worried him and inconvenienced him. So that night he told her, 'Did you hear mother coughing all night? She said she has fever. You sleep with her from today. I will keep the door open and call you.' And before he could finish, she said, 'There will not be any necessity,' so softly that he could not catch it. He thought she was in a bad mood and continued, 'What happened? You went to the doctor this morning? What did he say?'

'What he said would have carried me to the seventh heaven of happiness yesterday, but today it is no good news to me.' She said this again in so low a tone that he failed to catch it.

'Are you pregnant or not?' he asked bluntly. 'Yes,' she said in an indifferent tone, which he mistook for shyness. 'Well, I am glad for you, because you wanted children. For my part, I do not care for them. I have seen my sisters giving birth to brats all the time and I used to find the house too noisy. But I see that to you, a child means something. I only hope it is a boy, and a good boy, with a proper idea of morality like you. I hope he will take after you and not me.' With this he left for the office. Now Lakshmi understood why he said all this about the child. 'So at least he repents. Then, I can bring him around. Yes, with tact I will do it. And I am going to win. I am going to wean him away from this habit. He has had no proper guidance in youth. I shall transform him. See if I don't,' she vowed to herself and the sky seemed to clear and her heart lighten.

Though from that day Ramanathan slept alone and Lakshmi slept with her mother-in-law, she did not resent it. She tried to get into his heart by other means. Young and inexperienced though she was, she began to see that sex meant something to her and something else to her husband. To her, it must follow love. And to him it was just an obsession, something to be got rid of, no matter who the person was. All he wanted was relief, being an extraordinarily healthy man with vigour and full-blooded too. Lakshmi asked her husband one day to drop her at the university library on his way to the office. With the help of the librarian, she hunted out books on sex, scientific books on the sex habits of men (by Dr Havelock Ellis[22] and Dr Marie Stopes). And she hunted for books on child rearing—their ailments and nutrition. Laden with these, she got home.

Ramanathan's glance first fell on the sex books. 'Why did you bring them?' he asked while he picked up the books. He laughed aloud and pointed to a paragraph in Marie Stopes' book, where it was said that some healthy men had sexual urges even up to six times a day and it was not harmful if they could stand it. 'What is your opinion of it?' he asked. She felt wrathful at fate that had brought that particular paragraph to his sight. From that day, Ramanathan seemed to lose even his guilt and began to pride himself on his energy. But still Lakshmi did not lose hope. She read the books and dressed herself attractively in the evenings even though no one took her out. And when her husband appeared after his usual evening walk, she would take him a plateful of fruit and talk to him pleasantly, asking about his office problems, which he never shared with her. She made light and pleasant conversation and made comments on news from the papers. Although indifferent to her attentions, he listened silently—never commenting much. After sometime, she noticed that he did not even listen to her and was preoccupied. After the first few months of marriage, he clean neglected her. Her act of seeking him out in the evenings and picking up

---

22  Havelock Ellis (1859–1939) was an English physician who studied sexual behaviour and challenged Victorian-era taboos about public discussions of the subject.

conversations with him began to irk him. He stopped inviting her to bed even once in two months.

When the situation was like this, her confinement drew near. It was decided that Lakshmi would go to her grandfather's house for the delivery. Once again, Lakshmi entered her childhood home. The cook Chellammal and thatha vied with each other in making things comfortable for her. Yet she felt that the house was strange—it did not belong to her anymore. And suddenly it dawned on her how happy she had been during the sixteen years she had spent in that house. How carefree and how well-loved! Did anybody love her in Madras? How to live without love? And yet it was given to her to live without love.

Well, the baby was born and without much problem, for Lakshmi was a very healthy girl. It was a boy. Oh, how pretty he was, with dark hair and lovely eyes and chubby little fingers! From the moment Lakshmi set eyes on him, her attitude to life changed. She felt proud as a queen as if she and only she had given birth to a boy! She never for a moment took her eyes off the tiny little flesh nestling against her in the cot. It was supreme satisfaction to watch him sip his milk from her and the touch of his little head against her sides sent titillations all over her body. 'Here is heaven, here is some rare gift given by God to me in all his love and sympathy. It does not matter if the father of the child loves me or not. I will defy the whole world with this child in my arms.' Such was her passionate love for the infant.

In the story, Lakshmi takes both Chellamal and her grandfather into her confidence regarding Ramanathan's infidelity. Both dissuade her from ever leaving Ramanathan. The story continues …

'… If he wants to go to other women, he is welcome to. I have my baby and I am going to ignore him,' said Lakshmi.

But the wise Chellamal shook her head, 'You should not say so, Lakshmi. Perhaps in some years, he might change and give up his bad habits. Besides if you ignore him, he might leave you and what will become of you?'

'Why if he left me, I can be free of him too and come here and be happy.'

'But you forget—there is no school here and you must educate your son. And your son must have a father too. You are young and thatha will die in a few years. You will be without protection,' argued Chellamal. 'And grandfather has neglected to give me any education that matters. I am not even an S.S.L.C and who cares about my general knowledge?' thought Lakshmi to herself.

That night she opened the subject with her grandfather, who did not seem to be surprised at all. 'Two months back, I went to Kumbakonam where people who did not connect me to your husband gave me bad reports about him. I did not want to disturb your peace. I waited for you to find out'

'But thatha, how could you be so complacent about it? Don't you think it is a matter of life and death to me?'

'It should not be, child. I can understand your feelings being so hurt. But life holds the bad and the good and you have to compromise with it.'

'No, no I am not compromising and I do not care for an unjust, bad life in this world!'

But thatha continued, 'For your son's sake, you have to endure it. You are a Hindu woman, Hindu wife and mother. Remember Savithri, Sita and Nalayini.'

'If I had a husband like Sita, I would not fear even hell and patiently serve and love my husband. But I cannot pretend to love a rake and play Nalayini. She was invented by wicked men who wanted to pursue their own inclinations and desired obedient slaves for wives. This is the twentieth century and I am a modern girl,' came the rebellious words.

'No, you are not a modern girl in practice, but only in mind. Your mind is liberated by reading literature. But you forget, you are not educated enough to take up a job like the girls of Madras. And you have no brother, sister, uncle or anyone to lean on and ask for help and advice. And I want to warn you that your husband is not an ordinary fool who just goes after women. He is a very clever, cantankerous man who can be ruthless to his enemies and root out all obstacles to gain a good name. He wants to pass off for a moral, normal householder. You are no match for him in any way. So, you have to endure it. Endure it, forget about it, put up with it, carry on with your household chores and find comfort in your child.' Lakshmi saw the wisdom of her grandfather's words and wondered how he had understood her husband's character even without knowing him well. 'Well, perhaps thatha is right—there is no other way, at present at any rate. I shall think about it later and find a way out,' she thought.

'Thatha, I am going to try *saama, dhaana, bedha, dhandam*[23] ways to reform my husband,' were her words when she left for Madras with her baby. Though the child occupied most of her time, she tried to be pleasant to her husband, dress well and draw him towards the child. One evening, when she saw him start for his evening walk, she said, 'Please wait—I will come with the baby too. Let us push the pram and go together. Look at our neighbour— she and her husband always go together for walks.'

'Oh, you want to become a fashionable lady and parade with the baby and me. But you can go alone. I do not like to go with you.' But when he saw her face fall and the neighbours come along, he said 'Well, come with me today. But do not make it a habit.'

'Why not? All couples go together.'

'But I do not want you,' came the stern reply. And Lakshmi went silently pushing the pram.

---

23  Tactics of pleading, bribing, coax/cajoling and eventually punishing someone into compliance.

On this fateful walk, Ramanathan leaves Lakshmi alone on a park bench and proceeds towards a hut in a secluded corner of the park. Lakshmi follows him and catches him red-handed with a woman. The story continues:

It annoyed Ramanathan to be caught red-handed and he fell foul on her. 'Who asked you to come after me? Are you policing me? Come home—I will give you a good thrashing which you will remember for life.' When Lakshmi reached home, she found her husband standing in the doorway. 'Come upstairs, I want to thrash you.'

'Yes, I will come presently. Just wait till I leave the boy at my friend's house across the road. Do not hurt the child—do anything to me.' The boy was one year old but uncannily clever and too fond of his mother. She ran with the baby to her friend. 'Radha, please keep the baby. If anything happens to me, hand him over to my grandfather.' And she went up to her husband's room. He stood glaring at her and with his belt gave her two or three hard blows. She never so much as winced and stood smiling. She did not stir or evade the blows. After three or four blows, something in her eyes and her manner must have made him feel ashamed. He left off beating her and said, 'Go now. Never again follow me or you will have to leave this house.' And henceforth, he became bolder in his ways as he knew that she knew.

After this, Lakshmi never crossed his path. She ceased to care about where he went or what he did. She was absorbed in the child. One night, when her boy was one year and more, Ramanathan called to her to bring him water. When she left the safety of her mother-in-law's bedroom, she was frightened. He caught hold of her hand and said, 'Come to bed. We have not been together for over a year'. She thought quickly—yes, it was raining very hard. That is why he had sought her out that day for he could not go down to the tool shed or elsewhere. She pulled her hands away from him and said, 'No, I am sleepy—the child wants me.' But he dragged her to the bed. She pushed him vehemently saying, 'I do not want any more children.' She dared not say anything else or make a scene as her mother-in-law was in the next room. He mistook her unwillingness as not wanting children and said, 'Once in a year or so will not give you a child.' Seeing no other way, she succumbed to him, hating herself for her weakness and her wretched situation. Her whole body revolted. Was it rape? It was.

Lakshmi became pregnant again. Just because she lived under the roof of her husband, she had to occasionally subject herself to him, whenever he could not obtain sex from other sources. When it rained heavily or when she left for her grandfather's place once a year and came back after six months, this repugnant thing happened. One day, she even told him, 'You do not have to come to me once a year as a concession. I do not need your sympathy or pity. I am not a sex-mad woman. I do not want sex. I can get along without it normally.' She threw these words at him one day when he blocked her way and said, 'It is a long, long time since I saw you in my room. Come in.'

'Do not come to me because you imagine I am waiting for you every day. I never think of you or of sex. Is your brain capable of understanding this?'

He stopped and thought and said, 'Yes, I know you are not waiting for me—I know you do not care for sex.' But fierce came the reply unbidden from the depths of her heart, 'I do care for sex and it is a beautiful experience. But not lust. Love and loyalty must precede sex or it is only a rape.' He never tried to understand her words but just bent her to his brute strength whenever he wanted. He never could distinguish between lust and love. To him, everything meant sex.

Thus the years passed—Lakshmi becoming pregnant periodically. As her children grew, she understood that for their sake she had to be friendly with her husband and so did not repulse his occasional sexual invitations. She cooperated because she needed his cooperation and money to bring up the children in proper ways. They must be educated and the girls must be trained in the fine arts. So, she sold her body willingly to him for eight or nine years until all sexual relations between them came to an end.

# 23

## Can intelligence trump fate?

The story of Lakshmi–Ramanthan (hereafter L–R) stops abruptly after a few more pages of writing when Pankajam develops it to the point where Lakshmi's five children are teenagers. Pankajam has written 'This story is discontinued' on the top left-hand corner of the last page. The Meena–Subbu (hereafter M–S) story appears to have been abandoned halfway as well. No more pages of the Tamil story *Vidhiyum Madhiyum* (V–M) were available making it difficult for me to ascertain if more was written and lost or the story itself was abandoned halfway. What may we make of these painfully and even startlingly honest 'fictional' accounts of conjugal life in Pankajam's stories? Evidently, the literary device had made it possible for her to lay bare the swift unravelling of her own marriage. I had no idea of the existence of at least two of these three stories until I began my research for this book. While I do not recall having done so, I must have read the M–S story several years ago as I have made corrections (by hand) in one of the typescripts. This was the only one of the three that was typed and of which several photocopies were made.

I must at this point clarify that these auto-fictional 'stories' are markedly different from the other short stories (in English and Tamil) that Pankajam wrote and eagerly circulated among her family, pressing us all to read them. Those stories had a clear end—a resolution of a domestic drama in the lives of her protagonists. It seems plausible that these three stories, on the other hand, were stopped mid-way because they had served the purpose they were intended to. Writing them as she does several years after the events she recounts had transpired, we may reasonably speculate that she was writing in order to come to terms with her deeply troubled conjugal life and to make sense of the deck of cards that the 'gamble' of arranged marriage (as Meena refers to it) had dealt her. This impression is strengthened by Pankajam's use of the technique of recall-and-reminiscence, a story-within-a-story approach. In both the M–S and L–R stories, an older married woman with children and grandchildren looks back on her married life on her golden wedding anniversary after the day's chores are done and she has cooked the evening meal and fed her husband.

In writing these stories, it appears that Pankajam was seeking to map the fault lines that ran through her marriage and trace, as precisely as possible, the pathways that led to the ruin of the conjugal bliss that she had dreamt of as a young girl. There is an unmissable undercurrent of disillusionment that marks the writing and the tone of anger that surfaces now and again, in the L–R story in particular. And yet, Pankajam does not iron out of the narrative her husband's qualms of conscience (in the early months of their marriage) or his moral unease at his own conduct. Nor does she gloss over the intense romantic love and longing that she felt for his company in the very early period of their life together or the marital rape of the later years, when all love had evaporated. It appears that she wishes to capture the story in its entirety, sparing no detail and turning an unflinching eye on the 'dissolutions and mortifications' of her married life, as she writes at one point in the L–R story.

In all three stories, the central character Meena/Kamala/Lakshmi suffers misgivings and anxieties once the wedding is fixed. 'Even the sheep feel uneasy when they go for slaughter,' Pankajam writes mockingly of Lakshmi's joy on her wedding day. Like her protagonists, Pankajam too may have feared that the vagaries of fate may not guarantee the ideal union that she sought from marriage. A confident young woman, Meena soon soothes away her fears and comforts herself by resolving that she will turn any situation to her advantage by being 'perfect, clever and good'. Kamala firmly believes that the 'education, intelligence and character' (*kalvi, budhi, gunam*) that are hers to command will stand her in good stead and enable her to even defeat fate and 'bring her husband to line' should the circumstances warrant it. And therefore, it seems that Pankajam wrote these stories as a way to understand why she had failed so utterly in her efforts to seize the situation and redress it. Why, Pankajam seems to be asking herself, had the popular Tamil dictum that one may even defeat fate through intelligence (*madhiyai kondu vidhiyai velvathu*) not worked in her case? Why could she not triumph over wily fate and turn around the bad marriage that she was destined to have with the abundant gifts that Pankajam knew herself to possess, chief among them, a loving heart, a generous spirit and an intelligent mind sharpened on the whetstone of books and reading?

# 24

## An agenda of reform

As Pankajam's granddaughter, I was already aware of some parts of the L–R story that she had confided in me—Sivaraman's infidelity and reliance on transactional sex, the episode of the whipping when she accosted him and her refusal to cry or appear weak during the beating. I did not know that she had devised strategies and endeavoured to salvage her marriage and re-work its terms by winning her way to his heart and 'reforming' him. Perhaps she omitted mentioning this for, in retrospect, it may have appeared a foolish, futile and even embarrassing exercise to her. Reading the L–R story, I did not find it surprising that Lakshmi/Pankajam had robustly addressed the quandary she found herself in when faced with the shock of her husband's actions, rather than recoiling in moral horror and withdrawing into herself. During my growing years, I was witness to her natural optimism, fortitude in the face of adversity and faith in human goodness and kindness. I knew that she was drawn always to the idea of redemption and the possibility of new beginnings. I recall how moved she was by Leo Tolstoy's *Resurrection* (1899) and the dilemmas of his protagonist Dmitri Ivanovich, who strove to undo the harm and suffering his actions had caused.

In the M–S story, a newly-wed Meena, who is hurt by the business-like tone of her husband's first letter to her, resolves to understand him better before judging him. Pankajam writes that Meena's tender heart secured a pardon for Subbu. But I would submit that it was more than a matter of Pankajam's generosity of heart that was at work here. It was her capacity to situate people's actions in the social circumstances and material contexts that had made them who they were. We see this, for instance, in V–M when Kamala speculates that her husband's perplexing behaviour, his aloofness and disinterest in the world around him was a likely outcome of the poverty of his early years or even the absence of books in his life. In the L–R story, Lakshmi attributes her husband's infidelity to 'bad habits' that were a consequence of the lack of 'proper guidance' in his youth. Locating the root of the problem in nurture and not his nature may have helped Pankajam devise a strategy of intervention by which she could wean him away from his philandering ways and habits 'with tact' ('See if I don't,' Lakshmi vows to herself in the story).

Lakshmi's story suggests that Pankajam, shaken and shocked as she was, had chosen to interpret her husband's betrayal as a cautionary reminder that her knowledge of the 'real world' was still woefully inadequate. I can entirely believe that Pankajam had turned to books in her hour of crisis, seeking to arm herself with the knowledge they promised, in order to better understand the science of sexual life and what men sought from it (as Lakshmi does). It appears that Pankajam had crafted an agenda of reform in order to win over her husband and make him a companion worthy of her. How may we understand her endeavours in terms of the models of conjugality that were available to her? Historians note that the dominant vision of a companionate union was fashioned through an amalgam of older, Brahmanical values of pativrata (wifely devotion) and the Victorian ideal of women as cultivated helpmeets to their men. This was also reflected in the world of print media. In the Madras Presidency, the Tamil magazines that were targeted at women readers from the 1890s onwards, mobilised both pre-modern texts (Sanskrit or Tamil) as well as English habits and customs when disseminating idealised notions of domesticity in order to groom young women in specific, pre-determined ways (Sreenivas, 2008). For instance, wives were required to train themselves to manage the more expensive types of households that were being established and beautify the home so that their men would feel an attraction to it, as men did in the West. Called upon to exercise a limited and defined agency, women were to play their part in converting homes and residences into moral and affective units (Chakravarti, 1998).

The case of Pankajam helps us see the fascinatingly complex ways in which young women (of the upper castes and middle classes) were participating in the re-configuring of home and domestic life in India of the late 1920s and the 1930s. While Pankajam baulked at the servility and unquestioning subservience that the puranic tales extoling *pativrata* demanded of her, she was happy and more than willing to be an enlightened companion, drawn as she was to (some elements of) the companionate ideal. She desired to keep a good home ('a nice drawing room in the modern way with curtains and good furniture' as she writes in her autobiography) and fashion herself as a wife who shows her husband sympathy and tender care when he returns from work, striving to make her home a haven that a man might enjoy and find soothing. We do not know which, if any, Tamil or English 'ladies' magazines Pankajam had ever read. But in strategising ways to win her husband's heart, it appears that she was drawing upon a diverse repertoire of sources, including perhaps the counsel that the celebrated British author and advocate of birth control Marie Carmichael Stopes (1880–1958) offered the young women of her times.

In the L–R story, Pankajam describes Lakshmi as an 'innocent prude' who had stealthily read books on sex from her grandfather's library. While Lakshmi is an orphan in the story, her creator Pankajam was Subbalakshmi's daughter and had no reason to be clandestine about her choice of reading. Before her daughter's marriage, when the family had moved to Vayalur (close to Madras) in early 1929, it was Subbalakshmi who had bought Pankajam books on sex and childbirth from the Higginbothams bookstore of Madras. As soon as the marriage was fixed, Subbalakshmi decided that the time had come for her daughter, who must not remain ignorant as she herself had been, to learn whatever books could teach her about sexuality and procreation. I learnt this from my conversations with Ramachandran, Pankajam's oldest child. He recalls that Subbalakshmi's books for Pankajam also included one or two 'adult' novels forbidden to children during that period (Gustave Flaubert's *Madame Bovary*, maybe?) These wedding gifts from Subbalakshmi may have guided Lakshmi/Pankajam in her subsequent quest for books from the university's library.

Pankajam writes that Lakshmi brought home books by Marie Stopes and Havelock Ellis, among others. Perhaps it was Stopes' *Married Love or Love in Marriage* (1918) that found its way to Pankajam, who may have drawn strength and inspiration from it. *Married Love* had reportedly sold 2,000 copies within two weeks of its publication in March 1918. A runaway success, six more editions of the book had been published within a year. In flowery prose, Stopes' book emphasises the need for every couple to seek and find sexual and spiritual love within marriage in an age that has come to realise, according to her, the 'corrosive horror' of prostitution. Stopes (1918: 5-6) writes,

However much he may conceal it under assumed cynicism, worldliness, or self-seeking, the heart of every young man yearns with a great longing for the fulfilment of the beautiful dream of a life-long union with a mate ... The more sensitive, the more romantic, and the more idealistic is the young person of either sex, the more his or her soul craves for some kindred soul with whom the whole being can unite. But all have some measure of this desire, even the most prosaic, and we know from innumerable stories that the sternest man of affairs, he who may have worldly success of every sort, may yet, through the lack of a real mate, live with a sense almost as though the limbs of his soul had been amputated.

From what we know of Pankajam, these lines are likely to have resonated with her own yearning for a 'kindred soul' and a 'real mate' and she may well have associated Sivaraman with the 'most prosaic' and 'sternest man of affairs.' In any case, as Pankajam knew only too well, much hinged on her success in the venture to reform her husband given that the rules of conjugality allowed him to take what he wanted from the marriage, seeking his pleasures elsewhere, whereas she, the woman, could find romantic and sexual fulfilment only through the conjugal union. That Pankajam did not eventually succeed does not take away from the sheer heroism of her efforts to wrest from fate her one chance of conjugal happiness. For, if she did not succeed, it was certainly not for the want of trying, as her stories amply demonstrate.

# 25

## The moon and the sea

In *Vidhiyum Madhiyum*, Kamala regrets deeply that Sundaresan is a man who takes no interest in anything. For then, what could she, a woman who cared so passionately about the universe, possibly hope to share with him? She desperately hopes to acquaint her husband with the richness of the universe 'with all its countless wonders and its truths' and a sense of something to live for beyond the everyday and the mundane, by introducing him to books. And yet, for all her faith in reading and its redemptive powers, books could not save Pankajam's marriage, nor did they open a pathway to her husband's heart. Pankajam, as a young bride, sought to 'read' the man she had married (as she writes in her first-hand account of her marriage), get to know him and make herself known to him. However, Sivaraman insistently remained opaque to her and would not be pried open. He was 'a man who kept himself to himself' and did not need a companion or at least did not require his wife to be one.

Faced with a man who refused to open his heart to her or accept her love so unconditionally given, Pankajam writes heartbreakingly (in V–M) of the 'unspeakable grief' she endured when her husband spurned her affections time and again. In the story, when Kamala takes delight in the sight of the moonlit sea during an evening's outing to the beach, a baffled Sundaresan asks her, this 'strange girl' he has married, what it is that she sees in the sky and the sea? When his brusque manners, abrasive demeanour and disinterest in her company ruin the romantic potential of the evening, Kamala's pride is wounded. Evidently, Kamala's creator Pankajam could see much in the sky and the sea on a moonlit night. Here is a poem that Pankajam wrote in 1930, about a year into her marriage. Perhaps this was Kamala/ Pankajam's response to her husband's question, a poem that she likely never shared with him.

*The moon and the sea (1930)*

The sun is set and out comes the moon,
On her nightly march over the earth, soon,
She rises and darkness is banished
She lights up the mountains and the valleys,
A soft light penetrates the dark sea
The stars withdraw from the heavens
Saying, 'Let us away, let the queen be'
The moon in solitary grandeur reigns.

The sea watching her falls in love
'Oh beautiful queen, I love thee,' roars he
The moonbeams quiver with laughter
And the queen doeth avow,
'You, the slave of the earth, love me?
 Me, who roams freely over the sea?'
'But thou art eternally under the shadow of the earth
And often the earth hides and darkens you,
Why, oh why, should you then be proud?' replies the sea
Then with his myriad arms, the waves,
He tries to embrace and catch her.
In vain, he falls back and raves,
The queen on her path serenely sails.

Lovers are incensed by her gentle rays
Raising love in others, she is vain
For her heart is as cold as her light
The sea, he ever mourns and thunders
With passion his bosom seethes
Madly he rushes over the boulders
The moon, through countless ages, passes on heedless.

But what did Sivaraman make of this 'strange girl' whose hunger for books drove her to read his engineering college textbooks and his brother's insurance books? Did he realise that his wife saw him as something of an unfinished project and that she yearned to 'open the world to him'? Did he resent it or shrug it off as the foolish whim of a chit of a girl who dared to dream of remaking her husband in her image, always only a male prerogative? Sivaraman's autobiography, much of which is focused on the ups and downs of his career, provides little by way of an answer. On the topic of his marriage, Sivaraman briefly writes, 'I have nothing to feel sorry about my marriage. Almighty brought me in contact with really great and good people and I feel grateful to Him.'

After Pankajam adjusted so well to life in a joint household, Sivaraman seems to have wanted little else from her. However, we may surmise that the 'gamble' of an arranged marriage had likely served him an unpleasant surprise too. He could not have bargained for a wife who aspired for an equal relationship, sought companionship and fulfilment through marriage and thought it only 'natural' that the sexual/moral codes of chastity should apply equally to both parties in a marriage. Being ten years older to Pankajam, whom he married when he was in his late twenties, it would be reasonable to assume that Sivaraman's sexual self was already formed by the time he became a householder and that he did not see why he must change himself or what he was accustomed to simply because he had acquired a wife. If he was unwilling to relinquish his privileges or rethink his entitled behaviour as a man, within marriage and outside it, he was nonetheless concerned about keeping his family untainted by his actions. In the L–R story, Ramanathan expresses relief that his wife is an 'innocent', 'pure', 'unworldly' girl and that she could be trusted to bring up his children in a 'proper and protected way'.

Pankajam's stories do not speculate on the nature of her husband's relationship with the women whose sexual services he sought or who they were and what role, if any, they played in his life. She makes no further reference to the 'Raji' figure in the L–R story. The incident where she follows him to a hut during their walk to the park is presumably a reference to his encounter with a woman who may (or not) have been a sex worker. What we do know, however, from the L–R story is that the dynamic of the marriage changed irrevocably once 'he knew that she knew' of his infidelity. For Pankajam, her husband's retaliatory action against her for daring to express her disapproval of his actions, rather than looking away discreetly, effectively terminated the marriage. This does make us wonder what might have happened if Sivaraman had not been an unfaithful husband and yet had remained 'a man who did not need a companion'. It seems to me that the marriage would have still been a deeply unhappy one for Pankajam, who may have perhaps tried harder and over a longer period of time to re-fashion it in keeping with her vision of a companionate union. For what she was seeking (as her stories testify) was more than just a stable marriage with both parties remaining loyal to each other. Pankajam was seeking nothing less than a re-definition of conjugality in ways that would make her husband an ally and partner in her striving for self-actualisation and intellectual growth—a remarkable ambition for a woman of her times and not one easily realised in ours either. What her own parents did not have, despite their shared interests in literature and poetry, Pankajam sought for herself.

# 26

## Why couldn't Pankajam be like Jo?

At one point in the L–R story, Lakshmi's grandfather gently but firmly counsels an unwilling and disgusted Lakshmi to return to her husband and her 'wretched marital situation' after the birth of her first child, when she contemplates leaving him. He cautions her against making unconventional life-choices when she has 'no brother, sister, uncle or anyone' to rely on. In the words of the grandfather in the story, we may hear the echoes of PRG's counsel to Pankajam reminding her that she has lost her devoted Raja and a baby brother, besides her beloved maternal uncle, Ananthakrishnan. In the Tamil social milieu, a woman's brothers and maternal uncles are usually regarded as close relatives that she may turn to for assistance during a crisis in her life. The grandfather points out that Lakshmi cannot live independently or support herself financially 'like the girls of Madras' ('I am not even an S.S.L.C and who cares about my general knowledge?' thinks Lakshmi to herself). She is a 'modern girl' not in a practical sense, but only insofar as 'reading literature has liberated [her] mind', as her grandfather ruefully says. This moment in the story raises a question that may be asked of Pankajam's life, her mother Subbalakshmi's or that of countless other women in a similar situation viz., what can a mind liberated by reading do when it is trapped in a woman's body?

The grandfather makes Lakshmi see that her natural impulse to flee the marriage would mean taking a decision that is both socially unacceptable and economically unfeasible. In the M–S story, Subbu's mother rejoices that they have found an heiress for their son when they see Meena's house, the furniture and the garden on their first visit to 'view' the bride. However, Pankajam was no heiress, although it may have seemed so to her in-laws. Unlike the grandfather in the stories, PRG was no landlord and the large bungalows with well-tended gardens that he lived in were government property that he could avail only so long as he was in service. Moreover, besides Pankajam's marriage, he had to arrange and finance the marriage of four of the five daughters of his (by then) deceased older brother Seshan. In his (unpublished) autobiography, PRG writes,

> My brother's legacy to me was a few debts and four unmarried girls. He had not liquidated the debt incurred for the first girl's marriage, which was met by the little patrimony that fell to our share ... The last girl's marriage cost me a lot and I am repaying it in instalments through a bank.

I wonder if it occurred to Pankajam that her literary heroines were women who were, in essence, made by circumstances not very dissimilar to hers. Elizabeth Bennet, Jane Eyre and Jo March were not born into great wealth and were certainly not equipped with the means or the training to seek careers on par with the men of their age. The Bennet sisters (Elizabeth and Jane), along with their three younger sisters, stood to be disinherited from their father's home and estate which, as per the rules of entailment that prevailed in England then, could only be passed on to a male heir. Jane Eyre was an orphan, a poor governess who inherits money (at the end of the novel) through the kindness of an uncle who dies without children of his own. Jo March spent time (unhappily) as a companion to her wealthy Aunt March and inherited, after her death, the aunt's estate that became the residential home for the boy's school she runs.

Through their dazzling conversations, quick wit and presence of mind, these young women had the good fortune of securing husbands who valued them for their mind. Matrimonial arrangements were rather different in Pankajam's corner of the world. Pankajam's 'bad' horoscope, which apparently predicted early widowhood, limited her marital prospects and the likelihood of bagging 'good' alliances. As a young girl, Meena (in the M–S story) is determined to 'be like Jo and always fight injustice' and run away if faced with a situation detrimental to her dignity and honour, unlike 'poor Sita (of the Ramayana), who put up with everything'. Did an older Pankajam, disillusioned by her marriage that was falling apart, ever wonder what Elizabeth and Jane Bennet or Jo March would have done if Darcy, Bingley or Doctor Bhaer had turned out to be uncaring and callous husbands? If ever she did, maybe she consoled herself with the thought that while her literary heroines too had had their minds liberated by reading literature (as Pankajam writes of herself), they were yet, each of them, trapped in a woman's body, as was she.

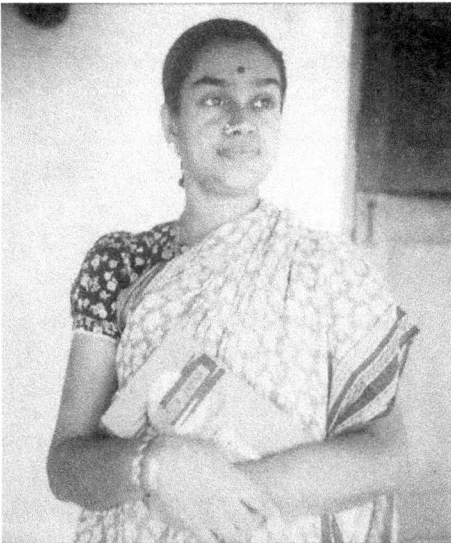

If Pankajam's 'mind liberated by reading' could not secure her escape from her marriage, it nonetheless enabled her to see her position within it with remarkable clarity. In the L–R story, Pankajam astutely places her finger on the banal and rather unexceptional nature of the sexual contract that many women, and not only those married to philandering men, may identify with. A wife too may sell her body within marriage in exchange for economic comfort and the bare necessities of life for herself and her children. When Lakshmi says that she sold her body 'willingly' for eight or nine years to her husband, Pankajam, using the alibi of Lakshmi, invites us to reflect on how a wife who may not refuse consent, may ever truly give it either. She appears to be asking us what value we may accord a woman's willed consent to the sexual-economic contract in a marriage such as the one she found herself in, neither exceptional for her times, nor even for ours. What I find exceptional, however, is that Pankajam clarifies to herself that she is as wounded by her husband's refusal to ever know her as a person as she is by any of the other cruelties he subjects her to. It is his unwillingness to link love and sex—it is unfeeling and soulless sex-as-rape and its indignities that diminish her, never the 'beautiful experience of sex' as Lakshmi describes it, which was always to remain the stuff of dreams for Pankajam.

Through her autofiction, Pankajam shows us how she stays true to her resolve to 'not pretend to love a rake' and never be a Nalayini under any circumstance, even while she remains married to her husband and bears his children. It was Pankajam's decision to eschew pretence that got her whipped by her husband and, more importantly, shifted the terms of her relationship with him. By showing him the contempt that she believed his actions deserved, Pankajam refused complicity in what might have otherwise been a sordid, if not unusual, marital pact—one where the man strayed and the woman looked away, feigning ignorance. In the final reckoning, Pankajam's stories speak to us not because of any extraordinary violence or drama or scandal, but for their immensely moving account of how a young woman courageously navigated the treacherous minefield of a profoundly unequal relationship and sought to hold her husband accountable for his actions, albeit with little effect.

# 27

## The song of life

During the years that Pankajam was waging her private battles with her husband, what were the public debates, if any, on the reform of conjugality? In 1929, the year that seventeen-year-old Pankajam got married, the passing of The Child Marriage Restraint Act or the Sarda Act (as it was called) by the colonial state made it illegal for girls less than fourteen and boys less than sixteen years of age to be married off by their families. The first legislation against child marriage in British India, the Act of 1929, brought the 'inner domain' of conjugality within the purview of state intervention, cutting across all religious and caste communities. The historian Mrinalini Sinha (2006) argues that the unprecedented involvement of women reformers and women's organisations in the public campaigns that preceded the Sarda Act constituted women as the key actors of social reform in India. Through their impassioned public speeches and writings, Indian women emerged as the subjects (no longer only objects) of public debate on the 'women's question' in India. This was facilitated by an autonomous, all-India women's movement that had begun to take shape and coalesce around the formation of three major women's organisations: the Women's Indian Association (1917) which was the first to emerge, the National

Council of Women in India (1925) and the All India Women's Conference (1927).

Public discourses around the status and condition of Indian women during this period were galvanised by the publication of the American journalist Katherine Mayo's book *Mother India* in 1927. *Mother India*, which declared Indians unfit for political self-government on the grounds of social backwardness and, in particular, the many social ills that women were subjected to, was widely read and publicly denounced by India's nationalist leaders. The largest protest meeting of Indian women against Mayo's book was organised by the Women's Indian Association (WIA) and took place in Triplicane (Madras) in 1927. The resolutions adopted by the meeting decried Mayo's cynical exploitation of the cause of Indian women in the service of the colonial domination of India. Simultaneously, they urged legislators to enact measures that prohibited child marriage, early parentage, enforced widowhood and the dedication of girls to temples. Elsewhere in India too, educated and articulate women, who had begun to organise themselves, mobilised public opinion in order to pressure the British government to pass legislations aiming to right historical wrongs committed against women (Sinha, 2006).

Historians have noted that the Sarda Act was no more than symbolic in its effects and produced little by way of a substantive transformation of material practices around conjugality. Child marriages continued to remain rampant and were hardly, if ever, prosecuted. In any case, nationalist reformers primarily defined consent with regard to the biological capacity of the female child's body to tolerate sexual intercourse and produce healthy children; their understandings of consent had little to do with the more radical question of women's willingness to marry or their agency in the conjugal relationship. It was activists and organisers from the nascent women's movement who wrote and spoke of women's bodily and emotional experiences of marriage, even as they took care to not reject outright the nationalist appeal to tradition and scriptural authority as the basis on which to ground calls for reform. For the most part, women desisted from attacking the patriarchal underpinnings of the nationalist interventions in marriage and conjugal life (Sreenivas, 2008).

During this period, more strident critiques of conjugality that were rooted in alternate visions of marriage were advanced by the followers of the anti-caste crusader and social reformer 'Periyar' E.V. Ramasamy. The self-respect marriage that Periyar and his followers conducted eschewed custom and convention, required only the approval of the bride and the groom (not their parents or extended families) and foregrounded a vision of marriage as a union of equal, consenting partners. As part of the self-respect marriage vow, the man and woman pledged to respect and heed each other's concerns, views and needs in the course of their life together. *Kudi Arasu*, the Tamil weekly magazine published by Periyar in the Madras Presidency, regularly carried articles written by women and men on women's status from 1928 onwards (Geetha and Rajadurai, 1998). Seeking to unite a Dravidian community of non-Brahmin Tamil speakers, the tracts and magazines of the 'Self-Respecters' were hardly likely to have found their way to Tamil Brahmin households. Pankajam could not have been aware that Periyar, in one of his more famous pieces of writing in *Kudi Arasu* in 1928, had debunked the 'myth' of chastity or sexual purity enjoined upon women, besides arguing that women have a right to desire.

Pankajam may have occasionally had the opportunity to attend a meeting or two organised by the mainstream women's organisations in Madras. In *Fragments of a Life*, Mythily cites a letter by Subbalakshmi to Pankajam in which she reacts with joy on hearing that her daughter attended a women's meet and displayed an 'original mind' in speaking with the women participants at the meeting. Subbalakshmi's letter was written in January 1948, when Pankajam's childbirth years were over and her youngest child about eight years old. We may confidently surmise that such occasions were but fleeting opportunities in Pankajam's life.

*Pankajam in a women's meeting in Madras (middle of second row from top), January 1948*

In the foreword to her autobiography in 1949, Pankajam declares that she dares to write of her life although she is not a 'society lady'. It is quite likely that Pankajam was referring to the elite, educated women whose personal and social circumstances had enabled them to access the public spheres of professional work, women's movement organising and anti-colonial, nationalist activism that Pankajam herself could not. And therefore, it seems to me that during the first ten or fifteen years of her marriage (1929/30–1945), the period that the extract from the L–R story covers, Pankajam was working out the meaning of her marriage and her position in it within her head for the most part. Not surprisingly, Pankajam turned to poetry and fiction as an outlet for the unsettling emotions, the hopes and frustrations that beset her.

*Pankajam as a young woman in the 1930s*

In a poem that twenty-eight-year-old Pankajam wrote in 1939 (*The Song of Life*), the year her fifth and last child Mythily was born, she traces the dreams of a young girl who imagines herself, at one moment, 'a Razia, a Sita or a Gargi' and at another 'a Chand Bibi, a Madame Curie, Madhavi the dancer or Meera the saint'. When the 'greatest crisis in a maiden's life' takes place (her marriage) she lays 'her youth, her beauty, the sacrifice of her ideals and freedom' at the feet of the man she marries and offers him the very 'song of her life' as a gift. But 'who knows that the groom can only strike discordant notes and turn the song into doleful tunes, a song of misery?' In the poem, Pankajam attributes the death of a girl's dreams, not to the actions of the man who was fated to be her husband, but to her 'parents, society, so-called friends' who 'give her advice in plenty, not to be stubborn and pursue her own inclinations'. When she sings as she weaves flowers, 'weaving fancies into her garlands', she is 'checked for being fanciful' and denied innocent, simple pleasures at every turn of her life. It is those who 'have her interests at heart' that play their part in snuffing out the potential of a girl's life. As the *Song of Life* shows us, Pankajam's 'mind liberated by reading' allows her to see well beyond the villainy of a husband or the vagaries of fate. It makes her see how structures of authority and control are intricately woven into familial and domestic worlds, constraining all that a woman may be and do.

# 28

## Ideals are chimera

In the M–S and L–R stories, the central character is an orphan being raised by her grandfather, to whom she has a strong emotional attachment. The dilemmas of the grandfather figure resemble those that Pankajam's father PRG is likely to have had when selecting a groom for his daughter. The grandfather in the M–S story speaks of high dowry demands from prospective grooms employed in the Indian Civil Service (ICS) and, by implication, from well-off families. Faced with a situation in which ICS grooms, or at least some of them, had come to expect wives with a college degree by the end of the 1920s, the grandfather's remorse that melts Meena's heart may well have been PRG's belated recognition that he had acted in haste by withdrawing his daughter from school even before she could secure an SSLC.

In the family album, there is a picture of sixteen-year-old Pankajam and PRG that was most likely taken during their year together in Marakkanam. Without his moustache and the long, flowing beard that he was to start growing soon after, PRG has a boyish demeanour and hardly looks like the father of the young girl beside him. By the time that he was re-united with his family in 1928, much had passed between PRG and Subbalakshmi—the domestic violence of the early years, the interference of the older brother that PRG had allowed, the loss of two sons that did not bring them closer, the years of estrangement and Subbalakshmi's condition that all sexual relations between them must end before returning to live with PRG in Marakkanam (Mythily calls them the 'celibate couple' in *Fragments of a Life*). Since his marriage was effectively over, it was with his daughter that PRG found companionship and camaraderie.

*Sixteen-year-old Pankajam with her father*

In Pankajam's early battles with her husband, it was her father who was her most dependable friend and ally. My cousin Padmavati recalls Pankajam's story of how weak she had become during her first pregnancy due to severe nausea. Pankajam's mother-in-law, seeing her son's indifference to his wife, remained neglectful as well. Pankajam's worsening condition prompted the neighbours to write PRG a letter, asking him to come right away and take her home as his daughter had barely any strength to get out of bed. When PRG showed up, he was appalled at the state his daughter was in. As Pankajam described it to Padmavati, 'My father lifted me up in his arms as if I were a little baby and carried me out of the house' besides directing some choice words at Sivaraman and his mother.

What I recall is an incident that Pankajam recounted about her father's reaction on hearing that Sivaraman had whipped her with his belt. Gathering a few of his friends, PRG had confronted Sivaraman and made it clear that he would not tolerate any further physical abuse of his daughter. During the early years of Pankajam's marriage, PRG occupied a senior position in government as an inspector of salt and customs, while his son-in-law was workshop supervisor in the Chennai Corporation. PRG's position in the higher rungs of the state administration could have somewhat offset the customary power and authority the son-in-law enjoyed in a traditional setting, enabling PRG to speak up for his daughter. It is ironic that PRG, a man who had beaten his teenaged wife 'often' in the early years of their marriage, as Pankajam writes in her autobiography, terrifying his little children 'when things flew out of the doors', should have intervened so vigorously to defend his daughter. It would appear that PRG, as a doting father, was driven by impulses and emotions very different from PRG as a husband.

While PRG was uncomfortable with the idea of a wife with an independent intellect of her own, he came to accept in his daughter what he would not in a wife. In a tribute to her father, Pankajam writes that she was 'as happy as the golden oriole that called from the mango tree' during the long, companionable hours of conversation with him in the coastal town of Marakkanam when she was gifted the *Book of Knowledge* by PRG. Having just left school in which she had excelled in all subjects, Pankajam must have discussed books and ideas with her father in Marakkanam. Clearly, PRG was no longer the man who had torn up his eight-year-old daughter's English primers (during their year in Ellore), insisting that she be taught Sanskrit instead. While Pankajam relied on her father's emotional and moral support during her troubles with her husband, I wonder if Subbalakshmi was ever fully aware of the extent of her daughter's marital distress. It is indeed plausible that Pankajam chose her father as her confidante and not her mother. It seems to me that Pankajam may have wished to spare Subbalakshmi, who had dreamed of educating her daughter to be a doctor, any knowledge that would have increased her mother's unhappiness and her sense of her own life as a failed enterprise.

Pankajam valued both her parents for having played quite different, if equally important, roles in her life. In the dedication of her collection of writings, *All My Yesteryears* (1987), Pankajam writes, 'My father was my best friend. He was my strength and solace till his end.' Of her mother, she writes, 'It is because of her tireless efforts and self-sacrifice that I am what I am today. Her ideas run through every cell of my body.' It was, after all, her mother who read to her the stories that made Meena/Pankajam (of the M–S story) a 'unique girl' and a 'unique woman'. During their years together in Madras, Subbalakshmi once asked little Pankajam if she would marry the artist Asit Kumar Haldar, an assistant of Rabindranath Tagore and a prominent artist of the Bengal Renaissance, when she grew up as 'he is so handsome' (Mythily writes of this incident in *Fragments of a Life* as an instance of Subbalakshmi's lack of prejudice). Later in her life, Pankajam may have pondered over what she too had lost when her mother was forbidden to take her to Shantiniketan (on the invitation of Sarojini Naidu, her sister Mrinalini Chattopadhyay and their sister-in-law Kamaladevi Chattopadhyay)[24] to explore the possibility of a different future for the two of them. Besides the opportunity of a college education, the chance to find love and a companionate marriage was also denied to Pankajam.

A poem that Pankajam wrote after Subbalakshmi's death in 1978 conveys a sense of how she saw her mother—a precious soul

---

24  Mythily writes about this lost opportunity in detail in *Fragments of a Life* (Sivaraman, 2006: 107-121).

who spoke of 'lofty ideals' to her daughter of 'little mind', whose dreams of happiness for her daughter would not countenance the boundaries of 'caste, creed and clime', and who was suffused with an impossible idealism.

*My Mother (1978)*

Strikes and demonstrations
Now your days filled
To the charka you turned
Spun yards and yards of it
To clothe your little girl
Khadi you wore
All your life
Dressed me in khadi too
When it did not catch my fancy,
Your nimble delicate fingers
Embroidered them
To make me happy.

I grew into a girl
Now your life's aim
My education became
You talked to little me
Of little mind,
Of lofty ideals—
Of wearing khadi,
Of simple living
And of sacrifices
All of which
Went over my head
I liked to imitate my cousins,
Wearing silk and jewellery
I did not care for prison
Nor of being sprayed with gas
But I loved Gandhiji

As much and more
As Rama and Sita.

As I grew into a maiden,
Grew your ambitions too sky high
You dreamed
Of an ideal groom,
Caste, creed and clime
You swept aside
Your heart regained courage
You visited painting galleries
Met artists Nandalal Bose,
Asit Kumar Haldar
Whose paintings you admired.
You even thought of Haldar
As a would-be son-in-law
Oh poor mother mine,
Ideals are chimera,
Real life is different.

# 29

# The madness of new love (1930–1939)

In March 1930, Mahatma Gandhi began a march to the sea and the coastal town of Dandi in the state of Gujarat, in protest against the colonial government's salt acts that prohibited Indians from collecting or selling salt. In the Madras Presidency, the Congress leader C. Rajagopalachari (or Rajaji, as he was called) led a similar march from Trichinopoly to the town of Vedaranyam on the Coromandel coast. The Salt Satyagraha launched a new phase in India's struggle for Independence— the Civil Disobedience Movement. If India's coastal towns were the hotbeds of revolutionary ferment and dissent in the early-to-mid 1930s, they were spaces of belonging, rest, refuge and recuperation for Pankajam, for whom this decade was marked by the regular arrival of a new baby every two years, in February 1931, January 1933, March 1935, May 1937 and December 1939. As sanctioned by custom and convention, Pankajam returned to her natal family for the birth of the children. And therefore, sprawling homes in coastal villages and towns (where her father was posted) remained a mainstay of Pankajam's life in the 1930s and must have provided an affective link to the familiar landscapes of her childhood years.

In the story of Kamala (the heroine of V–M), Pankajam describes her ecstatic reaction to the birth of her first child.

Kamala's heart that had remained unconsoled for seventeen years finally knew fulfilment on seeing the baby's little face. The pleasure she felt was akin to that of Vasudeva's when he gazed upon Sri Krishna, whose birth was heralded by divine augury. Her devotion was no less than that of the three magi who found the baby Jesus in his barnyard crib. Her house was a palace, her baby a gift from the divine and she the queen ruling over this blessed kingdom. Whether it was her milk or the affection she showered on him, the baby glowed and flourished. In his toothless smile, the gleam in his eyes and his cooing, she perceived the world's philosophies and truths. She embraced him with ardour and breathed in his intoxicating baby smell.

No one but Yashoda, the mother of Krishna, could have enjoyed a child as much as Kamala enjoyed hers. In her heart, she even teased Yashoda. 'I will not be jealous of you anymore. It is your turn to be jealous of me. For isn't your Krishna born to me now?' When the child slept, she would often watch him sleep in his crib, entranced by his plump cheeks, his rosebud lips, the beauty of his shut eyes. If she chanced to hear her mother-in-law and the cook laugh at her 'madness', she paid no heed to it. Hugging the child to herself, she would say to him, 'You will never think me mad. So long as you are with me, I am a queen and no one can say a (hurtful) word about me.'

After suffering a stroke in September 1994, when she was eighty-three years old, Pankajam wrote brief biographies of her five children. The following section, extracted from Pankajam's writing on the early years of her children's lives, gives us glimpses of the first decade of her motherhood.

*Pankajam with her firstborn child (two years old) and PRG in 1933*

I was pregnant and so proud of it. I often looked at myself and wondered how my baby was going to be. I would dream that my child would be as great as a king, or perhaps a Buddha or a Nehru. On the day he was born, there was a great temple festival of *Thaipusam*.[25] Towards evening, my grandmother and mother were observing the full moon rise, just as the child was born. I had too much milk in my breasts, more than the baby could drink and the doctor did not know what to do. We removed much of it with a breast pump and my grandmother suggested that we give it to a motherless child. My father was simply delighted with the birth of his grandson.

---

25  A Tamil festival celebrated on the full moon of the Tamil month of *Thai* (January/February).

When I was twenty-one, my second child Lalitha was born. My father was then posted in a village in Adirampattinam, a wilderness. The remarkable thing about my second baby was her big, round, black eyes that filled her face. When my husband first beheld her about two months later, his remark was, 'Oh what big eyes!' and then he said, 'She is chubby and fat and looks like Mrs Scott.'[26] And the third sentence was 'I have bought some land in a faraway place called Spurtank Road (in Madras). You know my brother has bought land and is building a house in his wife's name because the corporation does not tax ladies. So, I too have bought this land in your name.' After he left, my grandmother said to me 'Well, this girl of yours seems very lucky. She has brought lands to you—in your name.'

When the house in Spurtank Road was half-finished, we had a small house-warming function that coincided with Lalitha's first birthday, after which we moved in. The living room was all mud. My baby girl played in the mud, climbed the ladder after the workers and become very fond of a puppy that came along with them … According to superstition, the third child must be born in the father's house and not the maternal grandfather's. And so, we were in our home in Spurtank Road when the day drew near. I was playing football with my older children when I felt some discomfort. Before the midwife could enter the room, the baby was born. There was no pain. He was a bonnie boy who shone like moonlight. I named him Srinivasan, a name of the Lord.

---

26  This is most likely a reference to Mabel Besant-Scott (1870–1952), the daughter of the theosophist Annie Besant, whose financial help Sivaraman had sought when he was a college student. For a period of time, Mabel Besant-Scott assisted her mother in managing the affairs of the Theosophical Society, Adyar.

Less than three years old when her brother was born, Lalitha was fond of him, sang to him, changed his nappies and looked after him. By nature, Srini was quiet and reserved. He always stayed by my side. Stuck to my hip. My father and others called him the leech. Srini was so gentle and quiet the night his brother Sundaram was born. When my grandmother tried to move Srini and make room for the infant, he said, 'Let me move and I will go the bathroom myself, Amma and Paati. I can manage alone.' Everyone was surprised. In those days, the toilet, which was just a ramshackle thatched shed with a stone to sit on, was a furlong away from our bungalow in Kakinada.

When my firstborn Ram was about four or five years old, a lucky opportunity came my children's way. My father was promoted as Commissioner of Salts and posted to the coastal town of Kakinada in Andhra. He was given a bungalow surrounded by an acre of land which had a mango and cashew nut grove, all kinds of fruit-bearing trees and shrubs with lovely flowers. The huge Malabar squirrel, treepies, parrots and other fruit-eating birds and bats set up a cacophony around us. The house was surrounded by four huge artificial tanks. My children were delighted that they could bathe in one of the tanks which was not too deep and soon they had learnt to swim. Whenever I called the children to feed them castor oil,[27] they would hide behind the hundred short mango trees full of fruit and we had a tough time rounding them up.

My older children Ram and Lalitha went to a convent school in Kakinada for about a year, along with other children who lived close to us. When I saw so many children, my imagination was fired. When I was in school,

---

27  It was common practice to administer the bitter tasting castor oil to children as a purgative to periodically cleanse the stomach and intestines.

I was famous as an 'actress'. Now I wanted to make the children act. The other mothers helped stitch the costumes and make the screen props. The script writing and training the actors fell to my lot. I chose *Cinderella* first. The children performed many plays and even the adults would join the tableaux ... My last child was a girl we named Mythily. Soon after her birth in December 1939, my father retired from service and our life in Kakinada came to an end. I was loath to leave as I knew that I would never see the enchanting place again ...

During the first decade of Pankajam's married life (1929–1939), we see in quick succession her romantic love and longing for her new husband, the dashing of her hope for a happy and fulfilling marriage, her great joy at the birth of her first child and her overall contentment with motherhood, its rough edges tempered by her older children's undemanding nature, their joyful acceptance of their younger siblings and her father's reassuring presence in her life as a welcoming and gracious patriarch who was happy to host his only surviving child and grandchildren in his comfortable home. Apart from the bouts of severe 'morning sickness' that she would suffer, childbirth itself does not seem to have been an overly difficult or traumatic experience for Pankajam, as she was generally of robust physical health.

But how did Pankajam, a young married woman, manage to spend so much time in her parents' household, away from her husband? In 1935, Sivaraman added one storey to the house that he had built in Madras. The next year he began to invest in the stock market, suffering substantial losses when the market crashed in April 1937, and had to make monthly payments to the firm Kothari and Sons, one of the first firms in the stock and shares business in Madras. In order to reduce household expenses during this period of financial stress, he sent his young and growing family to his father-in-law's home in Kakinada for extended periods of time.

*The children in the garden pond at Kakinada, 1940*

Sivaraman had also received a more direct form of financial support from Pankajam's family on an earlier occasion. Towards the end of 1932, he bought 8.5 grounds of land (0.47 acres) on Spurtank Road (Chetpet), costing a little over Rs 3,000. As he was then a workshop superintendent and could not afford the investment, he made Pankajam ask her mother for the money. Subbalakshmi readily gave her daughter the sum of Rs 3,000 that she had saved from a monthly allowance (of Rs 50) that she had received from PRG during her years of living in Madras in the 1920s, evidently after the couple (PRG and Subbalakshmi) had made peace with each other. Subbalakshmi had saved what she could from this allowance after paying for Pankajam's school fees, her own medicines, books and other necessities. It was the land bought with this money that was registered in Pankajam's name in order to save on taxes, as Sivaraman informs Pankajam shortly after the birth of their second child Lalitha.[28]

---

28  Sivaraman repaid Subbalakshmi in 1946 when Pankajam informed him that her mother was asking for the money to be returned.

The bungalow across the road from the Coovum River on Spurtank Road was to remain Pankajam's home for over fifty-seven years (from 1934 to 1991). When Pankajam and Sivaraman established their household in Spurtank Road in February 1934, the area was deserted and their children shivered in their beds at night from hearing jackals howl in the moonlight. Across the Coovum, the forested area of the Women's Christian College (WCC) on College Road (Nungambakkam) was frequented by jackals that hunted crabs and frogs on the banks of the Coovum. As late as 1949, the family's dog Elsie discovered a jackal lurking behind a clump of bushes in the garden, looking to hunt the bandicoots that fed on the kitchen refuse dumped in the garden. On occasions of exceptionally heavy rainfall, the Coovum overflowed its banks and inundated the garden, reaching the steps of the house (as was the case during the Madras floods of 1943).

*Panchavati House, Chetpet, after it was fully constructed*
*(image taken in the 1980s)*

Any visitor to the household could take a city bus to Spurtank Road, buy a ticket to the bus stop of 'Panchavati' (as the area was called) and find themselves practically at the gate.

In 1950 or so, it was felt that the house must have a name, announced via a nameplate installed at the gate. Pankajam's son Ram suggested the name 'Panchavati House', putting an end to months of bickering between his parents, who could not agree on a suitable name. As a child, when I heard the Ramayana from Pankajam, she emphasised that Rama and Sita had shared years of devoted love (perhaps the happiest period of their life together) during their exile in the forest of Panchavati before the couple's separation.[29] Pankajam knew little of the idyllic marital bliss that her epic heroine Sita had experienced in Panchavati. Yet, Pankajam's Panchavati provided her sufficient material comfort and anchored her during her adult life in Madras.

---

29  In the epic, the Panchavati forest is believed to be located in the Nashik district of north-west Maharashtra.

# 30

# A city like a cemetery: Madras in the War Years

Despite the whirlwind pace of events in her life in the 1930s, when she had 'one child in the belly, the other in the hip', as she would jocularly say of her life during this decade, Pankajam wrote poetry intermittently. The poems showcase her moods—nostalgic and melancholic in one instance, and in another, soaking in the abundant natural beauty that enveloped her in Kakinada. In a poem, 'Mahatma Gandhi', written in 1930 (the year of the Dandi March), when she was a newly married woman living in a joint family and possibly pregnant with her first child, eighteen-year-old Pankajam exhorts her fellow Indians to heed Gandhi's call to action, even if she could not do so herself. In another poem, written in 1931, she addresses her former classmates in the context of a school reunion of 'old girls' that Pankajam must have missed attending.

*To My Classmates (1931)*

My classmates and friends dear
If you haven't forgotten me, just hear
Though my heart is fleet as light
My fate is, surely, slow of flight

So I cannot visit my Alma-Mater
On the Old Girls Day, but later
School girls, you are like bubbling water
Fond of mischief and full of laughter
Unhappily with school, I parted
Far away am I, sad-hearted
They say 'out of sight out of mind'
Do not observe the rule, be kind
Never from your hearts a true friend tear,
And all your thoughts nurse with care
Till we meet again sometime somewhere.

Pankajam may not have been able to thrown herself into the heady anti-colonial struggle of her times or even attend the occasional school reunion. But she fully used any opportunity she had to keep alive her passions, including her interest in the natural world. Staying with her parents in Adiramapattinam when expecting her second child in 1932-33, Pankajam began to cultivate a life-long interest in birdwatching, nurtured by her mother Subbalakshmi. The proximity of Adiramapattinam to the Vedaranyam Swamp (and the adjoining area that would much later become the Point Calimere Wildlife and Bird Sanctuary) made it possible for mother and daughter to sight a multitude of migratory and water birds. As her son Ram recalls, Pankajam methodically taught herself to identify birds using the British ornithologist E.C. Stuart Baker's book *The Game-birds of India, Burma and Ceylon*, published by the Bombay Natural History Society in 1921. Subbalakshmi had bought the book at the Higginbothams bookstore during the late 1920s.

Pankajam was a keen observer not only of exotic feathered creatures, but of the steady flow of quotidian life as it unfolded around her. Her long essay 'Madras' (written in the 1980s) is a rich and vivid account of the social life of the city during the 1930s and 1940s. Living in Madras all her adult life, Pankajam witnessed and wrote about a tumultuous chapter in the city's history. In the passage below, I also draw from her biographical sketches of her children to supplement her account of Madras during the eventful years of World War II.

… Ever since the Japanese captured Singapore [in February 1942] and their navy encircled the island, sinking British ships, the English got frightened at the prospect of losing India. They brought British and American soldiers to fight the Japanese as they did not trust Indian soldiers. Large contingents of European troops were marched all over our towns. All night we heard the sound of left, right, left, right of the military boots in rhythmic fashion—this was the background to our slumber.

When at last, as the British feared, some warships of the Japanese did enter the Bay of Bengal and were stationed a few miles facing Madras harbour and Fort St George, the order 'Evacuate Madras' was issued. All essential servicemen were to stay behind, while women and children were to leave. Schools were closed. The South Indian masses were reputed to be passive by temperament. So they fled the city in unbelievable fashion. At first, all the upper and middle classes left. Then came the dramatic bomb throwing by the Japanese somewhere near the Fort [on the night of 11 October 1943]. This was the last straw and the panicking people, the whole population of Madras, deserted the town in a hurry. Trains were full—people and children standing on luggage. Kothaval Chavadi, the huge vegetable market was empty. All hotels and shops, small and big were closed. All milkmen with their cattle left Madras and no coffee could be made at home.

For a few months after the bomb episode, the city was like a cemetery – dead silence prevailed. Those who were still in the city (like us) could hear people talking or shouting in other localities. No, I am not exaggerating! Anyone standing on Spurtank road in front of our house could hear the people in Egmore talking. The sea once again began to roar and the lions in the Madras Zoo could be heard in day time, frightening the children. At no time have I experienced the sudden eerie silence that descended on the city and not even in the remote villages where I grew up. This was when my father came to take me and the children to the town of Tindivanam where he was living post-retirement.

One day, my husband came from Madras and declared that he would like to take me back with him as he had no food and no cook either. I agreed to go. As the two young ones Sundaram (five years) and Mythily (three) began to cry, I suggested that they go with us. And so, we left for Madras with the younger children. I cooked for three days and on the fourth day, I was wondering how to sweep, wash and clean such a big house when my husband brought a young fellow to help me with the housework. After some days, I learnt that he was a prisoner who had been freed from the penitentiary when the city was evacuated! He was frank and I did keep him.

One day my husband was away and I was cooking when the young man came running and said, 'Amma, Amma, go upstairs at once and lock the door!' The garden was full of European soldiers—more than a hundred. Some were hiding, while others were in shooting position. I realised that the soldiers were rehearsing ambush and attack. It allayed a little my fear. Suddenly I noticed my little boy aiming his toy gun in shooting position at the soldiers. And, in return, they were pointing their guns at him! My poor husband got very frightened and immediately took me and the children back to Tindivanam.

As Pankajam's firstborn Ram said to me, a question that people commonly asked each other during the war years in Madras was, 'Where did you go during the evacuation?' Unlike the spacious homes that were the perquisites of government service, the house that PRG rented in Tindivanam was 'small, dingy and old-fashioned', as described by Pankajam's fourth child Sundaram. The children's chief entertainment was a tribe of monkeys that lived near the house and stole food from the kitchen. In keeping with the spirit of the times, the tribe leader and bully monkey was named 'Hitler' by Ram.

# 31

## Tutor, teacher, playmate, mother (1930–1940)

Sometime in the early 1940s, a young woman makes her way into the red-brick, Indo-Saracenic building of Madras city's reputed Moore Market, which takes its name from Sir George Moore, President of the Corporation of Madras, who laid its foundation stone in August 1898. Crossing the long inner courtyard, she says to herself, 'There is nothing in the world that is not here in this market.' She stops to look at the cutlery on display, the glassware and chinaware, the garments and textiles from distant lands, the silk, corduroy, satin, taffeta and lace. The cacophonous din from the pet market draws her attention—monkeys, rabbits, guinea pigs, Siamese cats, squirrels and cages and cages of birds. She makes a face. She hates to see birds caged.

All of a sudden, she stops gawking and reminds herself that her time is limited and so is her purse. Her household and children await her and she is here for a purpose. Somehow she has found herself with a little bit of money left over at the end of the month and knows what she wants to buy. She must also get her old flask repaired in one of the hardware shops at the back of the building where knives, spades and tools of every kind are hawked, sold and mended. But again she stops to stare at the mountains of tinned food, the preserved fruits, the prunes from California that make her mouth water ... the German-made Kohler's Chocolate catches her eye as it is a particular favourite with her children. To her horror, she finds that the price has gone up from twelve annas for a box of forty sticks to fourteen annas!

Deploring this unforeseen hike, she makes her way to the familiar corridor full of bookshops. There are old books on sale and classics of almost every country, science and philosophy books and so many more. She sighs with contentment. The Moore Market does not disappoint. It remains a treasure house for books at cheap prices. She is looking for children's picture books made of cloth which her young children cannot tear up and eagerly begins her book hunt ...

Pankajam's essay 'Madras' allows me to take the liberty of imagining a shopping expedition she might have undertaken when finding herself with spare cash and a bit of time to get out of the house. In the two decades preceding the birth of independent India, Pankajam was intensely engaged in building a home and raising her children, ever-mindful that she was doing so amidst a 'great cry and shout of independence'. I draw on the L–R story, my interviews with Pankajam's firstborn Ram, and the (unpublished) memoir of her fourth child, Sundaram, to show how Pankajam fashioned herself as an enlightened and progressive motherduring the 1930s and 1940s, one equally interested in the theory and practise of good parenting.

When the children came, Lakshmi was happy for she thought, 'They will not be alone like me. There must be sisters and brothers in one's life.' And she devoted all her days and nights to the care of them. She was their nurse, ayah, tutor, teacher, playmate, mother and everything.

The children responded to her love like flowers to the rain and grew and flourished in security and love. Lakshmi scoured the libraries and brought books on how to bring up children, their habit formation and other problems pertaining to older children. She read them avidly and acted on them. Soon, the news of her dedication to the children and her intelligent and loving ways towards them spread to their relatives, friends and neighbours. All stood in awe of such dedication and passionate love. And it bore fruit. All five children, three boys and two girls, became exceptionally good. They were gentle, sensitive, truthful and always eager to help anyone in need. It was never hard for Lakshmi to manage them for they had such faith in her words. They consulted her in everything. They had no secrets from her.

Pankajam took the business of child-rearing seriously and applied herself to the scientific study of child care, the diet and nutritional requirements of children and child psychology among other themes. As her son Ram reiterated, Pankajam was determined to raise her children well and, in particular, to not lose any of them to childhood illnesses. The loss of her two brothers not so long ago and the devastation it wrought in her mother Subbalakshmi's life rankled in Pankajam's memory during the early years of her own motherhood. Pankajam's diet for her children included Ovaltine (a malted drink), cod-liver oil supplements and Rowntree's cocoa. When the Congress leader C. Rajagopalachari (Rajaji) urged the public to substitute the 'foreign' Ovaltine with the homegrown ragi malt, Pankajam promptly did so.

Pankajam's enthusiasm for her children's well-being was tempered by her sense of herself as a patriot who must heed the call to arms of a nation-in-the-making. In 1939, the educationist Maria Montessori was invited by the city's eminent theosophist couple George Arundale and Rukmini Devi Arundale to move to Madras and implement her educational methods that recognised the creative potential of children, their drive to learn and the right

*Subbalakshmi (left), PRG and Pankajam (right) with three of Pankajam's children (1937)*

of each child to be treated as an individual. Intrigued by this novel method, Pankajam sent her oldest child to a kindergarten school which adopted Montessori's pedagogy and often accompanied him to observe the new system in action. Soon after, she sent him to a Madras Corporation-run Tamil-medium school, when the rising tide of the national movement (in the 'Quit India' phase of the struggle) triggered a turn towards vernacular languages.

> When Ram was about nine years old [1940], a great change came over the country—the cry and shout of Independence! Everyone's mother tongue became very dear to them and we were all encouraged to boycott the use of English or any other foreign language. So, like all other mothers of that time, I sent Ram to a Tamil medium school …

Pankajam's children did not always enjoy or appreciate her efforts on their behalf. In a memoir of his childhood that he wrote and circulated among his family in 2004, Sundaram describes his years of growing up in Panchavati House. He writes of how Pankajam would feed her children a daily diet of raw egg beaten up with milk in order to supplement their vegetarian diet, the repulsive feeling of the eggnog in the mouth and throat, and the sorry sight of his sister Mythily's 'miserable expression' as she struggled to swallow the 'slimy yolk' every morning for over an hour. But it was not only the physical well-being of her children that was of concern to Pankajam, as Sundaram makes us see.

My mother was shorter than an average Indian woman, but had a big heart. She was a kind, generous person who spent a lot of time with us, helping us with school lessons and homework. She managed to discipline us mostly with persuasive words and very little physical punishment. While waiting to be married, my mother persuaded her father to buy her a complete set of the 'Book of Knowledge'. So enthusiastic was she about these books, that when she became a mother, she shared all her knowledge about this planet and the universe with her children. She encouraged us to read a variety of books on different subjects to appreciate the complexity of life on this earth ... she was interested in flowers, watching birds and wild animals and she taught us to love these beautiful creatures. She left a strong impression on me and her interest in a variety of subjects encouraged me to get interested in several things in my life.

Pankajam home-schooled two of her younger children over several years. In the following passage, Sundaram writes of his home-school experience.

Mom's school: At the end of World War II, my mother and all her children returned [from Tindivanam] to live with our father in Madras. My parents tried to make me go to school at the age of six or seven. I was a very nervous and shy boy and would not take to school life. I protested and demonstrated. My dislike was partly because of the type of school I was sent to. The teachers were old-fashioned and rigid, and the students were quite rough and tough. Realising that I was not emotionally ready for school, my mother, who was always more sympathetic and considerate than my father, persuaded him to let me stay home and learn under her teaching. My home-schooling time was adjusted to suit my mother's free time. When she wanted to have a nap, she would give me some 'homework' to do on my own. This kind of learning in the relaxed setting of my home was thoroughly suited to my temperament. I was of course teased in the evenings by my father and brothers who enquired what I was learning in 'Amma college'.

Sundaram's aversion to school life and the 'rough and tough' students he encountered may have reminded Pankajam of her own unhappy experience with the 'thinnai' school of Sankaridurg (in 1918), where the boys took away her pencil box, pinched her and left her in 'mortal fear'. Pankajam's last-born, Mythily, a sickly and frail child, was also home-schooled by her mother. Nine-year-old Mythily was directly admitted to class five, as was Sundaram at the age of eight years. In both cases, the respective school headmasters reviewed and tested their home-acquired learning prior to admission. Evidently, the years of 'Amma college' did not set either Sundaram or Mythily back in their academic lives.

Towards the end of 1948, Pankajam gave her children moments of great fear and anxiety. In his memoir, Sundaram writes of his mother falling seriously ill with typhoid when he was about eleven years old, and of a poem that he wrote in his fear of losing her. Among Pankajam's letters, diaries and memorabilia, I found Sundaram's poem (dated 30 November 1948) neatly folded and tucked away.

*As a young mother with three of her children, 1937*

Dear Mother,

I am very sad, because you went to hospital. My self written a poem to you. There are many mistakes in it. Please don't mind it, and don't show it to anyone. Father said to me mother will be all right in a fortnight. But you must take rest for 2 months.

Yours loving son, S. Sundaram
JAI-HIND

Sweet mother, how are you?
Oh, what a beautiful mother you are,
Your lips are so red like red apple,
And your sharp eyes are green and blue,
Pray to god, he will help you; Be frank,
And don't afraid for anything.

In her autobiography, Pankajam writes of spending six weeks 'in a sort of stupor' with a very high temperature in the general hospital during a period when there was no treatment for typhoid (apart from cold compresses and a diet of porridge) and no antibiotics. After her third relapse into the cycle of fever and diarrhoea, the doctors, nurses and everyone else thought that she would die. Suffering from 'nursing neglect, the merciless fever and the absence of nourishment', Pankajam herself believed that the end was near. Her poem 'Hope' was written during her stay in the hospital, probably during one of the periods when the fever eased a little.

*Hope (1948, from the hospital)*

No sky, no sun I see
The four walls grim encircle me
The world to me has crumbled into this room
Books, my only friends, break the gloom
God hath deemed that I should learn
In the school of pain, for help to Him I turn
My freedom lost, the children from me torn
I feel like a bird, whose wings are shorn
Out of love, they say, 'Rest and be free of care,'
Who cares for rest?
In the strife I would ever be,
To tend, nurse, serve all whom I love.

To her children's great relief and delight, Pankajam turned the corner and recovered. For Pankajam, the business of 'tending, nursing and serving all whom she loved' included getting to know intimately well each child's distinctive personality, temperament and capacities. In a poem written in 1945 ('My Treasures'), when her oldest child is fourteen years old, Pankajam describes the singular qualities of each child that makes them who they are—'generous-hearted, eager and impetuous Ram growing to manhood'; 'star-eyed' Lalitha who is 'full of wit, humour and laughter'; Srini, 'a sensitive, shy, intelligent lad' whose mother cannot fathom 'what lies beneath his gentle heart'; 'capable, self-reliant and ambitious' Sundaram, who is 'mischievous and full of spirits'; and last-born Mythily, 'fragile and refined as the hues of dawn' with 'a head full of imagination and fancies wild'.

*Pankajam and baby Mythily (1941)*

*Pankajam with older Mythily (late 1940s)*

Pankajam remained her children's primary confidante, privy to their secret joys and disappointments as they transited from adolescence to young adulthood. In the following extract from the L–R story, the interaction between Lakshmi and her older son was likely modelled on conversations between Pankajam and Ram who opted to study geology in college, influenced by his mother's love of natural phenomena.

> 'Amma, I want to take up geology next year because my friends say we can surely get a government job then. Since father refuses to send me to the agricultural college, which I want very much, this is the next best,' said Ramu.

'Well, you join the geology class as you want. I hear they have fieldwork to do. Isn't it so?' asked Lakshmi. 'Yes, Amma, that will be very interesting. You used to tell us about how our earth and the mountains and rivers were all formed when we were children. Don't you remember?'

'Yes, yes. Do join it if you are confident about mastering the subject,' said Lakshmi. And so Ramu joined the BA course in geology.

The first day Ramu came home from college calling out to Lakshmi, 'Amma, Amma come here! What do you think they taught us today? All about the prehistoric animals like the brontosaurus that you would tell us about when we were young. Nothing but what I know! So I answered everything so easily. And master asked me, "Are you last year's student? A failed student?" Everyone thinks so because I already know so much about prehistoric lore from you.'

Ramu liked teasing his mother. One day when he returned from college, he said, 'Amma, what they taught me today in college, you surely do not know.' Lakshmi replied, 'Yes, I do not know. What is it? Tell me. Did I go to college? Surely you will all know more than me. What did they teach today?'

'About the hereditary cells in the body and ...'

'Oh, was the class about chromosomes today?' asked Lakshmi. Ramu was astonished that his mother knew about chromosomes. 'Oh yes, I know about chromosomes, the fibre, etc,' replied Lakshmi. 'Where did you read it, Amma? How did you know?' His mother showed him a book on heredity with the design of chromosomes on the cover. 'I bought it some years ago,' she said.

'Why did you buy it Amma?'

'Why, I was interested in hereditary problems and wanted to understand them,' Lakshmi replied.

Both her older daughter and son would tell their mother what happened in class each day as soon as they entered

the house. They shared their experiences with their mother
...

Pankajam (as Lakshmi above) modestly asserts that she has never been to college and cannot possibly guess what her children may learn. And yet, they could not surprise her (as the story of the chromosomes demonstrates), given her extensive curiosity and the knowledge she had gained thereby. Pankajam was, after all, the girl who had vowed to herself (as Kamala does in V–M on her last day in school) that, 'I will somehow study from home and become equal to the educated.' In V–M, the heroine Kamala dreams of a kingdom that stimulates and enthuses the mind and without which, 'a mind full of ideals and ambitions will shrink, lose faith in itself and lose its way in this barren world'. Being a tutor, teacher, playmate and friend to her children, Pankajam nurtured a 'kingdom of the mind' by which she kept alive the 'tender sapling of confidence' in herself, her intellect and her talents by giving of herself generously to her children. If Pankajam strove desperately hard and yet could not rework the terms of her marriage and conjugal life, she succeeded exceptionally well in redefining motherhood and making her children in her image by co-creating a universe of emotional intimacy and intellectual curiosity that she inhabited with them.

# 32

## But life is never smooth (1940–1950)

What was Pankajam's relationship with her husband like during their years of parenthood and co-habitation? I turn to the L–R story in which Pankajam narrates the unfolding domestic drama in the life of her protagonist Lakshmi.

Ramanathan got into higher positions at work. He had a telephone, a car and a big house. Lakshmi rejoiced for the sake of her children. Though she was wrapped up in her children and their studies, life was not smooth. It never was. For some years, when the children were still young, Ramanathan neglected Lakshmi, leaving her to have her own way with the children. He did not care to interfere, nor was he interested in them. He never knew in which classes they were. Did not know anything about their progress or shortcomings. Everything was attended to and taken care of by Lakshmi so much so that the children were frightened of him and even curbed their talk and laughter when their father suddenly entered the room.

By the time the children were nine years or older, all sexual relations stopped completely between the couple. Lakshmi now slept with all the children around her. Eight-year-old Ravi one day confronted her thus, 'Amma, can I ask you something?'

'Why not?' said Lakshmi.

'My friend Raghu and other classmates tell me that they never sleep with their mothers, that only fathers and mothers sleep together and children sleep with grandparents or alone in a separate room. I said we never do that and they did not believe me.' Lakshmi did not know how to tackle this. She said, 'True, what you said is true. That is how it is in every house. But your father prefers to sleep alone and I had no one to look after all of you when you were young. So I developed the habit of being with all of you.' But young as he was, he sensed that something was being hidden from him by his mother. His mother thought, 'Who knows what the other boys have told him? But he will not hesitate to question me if he knew.' And slowly the children began to feel the disinterestedness of their father towards them.

In the following passage, extracted from Pankajam's biographical account of her son Srini, she recounts an incident that reflects the 'disinterestedness' that she mentions in the L–R story.

When Srini was nine or ten years old, this incident happened. During the war, the government built deep and broad cement trenches. After the war, the trenches remained as they were for two years or so. Children often jumped across the trenches. One afternoon, my husband, his friends and my eldest son [Ram] were playing badminton. Outside the gate, Srini and his friends were playing. While trying to jump across the trench, my boy Srini missed by an inch and fell and hit his head against the edge. He had cut his forehead in a deep gash and was drenched in blood. The boys ran to the gate and called for help. Ram ran out and helped his brother out of the pit.

Everyone expected his father to rush to help the son. But his father standing with bat in his hand, amidst four or five friends, saw his eldest son call a rickshaw and at once said, 'Ram will take his brother to the doctor. Come on, let us play.' But all the gentlemen threw their bats down and shouted, 'Sivarama, go and take the boy to the hospital!' Though my husband's friends shouted, I got into the rickshaw with Ram and Srini. Meanwhile I tied Srini's head with cotton and ice and the three of us went to the general hospital for first aid. The doctor stitched the gash just above the forehead and gave an injection and sent us away. By nightfall, we returned home.

The Lakshmi–Ramanthan story continues below …

When the children grew up to be ten years or so, Ramanathan became openly hostile to Lakshmi. He saw that she was getting on well with the children and the servants and was busy and happy in spite of him. He became jealous of her peace of mind. He turned the servants (now there was a cook) against Lakshmi and revelled in her perplexities. He gave her insufficient money because he could not forget that she knew his secret. There were occasional quarrels, but Lakshmi put up with most of the problems thinking it would all end when her children became older.

Now the children had grown up and had come to the stage of college life. They saw with their own eyes how things were. They saw the misery their mother underwent. But they dared not comment on it and waited their time, while offering sympathy and love. Lakshmi was happy with their love, understanding and sympathy.

'Amma, it seems you have arranged for my dance performance at Rasika Ranjani Sabha at the end of the month. Vadhiyar [teacher] told me. How did you manage to get a performance at that sabha?' asked her older daughter Vimala. 'Yes dear, I meant to tell you. Why, I would have got this performance fixed long ago but for your father. During your last performance, the RR Sabha people asked us. As I was in the green room, they applied to your father, as people naturally do. Your father, it seems, refused. I did not know this until last week when I approached them. They told me about it and said he was a bit haughty about it all. However, they were kind enough to give you an evening,' added Lakshmi. It had become the habit of Ramanathan to prevent or stand in the way of whatever Lakshmi wanted to do, out of sheer cussedness and jealousy.

Lakshmi's eldest son Ramu was a very impetuous boy and fond of his friends. One day, as usual, Ramu called out to her on entering the house from college. 'Amma, do you know what an escapade I had today? I was coming fast on my cycle and I was racing a fellow. So, I did not notice a bus and a car on either side. Somehow, I wended my way between them and managed to get out unscathed. It was thrilling,' he laughed. But this scared Lakshmi and gently she said, 'You should not race in a crowded thoroughfare and how is it that you are so late today?'

'Oh, I am not coming from college, Amma. Today we all cut classes and went to a picture. Do you know our English Master began to take class in a dull, sonorous way? Most of the boys walked out after throwing paper planes at him. I too got out. I heard him saying pitifully, "Let all the medavis[30] go out. And I will take the class for the rest of you." And Ramu roared with laughter.

'But you should not cut classes like that, Ramu, even if the teacher is an uninteresting one. How will you understand your lessons?'

'Why, the notes are there and the book is there! The fellow who comes first in my class always cuts classes and goes to pictures, Amma. You do not know. After all, you are a woman. Do you know something, Amma? You told us

30  A sarcastic reference to intellectuals.

that smoking causes cancer. My college mates were smoking and they offered me a cigarette. And I said, "It will cause cancer." All of them roared with laughter and said, "Did your grandmother say that? Look at Churchill. He is eighty. Do not believe all the cock-and-bull stories of orthodox old people in the house." And when I thought about it, I agreed with them. I am going to smoke hereafter.' He prattled on like that.

Now Lakshmi knew that she should not vehemently decry him and persist with her own opinion. So she smiled and said nothing ... In all these tantrums of her children, Lakshmi had greater trouble than other mothers. Other women always appealed to their husbands who came to their help when it became difficult for them to control their children. But this could not be with poor Lakshmi.

Pankajam believed that dealing with teenage children and their declarations of independence warranted a mature response that involved gently nudging them towards responsible behaviour, rather than imposing her views on them. But in this endeavour, she did not have an ally in her husband. In promoting her daughter Lalitha's dance performances too, Pankajam wrote (in her autobiography) that, 'I stood alone, playing the part that fathers usually do' such as securing performances and approaching sabhas (arts organisations that manage performance auditoriums). As the L–R story demonstrates with abundant evidence, the marriage grew increasingly difficult and fraught as the years went by, with Sivaraman's treatment of Pankajam morphing from one of neglect and disinterest to open hostility and 'jealousy of her peace of mind'. The L–R story offers a complex psychological portrait of a marriage wherein the man resents the ability of his wife to pursue her interests and passions and retain a fiercely independent sense of self, while sharing all that she deemed important with her children, even if it suited him very well to remain aloof, disengaged and free of domestic responsibilities.

*Pankajam and Sivaraman*

Lakshmi's story shows us that Pankajam interpreted Sivaraman's notorious tight-fistedness and churlish reluctance to part with money even for essential household expenses as his ongoing punishment of her for having dared to show him that 'she knew his secret' (of infidelity). On the other hand, Pankajam's children saw their father's excessive frugality as an outcome of the fears and habits he had imbibed from the material deprivation of his childhood years. I propose that we may (also) read Sivaraman's parsimony as an effort to re-assert dominance over his wife, who sought to carry on with her life as if her husband did not matter a whit, by underscoring her economic dependence on him. The two antagonists of this troubled marriage drew on different resources and allies. If Sivaraman had control of the money and household finances, Pankajam had the 'love, understanding and sympathy' of the children, coming of age with a growing awareness of their parents' loveless and embattled union.

# 33

## A woman who stood alone

In her autofiction and her autobiography, Pankajam's account of her years as a mother and householder is not without strife or sadness. Her burden of caring for her children, planning their activities and managing the household budget without her husband's sympathy or support weighed on her particularly heavily during a crisis such as the debilitating illness of her oldest son who suffered recurring bouts of tuberculosis over three years (1951–53).

My son Ram was the noblest gift of God to me. So lively, kind, loving and helpful to one and all was he. When Ram was studying in the second year of college, he developed TB and could not write his final exam. He was in bed for several months. This was a time of great trial and misery for me. Though his father was earning well, his incapacity to understand another's suffering and feelings was beyond anybody's understanding. This, I thought, was because my husband was a very healthy man—never suffering an illness or sickness. Some healthy people cannot understand ill health in others. After a month, my husband began to think his son was pretending and evading the exams. He began to be angry with his son and then became insulting and accused him of malingering. He instructed the cook not to carry food to the boy upstairs.

I tried to plead with my husband and make him see the state of things. And yet, he kept scolding and insulting the boy whenever I was absent for a few hours from his bedside. My poor boy put up with it all, never complained, and hid these things from me. It seems his father used to say to him, 'Either mend yourself or end yourself, no bed and pampering.' I came to know of this later on and witnessed many such scenes. Though I was helpless, I did not give up. I vowed to myself that I would somehow save my son and make him well again. It was not an easy affair. The doctor had to be paid. And there were frequent X-rays and medicine too. Dr Sanjivi prescribed a tonic called Vincarus which cost Rs 20 a bottle.

All this I could not afford. I was a timid idiot and did not dare fight with my husband or shout before my sick boy and the other children. So I began to sell the gold jewellery that my father had made for my marriage, one piece after the other, at a Jain mortgage shop in Egmore High Road. During the darkest hours when Ram spat blood, my father came to my help. He was then retired, and because of his philanthropic habits, never could save money. But he had many sympathisers and admirers. A grateful friend in Triplicane lent him Rs 1000 which he gave me to help me cure my boy. With the money and my own devices and our prayers, my boy was saved from the jaws of death.

When the doctor advised a change of environment for Ram, God came to my help in the form of my husband's older brother. He had bought a farm in Tambaram near a village and was cultivating the land. When I met him one day, he suddenly accosted me thus, 'If I build a small place in my farm, will your son come to occupy it? Will you go and stay there?' I was so enthralled at the prospect that I immediately agreed without even asking my husband. I suggested that the building could be modelled on a *dak* bungalow, a hall with verandas on both sides. The small structure was finished in a month. My son and I lived on the farm for more than three months. I shuttled between Tambaram and Chetpet using the electric train so that I could attend to my house and the other children ...

The pure country air refreshed my boy and his health improved. He took private classes and completed his degree. Then came an offer of a job. Unfortunately, once again he developed fever and was unable to accept it. You can imagine my husband's wrath and all our frustrations. The next year (after months in bed), Ram became fit enough to take up the job ...

As her account of Ram's bouts of recurring illness and convalescence reveals, Pankajam's tenacious spirit, her resolve and capacity to seize the initiative and turn circumstances around in her favour enabled her to do what it took to overcome the odds and ensure her son's recovery. We see evidence of this spirit in her successful efforts to move her parents to Madras so that she could care for them better. A constant source of worry and guilt for Pankajam during the 1940s was the worsening health of her mother. Mythily has written of Subbalakshmi's recurring bouts of back pain, asthma attacks, epileptic seizures and her isolation and depression. Pankajam was painfully conscious that she had abandoned her mother to a lonely and loveless life when she left her parental home after marriage. Being a single child, she knew that she had to eventually bring her ailing mother and ageing father to Madras (from Tindivanam) and arrange for them to live close to her.

In the 1940s, Panchavati House on Spurtank Road had a ground floor and a first floor, with four rooms on each floor, besides the living room. Not surprisingly, the question of PRG and Subbalakshmi moving permanently to the Madras house created some tension between Sivaraman and Pankajam. In the L–R story, Lakshmi, an orphan raised by her grandfather, has the difficult task of bringing the old man to live with her in Madras.

In the extract below, she is in conversation with her older children (Ramu and Vimala in the story).

> One day, Ramu and Vimala, who were both in Presidency College, saw their mother packing when they came home from college. 'Why, where are you going?' came the query. They never could think of their mother going anywhere alone. 'Ramu, thatha is very ill it seems. I am going there to fetch him here so that he can be with us. But ...' she stopped and tears glistened in her eyes. 'Yes, bring him here, Amma. He can stay with us,' they both said eagerly for great-grandfather, who loved and doted on them, was a favourite with them all. Lakshmi continued, 'Your father says that thatha should not be put up in the rooms upstairs. He says he may rent those rooms and wants him to be put up in the tool shed room.'
>
> 'What a shame that grandfather cannot come and stay in our house! As if there is no room for him here.' Ramu and Kamala too were indignant.
>
> Lakshmi, with her grandfather's money, improved the tool shed and made it a small room. She brought her grandfather to live in it ...

Pankajam's son Ram could not recall whether Pankajam had explicitly asked and Sivaraman refused to have her parents stay in the bungalow on Spurtank Road, as the L–R story suggests. Lalitha's daughter Padmavati pointed out (to me) that it would have been socially unacceptable for PRG to live in the same house as his son-in-law and partake of his hospitality. He would have preferred his own place and a degree of independence, she insisted. This could well have been the case. However, while Lakshmi's grandfather (in the story) had some money to build a house, PRG had no savings beyond his monthly pension that was fully used up for household expenses and his patronage of assorted holy men. Pankajam, who decided to build a small house in the garden beside the bungalow in Spurtank Road, had to sell her maternal inheritance of land (or *manja kaani*, as it was called) that Subbalakshmi had inherited from her mother Kamakshi.

Ram recalls that Pankajam took him along with her to a village in Lalgudi (near Trichy) to arrange the sales and collect the money. 'Come with me, I need a man to accompany me,' she said to Ram. As Ram put it, the land was sold 'for a pittance' as neither Pankajam, nor seventeen-year-old Ram had any experience or assistance in bargaining for a good price. Moreover, the land was not contiguous but scattered here and there in bits and pieces. Finally, the lands were sold and a house built for approximately Rs 11,000 beside the bungalow on Spurtank Road in 1948. Pankajam's grandmother Kamakshi lived here for a while with Subbalakshmi and PRG until she passed away in 1950.

*Subbalakshmi (visibly aged and ailing), Pankajam, Lalitha and Lalitha's children, 1957/58*

While writing this section, I suddenly realised that this house that Pankajam had struggled to build had housed five generations of women in the family. After Kamakshi passed away, Subbalakshmi continued to live here for several years, until Pankajam finally moved her mother to a room in her own house. Sometime in 1981, Mythily moved to this house with her husband and daughter; I was then about seven years of age. A few months later, Pankajam moved in with us.

Sivaraman had passed away by then and Pankajam, no longer needing the extra space, chose to rent out the rooms in the large house. Until the old buildings were demolished in 1991, Pankajam, Mythily and I lived together, carrying forward our tradition of daughters who never strayed too far from their mothers, no matter where our life trajectories may have taken us.

*Mythily, Pankajam and the author in the small house Pankajam built for her parents, 1987*

# 34

## Sultry evenings, summer holidays and family democracy (1940–1950)

In her writing, Pankajam narrates several instances that account for why she spoke of herself as having lived out her life 'as a widow' for all practical purposes. (Pankajam had said this once to her grand-daughter Padmavati while wryly commenting that the 'bad' horoscope, which had limited her marital prospects by predicting an early widowhood, could not have been so wrong after all). As Pankajam came to realise, being married to 'a man who did not need a companion' also meant that she was married to one who would not *be* a companion to her even in her hour of need. While Sivaraman was not given to writing about domesticity, what of the children? How did they see the household, their parent's relationship and the daily humdrum of domestic life when they were growing up? As Sundaram describes it in his memoir, life in Panchavati House was unexceptional in some ways and included the household head taking the entire family to the Marina beach on 'hot and sultry summer evenings'.

... There we used to lie down on the sand and enjoy the gentle and cool breeze blowing from the sea and eat some munchies and gaze at the darkening sky. We would observe the stars and count the meteorites that streaked across the sky and almost fall asleep to the rhythmic sound of the waves. With great reluctance we had to get back home to face the hot and still night and the diving, ravenous mosquitoes.

On 15 August 1947, when Sundaram was ten years old, India became independent of British rule. Like other families that owned a car, Sivaraman took his family for a car ride around the city to see the 'decorations and illuminations' and 'the parades and speeches, music and dancing in the streets'. Holidays away from the heat and bustle of the Madras summer were not uncommon. Family holidays included getting away to Conoor, Kodaikanal or the Nandi Hills where Sivaraman would book a room for Rs 5 a day in low-cost travellers' bungalows during the 1950s. The children of Panchavati House also grew up in a domestic environment of fights and mutual recrimination between their parents. When Sundaram was a toddler, he would bring a big stick to scare off his father when Sivaraman raised his voice or his hand to hit Pankajam during an argument. Such instances may have reminded Pankajam of her little brother Raja, who brought a stick to hit their father PRG when he struck Subbalakshmi during the couple's quarrels. While Pankajam writes that she had the 'love, understanding and sympathy' of the children (in the L–R story), they nevertheless suffered, as children would (and as Pankajam herself did), from witnessing their parents' unhappiness. On this, Sundaram has the following to say:

My father and mother ... held different opinions and attitudes on almost everything and were not compatible partners. There were frequent disagreements, arguments and quarrels in front of their children. Although this had gone on throughout our childhood, my siblings and I never accepted these as normal, and we were saddened by them to some extent. These episodes always bothered us, but we kept out of their quarrels, and minded our own business. Even my oldest brother and older sister did not have the courage to interfere ...

In the Meena–Subbu story, when describing Meena's first meeting with Subbu, Pankajam writes that 'fate was scheming to bring together two entirely different but equally strong personalities'. And therefore, the confrontations between Pankajam and Sivaraman did not involve a wife cowering before her husband in abject terror or being brow-beaten into silence by him. When speaking of her parents' life together, the couple's last child (and my mother) Mythily, a strong champion of gender equality during her adult life, recognised that her mother's position in an unequal relationship made her the more vulnerable partner. Nonetheless, she said to me more than once, 'When I was growing up, I never saw my mother as a victim. She gave my father as good as she got from him.'

Whatever their differences, Pankajam and Sivaraman did not differ in one respect—the Panchavati household was one that allowed its inhabitants to discuss social and political issues in a free and unconstrained atmosphere. In his memoir, Sundaram explains how this came about.

During the work week, all of us ate at different times to suit our study or work schedule. So, every Sunday, my father insisted that the whole family should sit together to have lunch. Both my parents encouraged us to talk about and discuss any news, topic or subject that we liked during lunchtime. The topics discussed covered a wide range—friends and their families, political news and current affairs, philosophy and religious concepts, social problems, scientific matters, travel tales, university issues, and such others. Sometimes, since we were teenagers, our discussions turned into passionate arguments and rude criticism against each other's opinions. In those moments, my parents had to intervene to cool down the discussions. This freedom given to me to discuss during lunchtime, instead of eating gloomily without saying a word, stuck with me for the rest of my life.

As a teenager, I was an atheist, as I could not find convincing arguments and rational proof for the existence of a god … I enjoyed discussing philosophy and arguing against the existence of a god. I also liked debating with my family and friends why India did not progress as much as some European countries did in spite of its older history and civilisation, and also the damages and benefits of colonialism. I argued strongly against the unfairness of the Hindu caste system, which denied equal opportunities to all people. I passionately argued against the Indian arranged marriage and dowry system, equating it to a commercial contract, and declared my preference for two individuals selecting their own life partners. I ridiculed irrational religious beliefs and superstitious practices such as consulting an astrologer and horoscopes. I strongly believed that the joint family system would never encourage younger people to develop to their full potential because of interference from the family elders. My rebellious spirit made me disagree with the traditional thoughts and customs of the Madras society in which I was raised.

*The full family with PRG in 1949/50*

Animated by the headstrong opinions of argumentative teenagers taking sarcastic swipes at each other, the family's Sunday lunch discussions admitted the airing of worldviews that may have been considered heretical by orthodox Brahmin households of Madras in the 1950s. In some other respects too, the Panchavati household was an unorthodox one. Pankajam's oldest child Ram recalls that his mother would be 'put out' of the house during the days she had her periods. Sitting on a mat in the veranda, Pankajam did not seem unhappy as she had books and newspapers to read and kept herself occupied. Ram remembers that she appeared relieved to be spared housework. After the death of Sivaraman's mother in 1944, Pankajam stopped observing the ritual-prescribed social isolation of a menstruating woman. She freely entered the kitchen and the puja room, and did not impose menstrual taboos on her daughters either.

As Ram recalls, all major Hindu festivals were observed at home, but there was no adherence to the everyday practises of purity and pollution (*madi* or *aacharam*, in Tamil) that marked the texture of daily life in traditional Tamil Brahmin households. On this subject, I recall Pankajam's daughter (and my aunt) Lalitha speaking to me of the shock and astonishment of her mother-in-law who, soon after Lalitha's wedding, realised that the new bride had received no instruction in these matters from her mother or grandmother. Lalitha recalled Subbalakshmi's eminent unsuitability for this enterprise and how she had to be reminded by Pankajam to wear a more presentable sari, comb her hair and put on a bindi when Lalitha's prospective in-laws visited their home for the first time. As for Pankajam, Lalitha said, 'My mother had no interest and did not even know any of these rules ... She was a woman who would drop whatever she was doing in the kitchen or anywhere else and run out of the house if she happened to hear a bird call, trying to spot the bird. What did she know of aacharam?' And yet, neither Pankajam nor Sivaraman was prepared to break with tradition in matters such as arranging an early marriage for their older daughter or prioritising 'settling down' over novel opportunities that came her way.

# 35

## 'I am the queen,' said the princess (late 1940s–early 1950s)

In the L–R story, Pankajam writes at one point that she had to accommodate her husband or at least not antagonise him as she needed his cooperation to raise and educate her children well and ensure that her daughters were trained in the fine arts. That Pankajam had felt that her daughters' education was incomplete without an exposure to the arts was itself a sign of the changing times. When Pankajam was an adolescent, a young maiden in a Tamil Brahmin family may show off her skills in music amongst family circles or before a prospective groom during the customary 'bride-seeing' exercise as proof of her feminine accomplishments and appropriate acculturation. However, there was no question of any public performance whatsoever. For it was only in the 1920s and 1930s that Carnatic music and, subsequently, Bharatanatyam were deemed 'classical' art forms through a complex reinvention of what was formerly the artistic heritage of women and men of the Isai Vellala community of dancers, musicians and choreographers in South India.

Sadir, the dance of the hereditary women performers from non-Brahmin castes attached to temples or royal courts, had suffered a decline since 1892 when the anti-*nautch* (anti-dance) reform movement denigrated the women dancers' non-conjugal lifestyles as prostitution and their ritual activities as superstition. As historians have shown, 'classical' dance was reconfigured when a new generation of dancers and promoters of dance (all from the upper castes) rather successfully aligned it with the values of classicised culture, tradition, a pan-Indian heritage and a reformed spirituality. This paved the way for middle class 'family women' to perform on a public stage without compromising dominant notions of morality or propriety (Allen, 1997; O'Shea, 2007).

Pankajam's older daughter Lalitha was born (in 1933), a few years before Rukmini Devi Arundale (1904–1986), the founder of Kalakshetra, launched her efforts (in end-1935/36) to render Sadir 'respectable' by distancing it from its original community of hereditary practitioners and enhancing its appeal in the eyes of the upper castes and middle classes, who would monopolise its practise in the subsequent decades.[31] While Pankajam hoped to make her daughter a 'famous vocalist' when she grew up, Lalitha appears to have had other plans for herself. In her biographical sketch of Lalitha written in 1995 (a year after her stroke), Pankajam gives us a sense of this.

In Kakinada, I employed a music teacher for Lalitha when she was five years old as I wanted her to be a famous vocalist. Though the teacher was a good one, Lalitha hid in the huge garden whenever she saw him. A good race she used to give him! My father often used to get up sports tournaments with the peons, petty officers, sub-inspectors, inspectors, etc. Once he organised a big tournament at Gurznapalli. The whole town was there. My father took the

---

31 Rukmini Devi's efforts to sanitise Bharatanatyam and locate its history within a Sanskrit tradition were contested by T. Balasaraswati (1918–1984), a legendary dancer who claimed and celebrated the 'devadasi' legacy and traced the roots of the dance to Tamil/South Indian literature and music (O'Shea, 2007).

children and me. Lalitha was just five then. She suddenly ran from me and, with doll in hand, climbed the table with some help from people around. It was prize-giving time. And suddenly, she began to dance on the table. My heart was beating fast with fear, even as she kept swaying on the table. Many prizes rained on her. Clever child, she picked them all up.

My father's friend who got her down finally turned to me and asked, 'When did you teach her dancing and why did you allow her to dance on the stage when so young?' I replied that I had not taught her to dance and neither had I asked her to go onto the stage. She had started dancing ever since she saw Rabindranath Tagore's ballet give a performance at Madras when she was barely three years old. Back home, she would be engrossed in dancing movements the whole day. She was greatly inspired by the artists from Shantiniketan.

Lalitha began to learn Bharatanatyam in 1944 and had her debut performance (*arangetram*) in December 1946. Mythily's book on Subbalakshmi contains a piece written by (her sister) Lalitha on the views of her grandmother Subbalakshmi and great-grandmother Kamakshi on the question of girls in the family

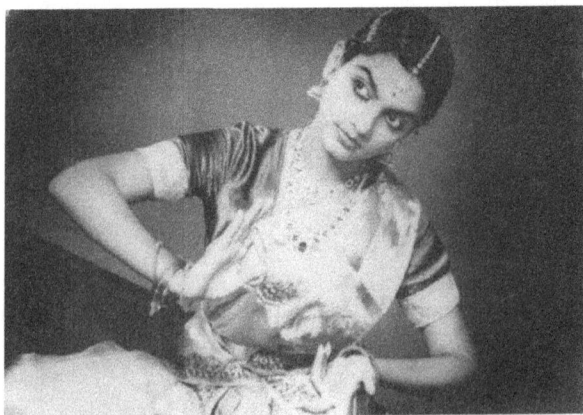

*Lalitha dancing (late 1940s)*

learning to dance and performing in public. Lalitha describes Subbalakshmi as 'flushed, excited and happy' when she saw 'the beauty and joy of the human body expressing the splendour of life' in her granddaughter's dance. Lalitha writes that she realised how different the women of her family were from other women of their own age and social standing only when her parents began looking for a suitable groom for her, exposing her to the 'rigid attitudes' of most other people of the time (Sivaraman, 2006: 141).

Lalitha's note in Mythily's book alerts us to the tensions that these new developments may have produced among Tamil Brahmin families, with some decrying them and others adapting earlier perhaps. These differences appear to have been consequential for the young women of these families who (like Lalitha) evinced an early interest in dance and had before them the options and performance spaces that opened up from the late 1930s. Lalitha, a vivacious, talented and outgoing girl, was regarded by friends and relatives as the beauty of the family on account of her large, expressive eyes. As Pankajam writes, the 'eyes that filled her face' were the most striking feature of the baby that Sivaraman commented upon when he beheld two-month-old Lalitha for the first time. In her autobiography, Pankajam describes Lalitha's talent and flair for dance, theatre and drama and the opportunities that came her way until a 'fateful halt' changed the course of her daughter's life.

> ... I sent to Lalitha to the school 'Vidyodaya' for some time where she learnt Manipuri. Although she left the school, the style and talent stayed with her. I sent her next to the Presidency Teacher's Training School (PTS) in Egmore. She acted in all the plays in school and took part in Kummi and Kolattam dances too. At that time, the famous dance teacher Chockalingam Pillai, the son–in–law of Pandanallur Meenakshi Sundaram Pillai[32] who had taught Rukmini Devi Arundale, parted ways with her and left Adyar and started a dance school of his own. Luckily, I was then looking for a dance master and I enrolled Lalitha in the school.
>
> Soon many girls joined as the rate was easy. Many famous people such as Bangalore Krishna Rao, Pandanallur Jayalakshmi and Indirani Rahman visited the school of Chockalingam Pillai. In one annual show, the master got up a pinnal kolattam performance with many coloured ribbons hung from a tall pole. Each girl sang a song and danced with the ribbons until the pinnal (braid) unravelled. This was a beautiful piece of work that was new and very attractive.
>
> Lalitha gave Bharathanatyam recitals at sabhas and won many medals and prizes. When she performed at

---

32  Meenakshi Sundaram Pillai (1869–1964), a revered dance teacher from the *Isai Vellala* community, was the chief exponent of the celebrated Pandanallur style of Bharatanatyam, which derives its name from Pandanallur village of Thanjavur district.

Coonoor, there was such a crowd that she collected Rs 5000 which she presented to the hospital to build a maternity ward. When she was a student in Presidency college, Lalitha danced at college shows and acted in drama and plays. Once she enacted a piece from 'Cilappatikaram' (Tamil epic poem) where the heroine Kannagi is angry with the Madurai king. She acted so realistically that she was overcome by emotion and tears ran down her cheeks. When Lalitha entered the college, a crowd of students would stand at the steps calling out 'Kannagi, Kannagi!'

*Lalitha in costume for a play*

Suddenly, one day, a very famous visitor (Ramagopal) came and met Lalitha's father. He requested that she be allowed to go with him and his group of dancers to America. He said that he was prepared to take my husband and me with the group. We refused and Ramagopal said, 'You don't know that with her eyes she can bring the world to her feet.' Once, Rukmini Devi heard about Lalitha and invited her to come and dance. Rukmini so admired Lalitha that she asked me, 'I am going to Europe with a group. Why don't you send Lalitha with me?' I said, 'Lalitha is studying in college now. After finishing college, she will go with you.' Rukmini Devi said, 'College? I did not go to any college. I am not the worse for it!'

Just when Lalitha was becoming a sought-after dancer, there came a fateful halt to it. When Lalitha was in the Intermediate class, we began looking for a bridegroom for her. But, as with most things, my husband and I disagreed about the various aspects of the affair. I was keen on certain aspects which did not mean much to her father. So, we agreed to stop till she completed college and secured a degree. And lo, just as we both stopped thinking of her marriage, providence intervened. One Mr S came to my husband suggesting an alliance with the son of a well-known lawyer of Mylapore. We were small fry and we thought it was too big an alliance for us. But as he insisted, we went to the boy's house with her horoscope and met the boy's mother. At first glance, I was not very impressed with her because she had worn her sari in the orthodox fashion.[33] But I found her very courteous, pleasant, knowledgeable and dignified.

On my visit to their house, I was taken to the boy's room where I saw a huge library. I glanced through it and realised that he must be fond of literature. And I was told that the boy was very fond of western classical music and had a deep knowledge of it. That decided it for me. I

---

33  Pankajam's reference is to the 'madisaru' or the nine-yard sari traditionally worn by Brahmin women. Pankajam wore the madisaru during special events such as a wedding of a close family member and not on an everyday basis.

thought to myself that the boy must be an extraordinary one since in those days no one knew anything of western music. Anyway, I was still scared of the alliance. But my fears were overruled as word came that the horoscopes tally well …

When the boy and his parents came to see our girl, we were ready with the customary tiffin and coffee. The boy's father plied a few questions to Lalitha about her college and studies. Then he took his son aside to the portico and in a minute he returned and said very unceremoniously to my daughter, 'Lalitha, my boy likes you and what do you say now? Would you like to marry him?' This was such an unforeseen question asked in an unorthodox way! Usually after seeing the girl, the boy's family departs and sends word of their decision. When confronted like this, my girl had the presence of mind to say, 'Whatever my parents say, I accept.' A diplomatic answer. But my husband, equally blunt, shot back, 'We have no objection.' He spoke both for his daughter and me without consulting us. Of course, none of us had any objection for, as I had said earlier, I was impressed with the boy. And now his good looks pleased all of us. Thus my daughter's wedding was settled.

Just before her wedding was fixed, an entertainment show came up in Lalitha's college and, as usual, she had a part in it. It was a poem by Rabindranath Tagore, where the queen (Lalitha) dresses up before the mirror. She is about to put a tiara on her head saying 'I am the queen,' when suddenly the little princess pulls the tiara away and puts it on her head saying, 'I am the queen.' It was like an augury for after that day, Lalitha never appeared on the stage—neither dance nor drama. As soon as her wedding was fixed, her in-laws, in clear terms, told her and us too that Lalitha should not perform on the stage. In return, I asked that she be allowed to finish her college degree— B.A. Honours in History. It was agreed.

Married in January 1952, Lalitha became pregnant soon after and had her child the next year. After the birth of her baby, Lalitha returned to college, attended classes, took her exams and got her degree, leaving her infant in the care of her mother. Pankajam writes, 'No one could have been happier than me when Lalitha got her degree. It was my ambition that she and later, her sister, secure degrees, for the sake of which I turned down wonderful, unbelievable offers to accompany dancers like Rukmini Devi.' In her account, Pankajam with her characteristic frankness reveals the considerations and pressures that shaped the decisions she and Sivaraman took with respect to their daughter's life. Like other parents of their times, Pankajam and Sivaraman began looking for a groom for Lalitha when she was still in college. Pankajam does not tell us what the differences of opinion were between her and Sivaraman 'on the various aspects of the affair', as she writes.

*Pankajam, Mythily, Lalitha and Lalitha's child (P's first grandchild), 1956*

From what we know of Pankajam, it is quite likely that she looked for signs of compatibility between the couple even within the traditional universe of a caste-endogamous arranged marriage. In the Meena–Subbu story, Subbu asks in a tone of bewilderment, 'How can books be called treasures?' when Meena drags a reluctant Subbu to her room to show him her bookcase. It is hardly surprising that Pankajam's fears were allayed somewhat after visiting the boy's room and discovering his love of books, reading and music. From her own and her mother's experience, Pankajam knew the costs of a marriage bereft of companionship and would not have her daughters suffer similarly. In her later years, Pankajam expressed contentment that both her daughters were married to men who valued and cared for them. And yet, the 'what-might-have-been' in Lalitha's case lingered with Pankajam as her autobiography indicates.

> ... dance and Bharathanatyam were not widespread then and a respectable family travelling with a dance troupe would scandalise everyone. Yes, I thought then as others like me during that decade ... Oh, what a future was before my daughter—what appreciation of her talents and looks which I, in my prudent and cautious ways, let go ...

In her biographical note on Lalitha written in 1995 (after her stroke), Pankajam writes that she was absorbed in 'housewifely chores' that included raising two children, cooking, managing her household and caring for her ailing and bedridden mother-in-law. She ends her note on Lalitha by writing, 'For all her intellect, fate has made her a housewife.'

# 36

## Nothing but ourselves

While caste-elite families had begun to allow their adolescent daughters to dance and perform on a stage in the 1940s, the professional performance of dance by adult, married women did not resonate with symbolic domesticity in quite the same fashion. And this had as much to do with the demands that the pursuit of a professional career (in dance or any other) would make of married women (O'Shea, 2007). And so, while Lalitha's in-laws permitted her to study and complete her degree, a career in dance was out of the question. When Pankajam's son Ram married in 1958, Panchavati House welcomed its first daughter-in-law, a Bharatanatyam dancer. Ram got married to the younger sister of his long-time friend (an arranged marriage) after the two families had known each other for several years. The girl Ram was to marry had made a name for herself as a dancer and had won a government-sponsored scholarship for promotion of the arts.

When Ram went to twenty-three-year-old Nirmala's house for the 'bride-seeing' ritual, he had a chance to speak to his wife-to-be in private. Ram recalls that he said to her, 'What are your plans, Nirmala? Shall we marry? You can continue to dance of course.' As Ram described it (to me), his family simply took it for granted that Pankajam would continue to manage the household and kitchen, while Nirmala would pursue her career. Pankajam supported her daughter-in-law's career without any reserve or bitterness, even though her own daughter, only three years older than Nirmala, had to stop dancing the moment she got engaged. Sometime in the late 1950s, a European magazine published a news feature on Nirmala with a photograph of Nirmala, Ram and

Mr. S. Ramachandran, his wife, Nirmala, and his mother in the sitting-room of their comfortable Madras home. At left, Nirmala poses in dance costume on the first-floor terrace off the sitting-room. She is a singer and classical dancer. He is an airlines executive. Although the couple live with his parents under the joint-family system, they are typical of modern India, in which, increasingly, marriage needn't end a girl's career.

*The magazine feature on Nirmala*

Pankajam in Panchavati House. Describing Nirmala as a singer and classical dancer, the report notes that, 'Although the couple live with his (Ram's) parents under the joint-family system, they are typical of modern India, in which increasingly, marriage needn't end a girl's career.'

Typical or not, Pankajam and Ram had played their part in creating a home environment that would nurture Nirmala's career during the 1950s and 1960s when dance was not much of a paying profession. As Ram recalled, dancers were paid no more than Rs 250 for a performance by sabha managers, and earned Rs 30 or less from a performance, after paying the musicians and other accompanying artists. Ram, who was then working as an executive in Air India, admired his wife's passion for dance and resolved to do what he could to support her. Their first child was born (in 1964) six years after they got married. This was an unusually long period without a child for a newly-wed couple in the early 1960s. A year or two into the marriage, Ram convinced his wife that they would do well to put off having children so that they could pursue other interests and, most importantly, Nirmala would be free to develop her career as a dancer. Not once during this period did Pankajam ask her son or daughter-in-law when or whether they intended to have a child.[34]

In the M–S story, when the grandfather informs Meena that a boy's family was going to visit them in order to 'view' her the next day, Meena protests by asking if she is a 'strange animal in the zoo' that she must be viewed. As a wife, a mother and a mother-in-law, Pankajam was part of several ritualistic exercises of 'bride-seeing' in her life in which she played the conventional part of the demure bride-to-be, the anxious mother

---

34 The story of Nirmala who danced and Lalitha who could not is what this book allows me to dwell on. Young dancers, who are hereditary practitioners of Bharatanatyam, have foregrounded the historical processes by which the women of their families were relegated to the margins of the dance world and remain unable to partake of the social and cultural capital associated with the practice of Bharatanatyam in post-Independence India (Pillai, 2022).

and prospective mother-in-law. However, Pankajam had also fashioned for herself a kingdom of the mind (the 'mano rajiyam' that Kamala speaks of in V–M) in which one may 'gallivant with freedom and autonomy'. It is in one such alternate universe that a 'modern girl' may participate in the bride-selecting ceremony on terms that Pankajam describes in an (undated) poem I found among her papers.

*Bride Selecting Ceremony by a Modern Girl*

The house was astir, everyone tense
'Why mother, I ask, who is coming?'
'The one to view you and choose.'
'View me and choose—certainly no'
'Send word, mother, we go there to view him.'
'It is not heard of,' says father
'No dad, in future, it will be
'To be exhibited—never
Am I an auction cow?'
Amidst protests, they come
I was called, I stare in anger
He requests a few private words with me
Unbidden springs these words from my heart
'If I choose, can we live alone without parents?
Can you help cook and manage a child?'
I ask questions too, why not?
'How am I less than you in status?
I have a degree too, am talented and beautiful
Shall I name the sum you should hand over?
Or we give nothing to each other but ourselves,
Both are equal in everything
Yes or no, quick, I have work to do!'

# 37

## Unusual guests (1950s)

In the 1950s, Panchavati House entertained unusual visitors. Chief among them was Swami Chinmayananda (1916–1993), the founder of the Chinmaya Mission, who began to deliver lectures on the Hindu scriptural texts in 1951. Pankajam's family met him for the first time in the summer of 1953. Pankajam's father PRG, who heard about a 'new' Swami visiting the city and lecturing in English, said to his grandson Ram, 'Go and meet him, he will explain religion the way you young people like. Call him home for *Biksha.*' Ram first met him at a crumbling old mansion in Egmore where he was then staying and meeting eager and curious visitors. Ram was taken aback to find a Swamiji accosting him saying, 'Hello young man, where are you from? What do you do? You work in Burma Shell, do you? Why, you must be seen with a tin of Goldflake in your hand! Where is it?' As Ram recalls, when Chinmayananda began his lectures in Madras in 1953, there was opposition to the idea of a non-Brahmin[35] performing and leading yagnas. Pankajam's youngest child Mythily, in a recorded interview, has also spoken of Chinmayananda's struggle in the

---

35  Named Balakrishna Menon, Chinmayananda belonged to a Malayali Nair family.

early years against the idea that, being a non-Brahmin, he had no authority to expound on the Vedas.

Pankajam did not care for the critics of Chinmayananda and admired his dynamic, forceful and articulate persona from their first meeting. With PRG's support, Pankajam invited Chinmayananda to stay with her family in Panchavati House whenever he visited Madras. Ram recalls a two-hour long discussion between his siblings and Chinmayananda one morning just after breakfast. Pankajam had organised the session so that he could address her children's scepticism and questions about religion and faith. Ram said to me:

> Mythily was always more of a believer than any of us. We did not care much about God and wondered how one can be certain about the existence of God, what is the proof and so on. We frankly shared our questions with Swamiji who began an impressive lecture on the body, the mind and the intellect. Suddenly, I noticed Sundaram slinking away from the house just as we began the discussion!

Ram was astonished to find that Chinmayananda remembered their breakfast discussion some twenty-five years later when Ram met him in Bombay on one occasion. Chinmayananda reportedly said, 'Hello Ramachandran! How is Pankajam? And how is your brother who would not speak to me?' From 1953 to 1956 or so, Chinmayananda took up residence at Panchavati House on his visits to Madras and held informal talks and meetings in the living room and under the *Magizam* tree (Bullet Wood) in the garden. When the numbers of listeners and visitors swelled, Sivaraman, never spiritually inclined, indicated to Pankajam that Chinmayananda would do well to stay elsewhere during his visits to Madras. Pankajam continued, however, to attend Chinmayananda's meetings when he lectured at Madras in the subsequent years.

It was in one of his lectures in the city that she met and befriended a young British woman in 1954 or so. Paxye

Thornhill's parents were British tea estate owners in Sri Lanka, who had left the country and relocated to England when the tea industry was nationalised. In 1952-53, Paxye, an adventurous and enterprising young woman, drove a van (named 'Biscuit') through Europe and journeyed to India. Starting from England, Paxye drove by herself through France, Switzerland, Austria, Turkey, Yugoslavia, Beirut, Syria, Iraq, Iran, Afghanistan, Pakistan and finally reached India. By fitting a bed inside the vehicle, Paxye lived and slept in the van during her long journey. An unmarried young woman who travelled alone, smoked openly and was in a relationship with an Italian filmmaker she had met in Madras, Paxye may have put off many people. But Pankajam was not one of them.

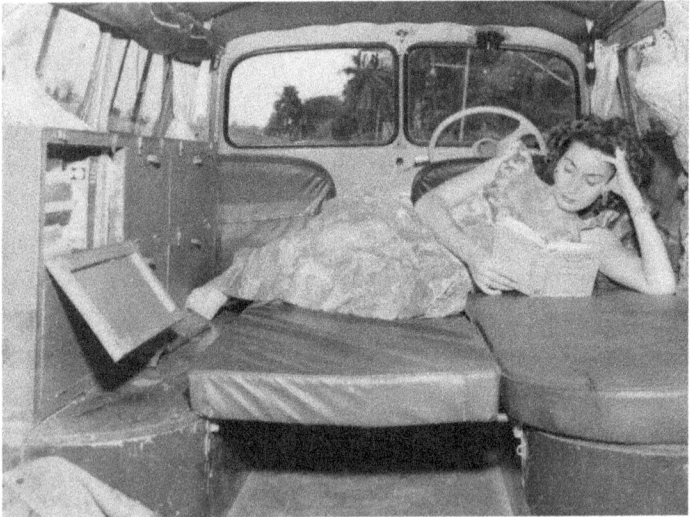

*Paxye in her van named Biscuit*

Sniffing out an interesting person, Pankajam immediately invited Paxye home to meet her children and get to know her better. Paxye got along fabulously with Pankajam and very soon after, became a friend of the family and a frequent visitor to Panchavati House. When Ram dropped in on Paxye some years later in Bombay, where she was then living, he was terrified to be greeted by a leopard that she had bought in Javadhu Hills (Tamil Nadu) and was raising in her flat! Pankajam's friendship and letter correspondence with Paxye lasted until the latter's death sometime in the mid-1990s.

# 38

## Friendship and camaraderie

In the late 1950s, Pankajam continued to remain the primary ally of her children, squirreling away money from the shoestring household budget that Sivaraman allowed her in order to help her children with their college-related expenses. In the case of her fourth child Sundaram, Pankajam supported his 'strong desire', as he writes in his memoir, to go to England even without a specific educational plan or job offer. Sundaram, who had spent three unhappy years studying for a bachelor's degree in commerce in the Pachayappas College (Madras), when he would rather have studied chemistry or chemical engineering, was keen to leave the country and start life anew elsewhere. Feeling sorry for her son, who had suffered ill health and depression from being pressured (by his father) to study a course he disliked, Pankajam worked on Sivaraman and gradually persuaded him to finance Sundaram's ship fare and buy him the winter clothing he needed 'without making a fuss', as Sundaram writes. As his ship pulled away from the Bombay harbour, Pankajam pressed into her son's hand some extra money that she had got by clandestinely selling household vessels.

Having to constantly manoeuvre between her children's desires and her husband's views on the right choice of study or career could not have been a pleasant experience for Pankajam. Besides her father, who were Pankajam's friends during these years? Pankajam's correspondence with Paxye from the 1950s to the 1990s gives us a sense of the rich friendship that the two women separated by race, nation and family circumstances had forged with each other. In her letters to Pankajam where she always addresses her as, 'My dear little Indian Mother,' Paxye comes across as a trusted confidante from whom Pankajam sought both practical advice and moral support. In her letter written in May 1958 from Bombay, Paxye responds to concerns that Pankajam appears to have expressed about her younger daughter Mythily. Pankajam seems to have considered taking eighteen-year-old Mythily to the Christian Medical College (CMC) hospital in Vellore and asked Paxye if she knows of doctors there and places to stay.

… Now if I might make a suggestion, I hope you will not take it amiss. I know that in the opinion of many doctors, 90% of the ailments of girls of Mythily's age are caused by frustrations, worry and nervousness. At the age when a girl grows into a woman, there are of course changes taking place, and new facts and duties to face. It is a time of struggle, of uncertainties, longings, fears, hopes, ambitions, etc, etc. These mental states are not usually acknowledged by the girl herself. So the worry spreads to the body as the only outlet … But these are only outward signs of the inner disorder … Now my advice to you, dear little mother, is to try and find out discreetly what it is that is worrying her. It may be her exams, or over-anxiousness, or a dread of being married off early like Lalitha.

Indian girls, who are blossoming out like Mythily into a new world, with new problems to solve and new situations to meet, have a lot of adjusting to do. They have one foot in the past and one in the future. She probably does not even know herself that she is worried. If you can find out her chief fear and help her recognise and solve it, she will be alright ... I suggest that she gets a good book of yoga and spends at least half an hour a day following them, fifteen minutes breathing, and fifteen minutes doing the asanas. If I were in Madras, I would force her!

... Your letter said nothing about yourself except you were nursing your mother and generally worrying about your large family ... Oh dear, life always seems to be taking from you and giving so little ...

In the early 1960s, Pankajam's father added to her worries on account of his growing senility brought on by the advance of Parkinson's disease and his stubborn refusal to take any medicines. Paxye's letter to Pankajam (of September 1963) was written after she received news of PRG's demise.

... I know how sad and despondent you must be feeling. That is the inevitable reaction of pouring forth your love day in and day out, exhausting yourself in service to someone you loved. Now that it is over, depression will set in, which is really exhaustion. That is why I hope and pray that you can get away from everyone for a real holiday ... You must go somewhere nice. You love and understand nature, and in return, if you can reach her, she will reward you by flowing into you, and giving you back your health and energy.

How I enjoyed being with you in Madras... You were so kind to me—as always. I love talking to you so much ... With you I know I can say everything as I feel it. That is a wonderful thing. I value your friendship so much. But it was awful to see you so exhausted, and with such a burden to carry. The strain of nursing your father must have been tremendous ... All my love and sympathy to you, my brave little Indian mother ...

Paxye's letter shows that the friendship meant a great deal to both women who could 'say everything as they felt it' without fear of disapproval or judgment by the other. Paxye's letters (this one and others) are strewn with insightful comments on the inextricable connection between physical and emotional states of being. Paxye appears to have been uncannily prescient in identifying the psychosomatic nature of Mythily's poor health (Mythily suffered from clinical depression that remained undiagnosed until the mid-1990s). In her letters, Paxye cautions her friend to be mindful of how depressed moods and depleted emotional energies can have significant bodily manifestations. She frequently urges Pankajam to put herself first, get away from her family now and then, seek solitude and the company of nature or make time for reading. Paxye expresses regret that everyone in Pankajam's life takes so much from her 'as people are wont to do with mothers'.

Pankajam was one who invested much of herself in 'tending, nursing and serving' all whom she loved (as she writes in her poem 'Hope' in 1948). Through her active years, Pankajam cared for her children, her parents and her grandchildren with passion and great generosity. For Pankajam, this was a way of life and her way of being in the world. As she saw it, the universe owed her no recompense for her labour of love, enriching and rewarding in and of itself. And yet, I would like to think that Paxye's counsel may have offered her a refreshingly different perspective on revaluing the labour of love and physical care that she so ceaselessly performed.

*Pankajam with her grandchild*

On 12 September 1963, the same day that Paxye was thinking of Pankajam and writing to her, another woman friend was doing the same. Among Pankajam's papers, I found a postcard written in Tamil that carried a brief yet pithy condolence note to Pankajam on the death of PRG. The writer was Pankajam's aunt Subamma, the widow of her maternal uncle Ananthakrishnan, in whose house (in Triplicane) Pankajam and Subbalakshmi had stayed during the 1920s. Subamma, a native of Madurai and the only child of her parents, was about six years older than Pankajam. Subamma's younger daughter Chella Kailasam, who I interviewed for this book, recalled her mother's description of Pankajam as an 'adorable child' with whom she had developed a close bond during their years together in Madras.

Immediately after Ananthakrishnan's death in February 1928, Subamma's father took his daughter and two little granddaughters back to his home in Madurai. Subamma lost contact with her husband's family thereafter. Sometime in the mid-1930s, Subamma received an unexpected visitor one day. This was Sivaraman, who had been expressly sent by his wife to re-establish contact with Subamma's family in Madurai. Sivaraman's visit led to a flood of letters between aunt (Subamma) and niece (Pankajam). Chella was about twelve years old when she and her older sister first spent a summer vacation at Panchavati House on Pankajam's invitation. As Pankajam's son Ram explained, his mother was always keen to have her young cousins stay with her and felt a deep sense of obligation to her uncle's family. 'We stayed in their house for six years and enjoyed their hospitality,' she would often say to Ram.

But it was more than a debt of gratitude or fond memories of a shared past that bound Pankajam to Subamma. As Chella put it, 'Whenever Pankajam wanted company, counsel, a cushion to lay her head on or a crutch to hold on to, she reached out to Subamma.' Pankajam's closeness to Subamma was also because she could confide in her and speak of her marital unhappiness openly and in a manner that she could not with her own mother. As Chella recalled, Pankajam would say to Subamma:

I can say all this only to you and not my mother. Do I have a mother like other mothers? A mother who will console me or even ask me, 'What does your husband say to you and what does he do and what sort of man is he and so on?'

When Pankajam shared her woes, Subamma offered her a counterpoint of view to the effect that Sivaraman was a good provider and a stable earner who had managed his finances well enough to build a big house and afford a car. He was not a dissolute who brawled or came home drunk to harass his wife and steal money wherever she hid it, as men were known to do. Chella recalled that her mother would say to Pankajam, 'Do not ever leave him or your credibility will be lost. If you leave your husband, people will say your mother did the same thing.' Widowed when she was about twenty-four years old, Subamma must have suffered the loss of status and the stigma that accompanied early widowhood in Tamil Brahmin families, even though her natal family was known to be very protective of her. She may have therefore seen the respectability conferred by the status of a wife, an auspicious *Sumangali* (married woman), as something that Pankajam must not scoff at or thoughtlessly discard.

If Paxye was the friend and confidante who reminded Pankajam to place her dreams, desires and needs above the demands of others, Subamma was the friend and confidante who cautioned her to be mindful of the social web of relationships in which she was embedded and not to fly against the face of established opinion. Located in the same social universe as Pankajam was, Subamma's support went well beyond counsel and a sympathetic ear. In the later years of Subbalakshmi's life when her health deteriorated, Subamma visited Pankajam often and helped care for her mother. As Mythily has written in *Fragments of a Life*, Subbalakshmi developed irrational fears and suspicions that Pankajam may have poisoned her food and wrote complaining letters about her daughter to her relatives. During this period of acute stress, the presence of a close woman friend and family member, who had known Subbalakshmi and had thought well of her during her younger years, must have been a great comfort to Pankajam.

# 39

## Two daughters, two destinies

The lives of Subbalakshmi and Pankajam and their hopes and aspirations for their daughters' lives tell us something of what was possible for girls and young women (in upper-caste and middle-class households) to *be* and *do* in colonial India and the first two decades after independence. Subbalakshmi had no formal schooling, while Pankajam had six years of schooling (owing to her mother's firmness of purpose and resolve), until she was forced to quit in the middle of class nine at the end of 1927. Pankajam's daughters Lalitha and Mythily both graduated from college with a BA (Honours) degree—Lalitha in 1953 and Mythily in 1959. Subbalakshmi was married when she was eleven years old (in 1908) and became a mother at fourteen. Pankajam was married at seventeen (in 1929) and was a mother at nineteen. Her older daughter Lalitha was married at nineteen (in 1952) and a mother at twenty. She graduated from college after the birth of her first child. Mythily married a person of her choice and outside her caste, when she was thirty-two (in 1972), twenty years after her older sister. Mythily's trajectory diverged from her sister's (and most other young women of her period) around the time that she graduated from college in 1959 and left for New Delhi to study for a master's diploma in the Indian School of

Public Administration (IIPA), Indraprastha in July 1960. How did this come to be?

*Mythily and Lalitha*

I distinctly recall from my conversations with Pankajam that her younger sons Srini and Sundaram had firmly dissuaded Pankajam and Sivaraman from ever 'doing to Mythily what they had done to Akka (Lalitha)' by subjecting her to an early marriage that would foreclose her options of further study and a possible career.

Letter correspondence between twenty-two-year-old Mythily and her parents when she was studying in Delhi (1960–61) reveal the positions that were taken by each of the three actors—Pankajam, Sivaraman and Mythily herself on the question of Mythily's marriage.

I reproduce extracts from Pankajam's letter to Mythily dated 10 June 1961.

You ask why I have suddenly thought about your marriage now when you are against it and why I was not so when you were inclined to it. If I remember right, I have never understood or heard you say that you ever were interested in marriage. When you were in college you used to say, 'Do not do to me anything as you did to Akka [Lalitha]. I want to take my degree.' When you finished your course, I wanted to start looking for a bridegroom for you … when came your results. It completely turned the tables.

You and I thought you will be going to America and I did not want to stand against such brilliant prospects. I thought maybe you are intended for greater purposes. I thought you will become a great woman wielding power and holding big offices. My second idea for not wanting to hurry you into marriage was that you had passed out just then and taken a high degree. I wanted to give you some more time to use your knowledge and the education I had given you by taking up a job and tasting freedom and power (which I had never known in my life). So I wanted you to know what they are before you finally give them up.

And I also thought you were too young then to marry as you were immature and maybe it was in the subconscious mind—the fear of parting with you (only a mother can understand this).

And lastly, or perhaps the most important reason which I should have given first, was your father's stiff opposition to it and evasion of the subject whenever I broached it … Do you not remember how many times I pleaded with you to say 'yes' to your father when I broached the marriage proposals in front of him? Has not your father called you many a time and asked you, 'Mythily, your mother says she wants you to marry. I know you are not such a fool. You have not said any such thing, is it not?' and you used to say, 'I never want to get married.' And how triumphant your father used to look. You always listened more to his advice than mine ...

I am perfectly convinced that you will be happy provided the man is alright. Only you do not know it and are unnecessarily worried because you have seen some unhappy marriages at home ... I want to see you perfectly happy ... You can be so, for I want to let you move with the man you are to marry and freely exchange your views. Besides I shall give you some more time—say a year or two. I shall wait as you are so emphatic now in denying the need ...

Pankajam's letter makes it clear that Mythily had resolutely set her mind against marriage during her college years in Madras (1956–59), and the 'unhappy marriages at home' (her mother's and grandmother's) had put her off the idea of marriage. While Pankajam was not one to force her daughter, Sivaraman allied himself fully with his daughter who, as he put it, was not 'fool' enough to desire marriage. When Mythily graduated in 1959, she topped the BA course in political science, winning the Candeth Medal for securing the first mark in her class.[36] Mythily had also held the top mark in Madras University the same year, securing a gold medal for her performance. This is what Pankajam was referring to in the letter when she writes that Mythily's (exam) 'results had completely turned the tables'. Mythily's academic performance meant that she had won herself the space to work

---

36  Awarded to students who topped the class in the history and political science department, the Candeth medal was instituted in 1944 in memory of Professor Candeth who had taught several years in the Presidency College, Madras.

or study further if she so chose to. It also allowed Pankajam to aspire to visions of 'freedom and power' for her daughter as 'a great woman wielding power and holding big offices' and maybe even going to America.

As Pankajam reiterates, she was keen that Mythily should have a taste of the independence that Pankajam herself had never known, even if it was going to be short-lived. At the same time, she reminds her daughter (in this letter) of the 'equal importance of psychological and biological needs' that must be met for her to be a 'normal, healthy person'. For Pankajam, the psychological needs included wanting to be 'loved, cherished and protected' and enjoying 'intelligent companionship' that would allow Mythily to share her joys and sorrows. This would make marriage necessary at some point, as Pankajam saw it, and Mythily must not therefore set her mind against it. Pankajam's letter was written just as Mythily was about to finish her master's diploma and return to Madras, rendering the question of 'what next?' salient.

Sivaraman's letter to Mythily, written a month after she left for Delhi to start her diploma, confirms that both her parents respected her wishes and saw her as someone who could not be trifled with. I reproduce an extract from his letter dated 7 August 1960.

My dear last child,

It is a month since you left. I am missing you every evening when I sip my quota when you used to have your stealthy sip. Well, you were telling me that Public Administration is the subject that you hated most and you have slipped into it finally—instead of returning home. Well, you are a child guided by fate and none of us can do anything to you, but look upon with wonder. I think the subjects you are reading will be useful in case you write the IAS exam … I would like to hear from you more in detail about the subjects you do and what your reactions are to each of them … I want you to play some games like tennis and badminton and learn swimming. I will be happy to learn of your progress in swimming and other exercise.

Sivaraman was described by his son Sundaram (in his memoir) as a 'domineering father' who expected his wife and all his children to follow his advice and wishes. Sivaraman, who had decided that Sundaram would do better studying commerce in college rather than chemistry (a subject he wanted to study), writes to his daughter, 'No one can do anything to you, but look upon with wonder.' I recall that Mythily always spoke of Sivaraman (to me) as a 'democratic father' who never imposed his views on her. It may have been the case that Sivaraman felt that he could dictate academic choices for his sons. But his daughter was stepping into a world of postgraduate study when it was not quite clear what professional careers young women of the middle classes could embrace with ease in newly-independent India. In Mythily's case, it appears therefore that Sivaraman would rather let his 'child guided by fate' find her own way.

In his letters to Mythily, written during her year of stay in Delhi, he repeatedly urges her to learn to swim, play a sport and get some physical exercise. He hopes she will decide to be a civil servant and prepare for the IAS examination. He enquires with great interest about the courses she studies, tries to keep up with the books she reads and sends her news clippings from *The Hindu* on her course subjects that she describes in her letters to him. In his letter (28 August 1960), Sivaraman writes to Mythily, 'My dear sweet child, I wish I was there with you so that I could also blabber something in the subjects you are dabbling in.' In a letter to her father (27 February 1961), Mythily writes,

Finally, as you have mentioned, I'm also equally glad that I'm not entangled in the matrimonial complications as yet. But I'm not very sure that I'll be wise for too long! (Please don't let your imagination run too fast. I'll give you a decent warning in advance).

In 1963, two years after returning to Madras, twenty-three-year-old Mythily left for America to study for a master's degree in public administration in Syracuse University (New York), having secured a scholarship that would finance her study. During the two years in Madras, Mythily remained 'wise' and free of 'matrimonial complications'. When Mythily was making her plans to leave India, there was no opposition from the family to her decision to make her way in the world as a single woman. In a farewell letter written to her sister from Karur, where she was then living with her husband and children, Lalitha expresses sadness at not being able to 'watch the Boeing's tail light vanish into the star-studded sky, taking with it our hearts' most beloved possession, while our lips mechanically chant a prayer for your wellbeing and happiness'. In her letter of 8 July 1963, Lalitha writes,

> As Srini remarked, you are the only one among the five of us who knew what you wanted and worked for it single-mindedly all along. You richly deserve this opportunity and I am sure it will be a year of fruitful learning and experience. Since all efforts were made by you, all credits should go to you. However, coming from a Hindu Brahmin family, you should consider yourself lucky and be thankful to father and mother for having been so frightfully decent about this trip of yours. You will realise it the moment you visualise the problems they could have created had they wanted ...

While Lalitha gives full credit to Mythily's initiative and efforts in carving out her own path in life, her letter reminds us that Pankajam and Sivaraman did make the unconventional choice of allowing their younger daughter to tread an uncertain path and pursue her dreams. In 1924, Subbalakshmi was refused permission (by her mother and brother) to leave for Shantiniketan to educate Pankajam and secure a fresh lease of life for herself. In the late 1940s/early 1950s, Pankajam and Sivaraman thought it too unorthodox to allow Lalitha to travel with dance troupes to America and Europe, even if they accompanied her. In 1963, they must have decided that orthodoxy had had its day and must give way to young women's dreams and aspirations, especially when they knew what they wanted and worked for it too, as Mythily had done. The letters indicate that Sivaraman no less than Pankajam (and perhaps even more) wanted Mythily to become a woman of consequence.

When looking back on her decisions regarding Lalitha's dance and marriage, Pankajam briefly mentions a college play in which Lalitha appeared as a queen when a young princess snatches her tiara declaring, 'I am the queen.' Pankajam writes that this play, in hindsight, felt like an augury given that it turned out to be Lalitha's last performance on the stage. If I may extend the analogy further, we may perhaps see Mythily as the princess who announces to the world her turn to wear the tiara in mid-1963 when she takes a flight to America. About a week or so before Mythily left, Pankajam took her to a photography studio and

*Mythily, 1963*

had a picture of her daughter taken in full bridal gear with her long hair plaited and decorated. In the picture, Mythily is seen wearing a silk sari and sporting traditional jewellery, including a girdle around her waist. As Pankajam told me, she had the picture taken as she suspected (rather astutely!) that this may be the last time her daughter would agree to dress in this fashion. Pankajam bid goodbye to her younger daughter, anticipating that she could not control or predict who Mythily may become in America.

# 40

## Bye-bye blackbird

In September 1957, Pankajam's sons Srini and Sundaram took off to England to study and to work, respectively. Her youngest child Mythily left for the US in July 1963. What was Pankajam's life like after her children flew the nest? Not surprisingly, parting from her children was difficult for her. Letter correspondence was the primary link between them since long-distance or 'trunk calls' were infrequent, expensive and unreliable. The first letter that Pankajam sent Mythily after her daughter left for the US was written on 16 July 1963.

> I was down two days in bed soon after you left but it may be psychological. Though I have not begun yet to understand or feel your absence with its full force for you seem to be just gone out and may return anytime as usual ... Your familiar figure seems to cling about the house and I frequently call your name—the dearest name in Christendom.

Though Pankajam keenly felt her children's absence, she did not cling to them, realising that it was through their experience of independent adulthood and self-actualisation that she may know the world better too. Wherever they travelled, her children wrote her letters that brought to life new landscapes, architecture, museums, churches, art and their impressions of everyday social mores and new cultures. Many of these letters were elaborate travelogues compressed into several pages of tiny handwriting, with after-thought observations and reflections scribbled in the margins. Pankajam's children knew that their letters served other purposes too. If their mother could not free herself from her familiar grind of cares, chores and worries, their letters may yet acquaint her with new sights, tastes and their own gradually-developing sensibilities, as they made their way in the world.

*Middle-aged Pankajam*

In an undated letter from London written sometime in the late 1950s, Srini writes of experiencing the 'peak of the entertainment season' including the Bertram Mills Circus and an opera (Giuseppe Verdi's *The Masked Ball*) staged in the Royal Opera House of Covent Garden. He describes spending Christmas with a 'very English family' in New Port (Wales), who were very kind to their visitor from India. Srini writes, 'Having been brought up in a society where your movements are informal and free, and when you come across people so formal, stiff and conventional with whom every movement means something, you feel rather uncomfortable ... I was surprised to see the number of presents exchanged!'. In his letter of August 1960, Sundaram, also writing from London, describes how a party of thirty-five boys and girls from different countries chartered a plane and flew to Paris. He writes, 'Mass at Notre Dame cathedral on Sunday left a greater impression on me than St Pauls' at London ... The French people are more human and not coldly polite and cultured like the English. Virtually, there is no colour bar in France.'

In the Meena–Subbu story, Pankajam writes of how listening to stories about American and British children made little Meena think of them as 'real people'. To an older Pankajam, her children's letters, pulsating with excitement at exploring unfamiliar pastures and expressing ambivalent feelings about being brown faces in 'white' countries, must have made other worlds even more real to her. How did Pankajam respond to these letters and the experiences they allowed her to savour? In her letter of 13 September 1965, Pankajam responded to the news of Mythily's cross-country drive across America with her friends.

> You cannot imagine how very proud I was to learn you were making a cross-country drive with friends. I was wild with excitement and following you with the map, all the places you must have crossed. Even you cannot have been as happy as I was in knowing you are enjoying and seeing things which seemed very familiar to me through books. Long ago, when I was a girl of sixteen, I had read in great

detail, wonderfully described [in the *Book of Knowledge*] about the Arizona desert, the Grand Canyon, Badlands and the beauties of Montana district. I was sure then that someday I would see Yellowstone Park and its Sulphur geysers and terraces ... Like an innocent child, I believed when I was a girl, I would be seeing them as sure as one expects to go from one class to the next!! I never counted the failures in life too. So, you can imagine my joy and excitement in seeing and enjoying them by proxy.

I have many queries to put to you ... Did you also drive and have you learnt their rules and regulations? You did not mention anything about Disneyland—did you see it— is it not somewhere in Hollywood? Did you meet any notables in your trip? Did you come across any writers, poets or artists? There must be talented youngsters also.

If Mythily's letters reminded Pankajam of her sixteen-year-old self's discovery of the *Book of Knowledge*, the sting of her disappointments and 'failures in life' was mitigated by her vicarious delight in her daughter's adventure. Pankajam's queries show us how meticulously she sought to relate her bookish knowledge of the world to her children's first-hand experience. We see this again in her response to Mythily's account of her first visit to New York city soon after reaching America. In her letter of 28 July 1963, Pankajam writes, 'It is interesting to hear about the City Music Hall and the stage show. May I hear in detail about the stage show—its back scenes and acting, whether the stage and actors are very like daily scenes or like got up things as they are here? Or is it like a cinema? What are its main striking features?' Intrigued by Mythily's reference to 'ivy-covered college cottages' in Syracuse University where she was enrolled, she asks her daughter to purchase a 'real nice camera with all modern adjustments and learn to take colour pictures' so that Mythily may have an album of memories and Pankajam may see what ivy-covered cottages look like.

Pankajam's activities in Madras were also influenced by her children's interests and involvements. After Mythily secured her degree from Syracuse University in 1965, she stayed on in America to gain work experience. In 1966, when Mythily was working and earning an income in the US, she informed her mother of her wish (and that of her American friends) to financially support the care and education of children living in poverty. Accompanied sometimes by her older daughter Lalitha, Pankajam visited charity homes and institutions in Madras and urged their founders and managers to send Mythily the information she needed to be of assistance to them.

> I visited Avvai Home, Mercy Home, Deaf and Dumb School, School for the Blind and Balamandir too ... I myself got so interested in the organisations and wished I had the money and freedom and time to be able to do some little bit for them. You are lucky in that you are free to help the helpless of your country ... All these organisations I saw are really doing much for the abandoned children of the streets and hospitals. Most of the institutions are kept running by Christian foreign mission money and some meagre Indian donations. They need more support ... (3 October 1966)

When Mythily financially assisted the care of a young girl in the School for the Blind, it was Pankajam and Lalitha who visited the child and brought her home to stay with them during school vacations. In her letters to Mythily written in 1966-67, Pankajam praises the 'steady work done for a long, long period of time' by the organisations, even as she decries their dire financial straits that leave the 'young ones in a very poor state, very weak and uncared for'. The tone of warm sympathy that underlies her description of the children's homes reminded me of Pankajam's wrenching narration of the story of Jane Eyre (the protagonist of Charlotte Bronte's celebrated novel) and her early years in an institution where she is cast away by her relatives. I recall Pankajam crying at each retelling of the death of the little girl Helen (Jane's best friend) from an illness brought on by poor feeding and care and her tone of outrage at the institutional neglect to which the girls were subjected. While Pankajam writes that she had not the 'money and freedom and time' to give as much of herself as she would have liked to these institutions of care, she appears to have valued the opportunities to visit, meet and interact with them, when Mythily's offer of financial support allowed her to do so.

# 41

# Metamorphosis (1960s)

Pankajam's children remained her primary allies and emotional anchor during their adult lives. However, their long stints of living and working abroad also gave them the means to look afresh at everyday life in Panchavati House and react in ways that posed new challenges to their parents. In the late 1950s and 1960s, Sundaram, Srini and Mythily, in their letters to one another written from India, England and America, occasionally commented with sadness on the atmosphere of troubled peace and disquiet that prevailed at home. In his letter (of 13 March 1961) written from Manchester to his sister, who was studying in Delhi, twenty-four-year-old Sundaram writes, 'I am glad you are enjoying yourself and far away from 45 Spurtank Road, the hotbed of domestic politics and where things make no progress and people never change.' After four years of living in England, Sundaram returned to Madras in mid-1961 and took up residence at Panchavati House again. In his memoir, he discusses his changing reactions to the situation at home.

My parents quarreled more when they became older. After I returned from England, I reacted more emotionally to their shouting matches ... One day, they were shouting at each other loudly again ... I lost my patience this time, and I decided to do something to pressure them to calm down and control themselves. When my father went into his room, I closed the door behind him and padlocked the door. Then I took my mother by her hand and led her to another room and padlocked the door of that room also. Thinking that I was sympathetic to my father, my mother got angry with me and asked to be let out. I told her that I am not taking anyone's side. And that until they agreed to behave better to each other, I would keep them locked in their rooms ...

My father was very quiet in his room and did not order me to unlock the door. It was lunchtime. He calmly said in a low voice that he was hungry and would like to eat lunch. Realising that I had accomplished what I wanted them to learn ... I let them both out, and they quietly went their way without saying anything to each other or to me ... They never referred to this incident later, or complained to me about my insolent behaviour anytime ...

This passage in Sundaram's memoir reveals that the animosity between his parents had not dimmed in their later years of co-habitation. What had changed instead was that their adult children, or at least one of them, was holding them to account for the emotional toll that the couple's acrimonious habits and patterns of interaction, took on them. In his memoir, Sundaram describes other conflicts with his parents during his period of stay (of three years) in Madras in the early 1960s. He writes of feeling 'angry and let down' when his parents, concerned at the single status of their twenty-five-year-old son, conspired with each other to make Sundaram call on a family friend, without revealing that the real objective of the visit was to arrange a meeting with a young woman in the hope that a marriage may come of it. Another attempt at matchmaking also came to naught when Sundaram 'escaped' (as he writes) from his parents' efforts to 'trap' him.

However, Pankajam did appreciate that her son's period of stay outside the country had altered his views and needs. When Sundaram complained that the vegetarian diet at home did not satisfy him any longer, she immediately approached their Anglo-Indian neighbours and offered to pay if they would send their cooked meals (meat dishes) every evening for her son. Pankajam writes in her biography of Sundaram, 'They agreed and sent their meals. Everyone at home was surprised.' The most difficult and painful dilemma that Pankajam grappled with had to do with Sundaram's wish to emigrate and build a life for himself elsewhere.

> When I talked about my wish to emigrate to Canada, my parents reacted negatively, as I had expected ... When my mother realised that she could not persuade me to change my mind using practical reasons, she mentioned how insecure she would be in India without me ... Her relationship with my father being bad, she had to rely on her sons to protect and support her. Such a pathetic appeal made it very difficult for me to make up my mind because I deeply loved my mother. There was a conflict of interest between my mother and myself ...

Eventually, Pankajam did not persevere in clinging to her son. In her biographical sketch of Sundaram, she writes of how her son's state of mind convinced her to change her own mind. She writes, 'One day, I was feeling unhappy thinking of Sundaram and his unhappiness. Suddenly I decided that we must let him go. So, I told him that he can go anywhere.' In April 1966, a year after Sundaram moved to Canada, he wrote to his parents announcing his decision to marry a French-Canadian girl he had met at work. How did Pankajam and Sivaraman react to the news of their son's impending wedding which was to be solemnised in a parish church as the girl's family was Roman Catholic? Sundaram writes, 'I received a prompt reply from my parents congratulating me, and expressing their happiness to know that I had finally found someone that I really liked and loved ...'

Pankajam, who soon grew very fond of her Canadian daughter-in-law, found her earlier certainties unsettled by her adult children's experiences. In the early 1960s, when Mythily was studying in Delhi, Pankajam sought to convince her daughter that she could find happiness through a marriage judiciously arranged by her parents. But this too was to change. In a letter to Mythily in 1966, Pankajam writes, 'But do not fear that I will choose for you here. You are too clever and experienced in life and capable too. You can get a husband on your own ... I dare not interfere.' This did not, however, keep Pankajam from occasionally expressing the wish that Mythily would do something about it and find herself a 'man of noble character'. As the years passed, Pankajam grew mindful of the boundaries her daughter may have drawn around herself, even as the mother and daughter kept up a regular correspondence. A letter from Pankajam to Mythily hints at this.

> Well, my dear, I am afraid I have offended or annoyed you by my letter in which I had alluded to certain private matters of yours ... For everything, please pardon me, my darling, and do not be angry with this silly mother of yours. I know I am silly, but I am not bad, I hope. I will understand and obey you and respect your wishes always, be sure of it... So do forgive this once trespassing in your affairs. My only intention was to sympathise and be of some help and relief to you—if it is relief to unburden yourself to me (dated 15 January 1966).

During the 1960s, when making important decisions, it appears that Pankajam chose to put her children's happiness and their freedom to pursue their dreams above other worries or concerns she may have had for herself. While offering her empathy and understanding, she simultaneously acknowledged that her limited practical experience of the worlds they negotiated, left her unfit to make their decisions for them. Her letter to Mythily (of 5 September 1967), who had decided to return to India, sums up Pankajam's attitude rather succinctly.

Father and all of us are glad to hear you are coming back. Come with a lean there, in case you find your plans and ambitions do not work out, you can always get back. But in these matters, I am very ignorant and you know what you want. Do what you think is best for you.

# 42

## A dependent woman and her penurious mother (1960s)

In India of the mid-1960s, an alarming food crisis threatened the optimism generated by the developmental promise of the post-Independence years. Manifested as spiralling food prices and the import of food grains, the crisis was brought on by a food grains deficit that grew from the late 1950s and was worsened by the recurring droughts of 1965-66 and 1966-67. Besides casting a shadow on India's fifteen years of experience in development planning, the crisis also appeared to jeopardise the country's political sovereignty. During this period, Pankajam's letters to her children contained references to the national economic crisis and its oppressive weight on the household economy. In a letter to Mythily (22 January 1967), Pankajam reassured her daughter that Sivaraman's health had improved rapidly (from a bout of illness) and that Mythily must not worry on his account.

If at all anyone's life is feared, it is my mother's. But she too may last till 1968!! Of one thing I am sure. Before she dies, I will be half or three-fourths dead and will follow her soon. So much trouble and problems I have because of her and the general condition of the country, its food problem, money problems, all are crushing one's spirits.

What were the troubles and worries that Pankajam feared may send her to an early grave? The death of Pankajam's father in September 1963 terminated his retirement pension that had financed the expenses of her parents' independent household within Panchavati House. This blow was compounded by the fact that PRG had made no provision for his wife. He had bought no land or house when he was employed with the colonial government. Nor had he invested in a pension that might have supported his wife. PRG's will (prepared in September 1952) contains the following lines:

> One may wonder what I have to will away. Of real property,
> I have none. Of the movable kind, there is only one which
> requires disposal, my body.

PRG's failure to leave anything behind but his mortal remains cost his daughter dearly. For how was Pankajam, herself a dependent woman in a conflict-ridden marriage, to financially support her mentally ill, widowed and penurious mother? Drawing on letters from Pankajam, Mythily and Lalitha to one another, I show how the affective ties between a mother and her two daughters allowed Pankajam to finance and organize the care of her ailing mother Subbalakshmi. On 16 February 1966, Lalitha writes to her sister Mythily:

> I was happy to see your letter to mother. I never knew you had offered to send her money previously and that she had refused. Any amount that you can spare, ten or fifteen dollars will be a great help to Amma for I am ashamed to say that she is still having financial problems. When Thatha [PRG] died, leaving Gamma[37] on her hands, father refused to give her any extra money to maintain Gamma. Mother was spending Srini's monthly Rs 100 on Gamma.

---

37  Subbalakshmi was called 'Gamma' by her grandchildren.

When Srini left for Scandinavia, it looked as though there would be a crisis. But somehow, I managed to ask him to leave his savings with Amma. With that money, she built two rooms for Gamma upstairs and let out the portion downstairs. Now it fetches Amma a monthly rent of Rs 230 … Srini has been exceedingly kind and his savings helped mother at a very opportune moment.

If your money comes, she will use it to meet any out-of-the-way demands of Gamma and also to buy tonics and personal items like slippers for herself. I am sorry to write about all these trifles. Mother would never ask for money, especially from daughters. So, you have to offer even if she refuses. Please forgive me for being such a useless thing ... Except for talking to her, I am unable to give Amma any financial help. You are privileged—you can help her in her time of need ...

Father has given Srini a Fiat car and Ram a Herald car. He has deposited Rs 10,000 for Sundaram as his share. For you also, he has put by something. Only towards Amma he is still uncharitable. He cut her monthly household allowance when the rent from Gamma's house started coming in!

Resourceful as ever, Pankajam had tided over a crisis by adding an upper floor to the small house she had built for her parents (in 1948), moving her mother upstairs and managing to earn a rental income to support her mother. Lalitha's letter enables us to perceive Pankajam's situation with stark clarity—she was a non-earning woman married to a man who had earned comfortably and (in contrast to her own father) had planned his finances well, always striving to do justice by his five children in equal measure, sons and daughters alike. If PRG had not the foresight or capacity to provide for his wife, Sivaraman did not have the generosity to assist his own. And it was Pankajam who suffered from the ineptitude of her father and the unkindness of her husband.

While Lalitha urged her sister to financially assist their mother in February 1966, it appears that Pankajam accepted Mythily's offer only a year later. In her letter of 13 February 1967, Pankajam writes,

> My dear girl, it is kind of you to want to send me some money. Once, you offered a year or so back, but I refused. Now my condition has worsened and I think I shall accept your offer of help. For I need it for my mother. Next month, I have to pay tax for her house. The rent from her house is used up for her maintenance, two ayahs, doctor, medicines, clothes and food. I am unable to save even for its tax. Father keeps on cutting from my monthly expenses and the soaring prices have made my position precarious …
>
> You can send me $15 every month to Lalitha's address. I shall spend half the money and save half … Next year my mother may fall seriously ill and be hospitalised or require a trained nurse. I do not want her to suffer at all. I shall hide away your money in a different bank where Lalitha has an account, so that no one need know I have money there … I wish I could say I would pay you back, but I am not sure … I only wish God gives me life and strength enough to be able to serve you and yours, the only way of returning your love.

Besides the challenge of marshalling resources, Pankajam had the additional stress of concealing Mythily's money so that no one would ask her to spend it on 'the ocean that is called the household' as she writes in a letter to her daughter. Caring for Subbalakshmi was an exacting task for other reasons too. In her letter (13 September 1965), Pankajam writes of her mother,

> She is very ill, confused, very irritable, quarrelsome so much—so no ayah is willing to serve her. I have to daily bribe and coax them and appeal to their sympathy. But for me no one can manage the situation. All are very angry

with her and since your grandfather's death, your father is openly against her. So poor thing she has no one but me to stand by her in her hour of need.

In a tone of despair and fatigue, Pankajam writes (in 1967) that Subbalakshmi's life may last till 1968. Subbalakshmi's longevity exceeded Pankajam's expectations, and partly because of her daughter's devoted care-giving, Subbalakshmi lived till 1978. Pankajam had been charged with the responsibility of looking after Subbalakshmi (by her grandmother Kamakshi) since the time nine-year-old Pankajam found her mother lying unconscious in a garbage heap behind the house. When Lalitha was seven years old or so, her mother prepared her (and subsequently her younger siblings) to remain vigilant and watch out for Subbalakshmi's epileptic seizures and fainting spells, prevent her from falling if they could, immediately send word to Pankajam and stay with Subbalakshmi until help arrived. Pankajam's protective nurturance of her mother was enhanced by her perception of her as an otherworldly being who had lived out her life in conflict with dominant social conventions and had suffered much for being at odds with her world and her times.

When Pankajam weathered storms in the 'ocean that is called the household' in the 1960s, her fellow sailor was her older daughter Lalitha. In her letter to her sister, Lalitha begs Mythily to forgive her for 'being such a useless thing' in matters relating to their mother. In self-deprecatory fashion, Lalitha undervalues the moral and emotional support that she provided her mother during a difficult period. As her letter reveals, it was Lalitha who arranged for Srini to leave behind his savings when he left for Scandinavia. It was Lalitha who kept Mythily informed of their mother's financial troubles. It was Lalitha who did what Pankajam would not do—appeal to a daughter to help her mother financially ('even if she refuses') in a social context where such a thing was anathema. Lalitha also helped manage both Panchavati House and Sivaraman's flaring temper when Pankajam did eventually travel to visit her children in their homes abroad.

# 43

## Can a woman travel?

The letters that Pankajam's children wrote her from London, New York and Montreal during the 1950s and 1960s stoked her desire to visit them and see a bit of the world for herself too. But can a woman cut herself adrift from the household and travel without a care in the world? Pankajam was, after all, a woman without 'money or freedom or time' as she wrote of herself. From a letter to Mythily written in June 1961, we know that Pankajam had missed a chance to visit her sons Srini and Sundaram, who were then living in the UK. An airfare concession of sixty per cent was available through her son Ram who was working in Air India. But, as Pankajam writes, 'I know I cannot find the money' for the balance fare (of Rs 1,600) since Sivaraman had erupted with anger 'at the very idea and shouted so that all began to talk of me going later on'.

A second travel plan in 1965 did not materialise either. In a letter to Mythily, Pankajam described the arrangements she had made for the care of her mother since Ram had been 'tempting', 'threatening' and 'pleading' with her to use his two free passages available that year and travel to New York (Two passages were required to make a single free trip possible). Lalitha and Subbalakshmi's doctor had both agreed to call on Subbalakshmi daily, while Pankajam's aunt Subamma had consented to stay a month to care for her. But in July 1965, Subbalakshmi had suddenly taken very ill with 'terrible pains' in the stomach. Pankajam writes,

> Now how can I ever countenance the idea of leaving her at such a time of her life! There is no one else to whom I can for a moment give the burden ... Despite all arguments about my losing such a wonderful opportunity, I am not moved or sorry for myself. For what does this disappointment mean to one whose life itself has been a lost one? I have missed my life... (13 September 1965)

About two years later, Pankajam was planning again to visit Mythily. Her worry this time was something else.

> Father thinks he may join me and travel to see you [Mythily] in the US. Has to be tactfully handled. If he comes, it will be additional responsibility for me and I will not be able to enjoy myself, nor have quiet and peace ... (17 April 1967)

Fortunately for Pankajam, the situation was tactfully handled and Sivaraman did not accompany her on the trip. When Pankajam did finally travel for two and a half months in 1967, Ram's free passage enabled her to visit New York, Montreal and even London on her way back to India. Lalitha's letter to her mother gives us a sense of what it took to keep the peace in Panchavati House and facilitate Pankajam's extended absence:

> Don't keep writing about how happy you are in superlatives for it upsets father very badly. He keeps lashing out at Anna [Ram] unjustly all the time ... Father is terribly restless and disturbed that he has missed this chance to visit Mythily and Sundaram ... He kept chasing away cooks

who came there ... I have been sending cooked meals for
the night ... Do not worry about anything ... (6 July 1967)

Pankajam began her travel during the Six-Day War or the Third
Arab–Israeli war that lasted from 5 to 10 June 1967. Mythily
does not seem to have been aware of her mother's date of arrival
owing perhaps to poor communication created by the international
situation. Pankajam writes of surprising Mythily by calling her on
the phone when she was at an office meeting and then 'somehow
managing to reach her apartment' in Manhattan where she was
welcomed by Mythily's good friend and housemate Reeva Singh.
When Mythily was a master's student in Delhi, Pankajam wrote
that she envisioned her as a 'great woman wielding power and
holding high offices' and 'tasting [the] freedom and power' that
Pankajam herself had never known. It was during her travel to New
York in 1967 that Pankajam could finally see what Mythily, who
was then working as research assistant in the Permanent Mission
of India to the United Nations, had made of herself in America.

*Pankajam in New York*

When Mythily took her mother to her office, she introduced her to G. Parthasarathy, educationist, diplomat and Permanent Ambassador of India to the UN from 1965 to 1969. On meeting Pankajam, he reportedly asked her whether she had come to New York to get her daughter married or take her back to India with her. A surprised Pankajam hastened to clarify that this was certainly not the purpose of her visit. Pankajam may have wondered at the irony of it—here she was enjoying a hard-fought escape from her familiar every day and being asked if she planned to entrench her daughter in another version of it!

*Pankajam in New York*

In Montreal, where Pankajam stayed with her son Sundaram, she visited daily the 'fascinating' Montreal Expo '67 accompanied by her daughter-in-law. The 1967 International Exposition held in Montreal was Canada's principal celebration during its centennial year. With themes such as 'Man the Explorer (of

Planet and Space, the Oceans, the Polar Regions)' featured in ninety pavilions, it was hardly surprising that Pankajam was wonderstruck. In her autobiographical notes written in 1995 after her stroke the previous year, eighty-four-year-old Pankajam recalled the expo:

> There was a large crowd but the milling crowd found in Indian fairs was absent. I saw a wonderful thing there, i.e., the previous evening there was no grass or tree. However, the next day, the whole area was covered by a carpet of velvety grass and huge trees stood here and there. I told Danielle that we had come to the wrong place. She laughed and explained that grass was grown on a thin iron mat lined with soil, carried around and spread wherever wanted. Saplings too were planted in huge tubs and when fully grown were carried and placed elsewhere. Talk about handy stuff!!

*Pankajam with Danielle in Canada*

In August 1967, Pankajam left New York for London on her way back to India. She had grown very fond of Reeva and her first letter from London was addressed to both Reeva and Mythily. In the letter (7 August 1967), Pankajam writes, 'I do not know if you could spot my window [in the plane]. I kept on waving the handkerchief and I saw you, Mythily, waving too. The two dear forms standing there would ever remain before my eyes.'

*Mythily, Pankajam and Reeva*

When Pankajam reached London, she found that Sivaraman's nephew, who was her host, was scheduled to leave soon on a holiday. She was, however, given the full use of his room (outside the city) with access to a kitchen shared by five people. The landlady lived downstairs. Pankajam initially reached out to two women contacts to help her tour London. Neither appeared friendly or interested. Undaunted, Pankajam resolved that she was 'not going to depend on anybody but [herself] for sightseeing'.

Her letter to Mythily (18 August 1967) describes how she set out by herself to discover England—a land, at once, new and familiar to her from her childhood books.

... I go to the city by tube alone with the map. The underground map is my only friend and guide. It is easy to find your way in the tube stations, for unlike New York, the instructions and maps on all the walls are very clear. But the buses are more difficult. So I avoid them altogether. The tube station from this house is as far as our house from Egmore railway station [2 kilometres]. Rather long for me to be doing it twice a day, in addition to walking and sightseeing in the city daily ... The weather is like Kodai [Kodaikanal]. And the cold agrees with me ... It has started raining every day. I am going out daily getting wet in the mornings and getting dry while inside museums. I have not cared to even buy a rain coat.

This is my daily routine here: I get up at 7 or 7.30 and have my cornflakes and cook rice, sambar and some vegetables. I bathe and dress before 9 and I take my food, pack a few sandwiches, an apple, a bar of chocolate and walk to the station. After going about the town, seeing whatever I want, changing trains frequently to go in different directions, I return home by 7.30 PM. You have to be studying the map always. Yesterday, I even directed some Americans, would you believe it? Of course, on the first day I made a few silly mistakes, but I soon found out and re-traced my way. Since then, I am very alert.

I took a conducted tour only to go to Stratford-upon-Avon and Oxford because I do not like the way they do it, which I saw at Westminster Abbey. You know how I like to see things, tarry at places to see, wonder and delight and I do not want to be rushed around with a crowd. Of course, all around me were the tourists. Mostly Americans, a few from the Continent, the Scots and various others. I made a few friends too with some whom I met thus.

Well, I saw the British museum. It took me a whole day. I nearly fainted with fatigue ... I have been to the zoo (better than the Bronx), the Kew Gardens, the Hyde Park, Petticoat Lane which is like our Moore Market—open market on the road where everyone shouts and bargains ... I could not control my emotions when I stood at the Poets' Corner before so many busts and inscription of souls that I have loved and revered, having felt with them through their literature ...

I did enjoy my London stay, it was packed with sightseeing which I did alone, all on my own! I overdid it, for on the last day, I felt very weak and tired. But I never gave up going out because there was little time at disposal ...

In her letter to Mythily, she exclaims in a tone of satisfaction that she had done it 'all on [her] own!'. Pankajam knew that she had thrived in the face of the challenge she had taken on and made the most of her precious days in London. In her brief autobiographical notes written in 1995, Pankajam has more detail on the friends she had made during her travels.

One day when I was going to the British Museum, a middle-aged couple, husband and wife, were also looking for the museum. So, we became friends. In the evening, when we came out, they invited me to travel with them to Scotland. I laughed as I was overjoyed. But since my financial situation would not permit my acceptance of their kind invitation, I turned it down despite their entreaties. Just before I left London, on the day I visited Shakespeare's residence, I returned as late as 10 p.m. I had not eaten and wanted to go to bed. But the landlady [from Gujarat] would not let me sleep without eating. She offered me chutney and rasam and asked me if her caste status would serve as a deterrent. I embraced her and thanked her profusely for her concern.

The news of Pankajam traveling alone in London greatly amused Reeva, who joked about this often at Mythily's expense. When Pankajam was in New York, Mythily had taken to locking her mother in the apartment every morning when she set out to work. An anxious person, Mythily feared that her mother would wander Manhattan by herself, lose her way and come to harm. In a conversation I had with Reeva a few years ago, she said to me, 'I laughed a great deal and asked Mythily what was the point of trying to keep her mother safe in New York when she did all this alone in London?!' In her autobiographical note, Pankajam's reference to her 'financial situation' reminds us that she was, as always, stretching a limited budget. After buying Sivaraman an expensive gift (an electric shaver costing nine pounds) as peace offering to placate him, she returned to Madras with two pounds and ten dollars in her pocket.

# 44

## The nausea of the familiar

During her travels overseas, Pankajam experienced a delightful reversal of her role as the primary carer and nurturer of her family in Madras, having spent 'priceless days' with Mythily and Sundaram in an environment where she was not a harried housewife on a shoestring budget, walking on a tightrope between the tantrums of an ailing mother and a hostile husband. Back home in Panchavati House, Pankajam had to readjust herself to the quotidian after two and a half months of absence. In her letters to Mythily, Pankajam closely observed and commented on the effects of her trip on her mental state and her physical condition, the two being intertwined as she knew them to be.

I am happy to know that all your friends appreciated what little there was in me. I came to you in my old age and I could have done much more, been more active and useful, if I had come ten years earlier. The best weeks in my life of fifty-six years were those that I spent with you in New York … When I came back, I felt a sudden revulsion at everything and a feeling of nausea came over me … Of course, the feeling is slowly disappearing and I may forget

it myself. Since I felt it, I have recorded it ... (5 September
1967)

My stomach has lost its old irritation and acts normally
now ... with the result I have added some pounds which is
a nuisance, for none of my jackets [saree blouses] will go
into my limbs any more ... The peace and happiness given
to me in New York and Montreal have been a balm which
has soothed my soul, and as a consequence, it has soothed
my stomach too. I feel strong and well ... (1 October 1967)

The words 'nausea' and 'sudden revulsion' suggest that Pankajam
may have experienced the visceral shock of returning to an
everyday routine that remained unchanged and depressingly
familiar, after immersing herself in a radically different way
of living and being. Pankajam knew that the 'old irritation'
of the stomach to which she was habituated, had its origin in
the mind and that emotional well-being (or its reverse) flowed
from 'soul' to 'stomach'. She had, after all, spent a lifetime
negotiating 'the hotbed of domestic politics' as Sundaram once
wrote of Panchavati House to his sister Mythily. In her Tamil
story *Vidhiyum Madhiyum*, Pankajam's protagonist Kamala is not
allowed to join her classmates on an evening's outing as part of
a school-sponsored excursion. A deeply dejected Kamala, who
yearns to 'go out [of the house] ... and experience everything',
vows to herself that she will go anywhere freely, even travelling
to Europe one day. If Pankajam, as a young woman, had fashioned
for herself a 'kingdom of the mind' (mano rajiyam) where one
may 'gallivant with freedom and autonomy', it was during her
travels from June to August 1967 that she had the opportunity to
actually do so for the first time. How transient this freedom was
and how completely she was to lose it was made brutally clear to
her within weeks of her return to Madras.

In October 1967, the Sarada Sangh (of which Pankajam was a
member), the sister organisation of the Ramakrishna Mutt, decided
to hold its annual conference in Guwahati. Conference delegates
were to be taken to the Kaziranga Game Sanctuary and Shillong

on excursions as part of the two-week trip. Since Sivaraman did not raise an objection and a newly-hired cook had offered to take care of Subbalakshmi, everything was set for Pankajam to accompany the delegates from Madras. The programme schedule, printed and ready to be circulated, included a slot for Pankajam to speak about her trip to America and England. However, just when the ticket had to be bought, Sivaraman turned stubborn and refused to let her go, forcing Pankajam to apologise to the conference organisers and withdraw at the last moment, as her letter to Mythily reveals.

> … Father's surprise attack has made us all very frustrated. I have learnt only one lesson out of this, that I must pull myself out of this family bondage and obligations. After thirty-seven years of slavish married and householder's life, I want to throw away my shackles and be free. Even in the Shastras, Vanaprastha is accepted. One need not forever wallow in family life … (5 October 1967)

Vanaprastha is the third of the four age-based, sequential stages of life prescribed for a Hindu upper-caste man by Hindu scripture and philosophy. In the Vanaprastha stage, the householder prepares to relieve himself of family responsibilities and withdraw from the world as a precursor to the final stage of sanyasa. The woman, on the other hand, is enjoined to submit lifelong to the three stages of protection by her father (as a child), her husband (as a married woman) and her eldest son (as a widow or after her husband seeks sanyasa). In her letter, Pankajam invokes the renunciatory ideal of Vanaparastha to seek liberation for herself from a 'slavish' householder's life. If she could not break away from the 'shackles' of household or husband, she could, at the least, threaten to reform the first in ways that were disconcerting for the second. Sivaraman comments on one such occasion drily in a letter to Mythily, written after his wife visited Singapore in 1966 (her first travel abroad) to stay with his relatives.

Your mother who had been to the Far East for six weeks is considerably enlightened. She has gathered a lot of progressive ideas and wants to revolutionise the household system. She thinks TV is for the better... Had she come to the States, she will be a live wire now. Visit to the Orient has changed her vision ...

# 45

## The epistolary self

Pankajam's letters to my mother Mythily, most of which I had access to, served as rich source material in a manner similar to her autobiographical writing and her 'fictional' short stories that covered earlier phases of her life. Letter correspondence was a deeply meaningful activity that allowed Pankajam to share her life, her thoughts and her passions with those who mattered to her. Through her letters to Mythily, Pankajam kept her informed of the books that she read and enjoyed and urged her daughter to read, travel widely and experience as much of the world as she could.

> I feel you ought to see Mexico sometime ... For I saw much to interest me about Mexico both in the Montreal Expo and the London museums. Besides, they say the city is built on sinking soil. I want you to see the city and understand the people ... (5 September 1967)

Pankajam had passed on the trait of writing expansive, self-revelatory letters to her children. In one of her letters to Mythily (of June 1966), she gently chides her for being tardy in writing to her sister Lalitha. Pankajam writes, 'After all, you are the only treasure we possess, and Akka [Lalitha] and I are equally happy to get a letter from you. In fact, we long for a letter from you.' Letters sent to Panchavati House by family members living overseas were circulated among everyone. About a month after Mythily left for America in July 1963, Sivaraman wrote to his daughter that her letters were first read by everyone in Madras and then sent to Karur (where Lalitha lived with her family) and onward to Poona where her brother Srini was working. Given the peregrination of her letters, Sivaraman advised Mythily cryptically, 'So, you would do well to draft your letter to cater to the taste of all.'

To Pankajam, the act of letter-writing was an occasion to take stock of her life and ask questions of herself and of how she found solace and comfort in everyday life rendered difficult by her husband's cussedness, her ceaseless caregiving and her financial troubles. In a letter to Mythily (1966), Pankajam writes of what her weekly visits to the Sarada Mutt brought to her life.

> There is a Bengali Sanyasini lady there who gives religious lectures. I go there more to see her and be with her, than hear her. For she is such a sweet, holy person from whom benign peace, love and joy radiate. She is doing me much good spiritually, pervading my heart with peace and patience and love too. She is with shaven head, wearing the ochre robe, shining with childlike innocence and inspiring worldly people, to something unknown to them.

When she suffered the bitter disappointment of losing an opportunity to travel to New York in September 1965 due to her mother's illness, a heartbroken Pankajam wrote (to Mythily) of how she yet managed to find 'cinders among the ashes' of her heart.

> Two things still I desire and they are seeing nature's work and hearing good music ... These two find some cinders among the ashes in my heart. And another thing which

is equally holy and sweet is the infant smiles and wiles. Do you know how little Raja loves me? He loves me more than his parents and is always seeking me out ... I know children are fond of one when they are helpless and when they grow, they throw it off with their independence. But the short span of their innocent, trustful childish days is divine to experience ... (13 September 1965)

*Pankajam playing the violin*

In January 1953, when Lalitha had her first child, forty-one-year-old Pankajam became a grandmother. In the letter above, Pankajam refers to her eighteen-month-old grandson (Ram's son), whom she called 'Raja' in honour of her younger brother after whose death, seven-year-old Pankajam had marked the days of grief and remembrance, counting more than 500. Pankajam alludes to 'nature's work' as cheering her heart. Her love of bird-watching had not diminished as she aged. In a short piece 'The

Pied Crested Cuckoo' written in 1970, Pankajam paid tribute to her 'handsome visitor on the hedge'.

We had a large garden in our house. Many kinds of birds inhabited it. Some built nests regularly and lived there—they were resident birds. Some others came occasionally. The occasional visitors must have been migratory birds, I concluded. I know of two such birds—the ground thrush and another, a pied crested cuckoo. I was very much interested in the latter, for it made its appearance punctually every year in our garden.

Every year on 14 January (Pongal day), we performed puja for the Sun God 'Surya' on the open terrace. From our terrace a portion of our garden was visible where a barbed wire fence separated our compound from our neighbour's garden. Along this fence, thick bushes of yellow flowers bloomed. On this oleander hedge, I first noticed the pied crested cuckoo. It made its appearance exactly on Pongal day year after year just when the puja was proceeding.

The Puja used to begin by 8.30 and ended by 9.30. Thus it became a habit with me to watch for the arrival of this bird with excitement on Pongal day at puja time. This happened from 1961 to 1969 or I began to notice it only during this period. It could have come in the previous years too. But from 1961–69, I wrote down the date and time of its arrival on puja day. I am ashamed to say that my attention wandered from Lord Surya towards my handsome visitor on the hedge. My heart would miss a beat when I spied the bird alight on the hedge as usual, exactly at the time of the puja performance.

I know that this exact timing of the arrival of migratory birds is known to bird watchers. What clock sets the time for them, I wonder? After 1969, the bird ceased to appear in our garden for its location has been disturbed. Our neighbour has built a huge flat there and frightened away the bird. I have never ceased to regret its disappearance.

In her letters, Pankajam chronicled changes in the everyday life of her household and probed her own reactions to these changes with honesty. Her son Ram and his wife Nirmala had set up an independent household in the first floor of Panchavati House in 1967. In a letter to Mythily (5 September 1967), Pankajam appreciates the change (of Nirmala cooking upstairs) as 'there is less worry and bother and no need to hurry for no one goes to office. It is a relief to be free from catering to the demands of so many, all with different tastes and views.' Yet, there is a wistful tone in her voice when she writes that 'only Raja is the old faithful' who seeks out her company in the evenings. Pankajam continued to reflect on this new phase of her life in her subsequent letters. 'It is rather strange to have only me and father here, as I have forgotten in the course of thirty-eight years of married life with a house full of children, how to be alone …' (22 September 1967) Through her letters, Pankajam contemplated the loneliness of advancing age and a growing need for companionship.

> Nothing counts but people … I feel it more now, when old age is creeping … Mrs Spalding is still in the same house next to ours. We are both very close friends now, closer since her husband died. We run to each other every day and are very happy for she has begun to read much now and we share books, ideas and views. She has begun to get interested in philosophy books of all sorts—Hindu, Islam and Western as well … (1966)

Ram recalls that the Spaldings, an Anglo-Indian couple, were the family's neighbours for about a decade or longer on Spurtank Road. The rasam made in Panchavati House was a great favourite with the Spaldings, who would ask for it often. When her husband died in a car accident that she survived, Mrs Spalding appears to have drawn closer to Pankajam and developed an interest in reading and philosophy. Besides capturing the shifting rhythms of the household, Pankajam's letter-writing enabled her to reflect on the big changes in her life even as they were unfolding. In one of her letters, Pankajam described her struggle to feed her father, who was stubbornly refusing to eat and whose end was drawing near.

> The usual humdrum life goes on in spite of the truth that a great and unusual personality is soon to pass on leaving us. Yet, I do not even have time to wonder at and inquire into this intimate and profound experience of mine, but must be forever submerged in the tawdry affairs of life. Life seems trivial compared to death, which has some nobility about it—perhaps the nobility comes from what lies beyond it (13 August 1963).

Pankajam's letter-writing enabled her to undertake what we may see as an ethnography of the self, an exercise enriched by anecdotal vignettes of everyday life, clear-sighted observations of social relationships, philosophical ruminations triggered by rite-of-passage events and, underlying everything, Pankajam's sense of herself as a traveller teasing out the 'riddle of life' (as she writes in the foreword to her autobiography) so as to illuminate the way for those who may be 'groping in the dark, seeking light and understanding of this world' as she herself was doing.

# 46

## An Indian type of mother

In the final reckoning, Pankajam's letter-writing was time and
effort spent in a worthy endeavour of maternal love that could
not be denied her, not even in the 'stifling atmosphere' she found
herself in. In one of her letters, Pankajam apologises to Mythily
whom she appears to have annoyed by offering (in her previous
letter) what her daughter saw as gratuitous advice regarding her
plans for travel in Europe before returning to India.

I do feel I am a very silly worrying Indian type of mother.
Please do forgive me and bear with my follies … I agree
with you perfectly that I should do something better
and useful than worry about my children—who are no
more children. I did try to go and do social service in the
evenings and your father frowned awfully on it. Even once
a week visiting Sarada Mutt makes father very angry. I
have purchased notebooks to write articles, stories and
other things I want to say to the world. But whenever I
sit down to read or write, I am bidden to get up and do
something more useful than read and write. Father thinks
pottering about the kitchen is more useful. You think
something else is.

I do want to get away from my stifling atmosphere and go and work where my services will be accepted and which will make me less selfish and more detached and less doting. But I am under house arrest and, as such, I find I am thinking more of you all than necessary. However, I shall learn to take off my mind from its useless grooves, but to channelise it how and where I know not ... (6 March 1968).

Although Pankajam begins her letter on a note of apology for being a 'silly, worrying' mother, she manages to succinctly convey to her daughter the circumstances in which an 'Indian type of mother' broods more about her adult children than she needs to. Notwithstanding its conciliatory tone, Pankajam's letter was a pointed reminder to Mythily that, while she may advise her mother on possible useful occupations and ways to spend her time, she could do little to help her mother exercise these options. Pankajam's letter also speaks to the tensions and conflicts of our pandemic times marked by the blurring of boundaries between work and home. While many (women and men alike) have tasted the 'house arrest' that Pankajam refers to, it is more likely women who have endured a 'stifling atmosphere' where they must constantly suffer interruptions of their own work and pander to the needs of their partners, children, parents and the elderly, all seeking refuge within the home from a raging pandemic.

Most of Pankajam's short stories (in English and Tamil) were romances on the themes of unrequited yet faithful love or the happy union of young lovers. However, her fictional depiction of the social experience of mothering was devoid of any romantic gloss. In her Tamil short story *Ammavin Piranthanaal* (Mother's birthday), Pankajam writes about one day in the life of a mother of five children.

At the start of the story, the eponymous mother exits the kitchen after cooking the Sunday lunch for her family. Chatting with their mother, the children discover by accident that the next day is her forty-fifth birthday. The children want to get her a present, but realise they have no money to do so. When the husband finds out, he asks his wife to prepare a good dinner on her birthday since he has been waiting for an occasion to invite two friends from his office. When the children realise that a special meal is in the offing, each of them wants to invite a favourite friend. Seeing that the children are getting competitive and upset at each other, the mother reassures them that each can invite a friend for her birthday meal. The number of invitees swell when the mother reminds her husband to invite the older daughter and son-in-law as well.

On her birthday, the mother begins her day early and bustles about, getting all her work done. The house resonates with her enthusiasm, good cheer and laughter. She runs about serving everyone lunch 'ready for everything and willing to please everyone'. When father settles down to play cards with his friends post-lunch, mother prepares a big jug full of coffee and serves snacks to the card players. The children are keen that father take them to a movie in the evening. Busy with the evening chores that include combing and plaiting her two daughters' hair, mother barely manages to change her workday sari and get ready for the movie, earning her husband's rebuke ('*Podi*, you women are always like this. Taking forever to doll yourselves up.')

When all gather excitedly around the car, father asks, 'Is this a bus? How can we all get in?' At once afraid that the son-in-law and older daughter may get left behind, the mother asks her husband to take the two of them in the car. The other children will follow by bus, she says. She offers to stay at home and take care of the grandchild. When the family gets back home, her husband complains, 'The movie was so bad. I should have gone to my friend's house to play cards and sent your mother instead!' Mother packs coffee powder and the evening tiffin for her married daughter to take to her home. She prevails on her husband to allow the son-in-law to drive his wife and child home in the former's car. 'Does the car run on water?' her husband grumbles. The day comes to an end with all the children shouting in chorus, 'Amma's birthday was super!'

With gentle irony, Pankajam shows us how the birthday of a married woman and mother turns out to be a busier day than usual with no rest or break from the routine of a household. She is expected to supervise the preparation of a special meal for more than twice the number she usually feeds. Ever-mindful of the social obligations owed to a married daughter and son-in-law, the mother gives up her outing, also realising that the grandchild must be taken care of. Not even on her birthday, Pankajam reminds us, can an 'Indian type of mother' lay aside her habitual cares and concerns. In the space of a short story, Pankajam deftly shows us how the children who love their mother as well as the husband who does not care for his wife, take her for granted and share a certain casual thoughtlessness with respect to her situation.

While Pankajam gave of herself unstintingly to the people in her life, she was not as self-effacing or sacrificing as the mother in her story. Lalitha's daughter Padmavati recalls an incident when Sivaraman, exerting his control over the car and driver, unceremoniously left behind his wife who was changing out of her workday sari in order to leave with him on an evening's outing to Lalitha's house. When a hurt Pankajam called up Lalitha sobbing, it was her granddaughter Padmavati who answered the phone. Plonking herself in the portico of her house, she confronted her grandfather, forcing him to send the car back to fetch his wife. This episode earned her the title 'What if and why not' from Sivaraman, an apparent reference to her argumentative nature.

# 47

## Writing of the 'merely' domestic

If a woman is to write fiction, she must have money and a room of her own to write in, Virginia Woolf famously argued. In '*A Room of One's Own*', written in 1929, Woolf describes the social conditions in which women wrote novels in the early nineteenth century. Woolf reminds us that when Jane Austen wrote her novels for instance, the English middle class family had but a single sitting room. Woolf quotes Jane Austen's nephew, who speculates that she must have been subject to all kinds of 'casual interruptions' when working in the common sitting room since she did not have a study to retreat to. The interruptions that Pankajam suffered were as likely to have been willed (by her husband) as casual since, as a married woman, she controlled neither her person nor her time, even if the large house her husband had built did have a spare room for her to work in.

What sorts of experiences informed and inspired the work of women writers? Woolf observes that the limited social universe of the woman writer in the early nineteenth century, in effect, meant that her sensibilities were schooled for centuries by the influences of the sitting-room where she spent most of her time. And therefore, the only literary training that she had was in the observation of character, the analysis of emotion, people's feelings and personal relations. Woolf wonders how the writings of Jane Austen, George Eliot, Charlotte Bronte and Emily Bronte (all incidentally Pankajam's favourite novelists), may have been transformed had they possessed more practical experience, acquaintance with a wide variety of characters and more knowledge of the world than was allowed to them. Responding to Woolf, Joanna Russ, writer and literary critic, makes the important counterpoint that Victorian women writers did not know *less* than what their fathers and brothers knew (as Woolf appears to suggest), but *other*. She writes, 'And if women did not know what the men knew, it was just as fair to say that the men did not know what the women knew and what they did not know included *what the women were.*' (Russ, 1983: 42)

In finely-etched detail, Pankajam's fictional writing shows us what she was and what her life-worlds were like during successive life-cycle phases. In her autofiction (*Vidhiyum Madhiyum* and *Ammavin Piranthanaal* in Tamil, and the Meena–Subbu and Lakshmi–Ramanathan stories in English), Pankajam writes of familial domains where young girls came of age with dreams crowding their heads, marriages were arranged, intimate relationships lived out and fought over and children birthed and raised. In V–M, a schoolgirl, who dreams of the autonomy that adulthood and a loving family may bring her, experiences her first year of marriage, her husband slowly turning cold and neglectful. In the M–S story, a marriage is arranged between an idealistic, book-reading, nature-loving, poetry-writing girl and a man who wonders how books may be considered treasures. The story hints at the social class and cultural differences that frame the marriage, even as it acknowledges (through the central character Meena) that an arranged marriage is always a gamble. The story ends with the young girl readying herself to 'meet womanhood and face family life with hope and pride'. The L–R story dwells on betrayal, infidelity, a young woman's (futile) efforts to win her husband's heart and companionship and reform him, the marital rape that makes a woman's situation wretched and yet begets children, and the blossoming companionship between a mother and her five children, whose minds she cultivates with ardour. *Ammavin Piranthanaal* revolves around a woman's invisible labour, both physical and emotional, that nourishes, sustains and holds together her household.

What are the images of manhood, of men as partners, husbands and fathers, that emerge from Pankajam's stories and the autobiographical accounts of her life? In the L–R story, the man who could never grasp the prospect of a meeting of hearts that a woman offered so eagerly and with so much love, and could not see a woman as a companion whose mind and body he could be invited (or not) to share, was, ultimately, to be pitied. In Pankajam's narratives, her husband remains a man who could not escape the 'thraldom of his body' (as she writes in her autobiographical account of the first year of her married life) and its tyranny over him. Trapped by his bodily urges and thus limited in fundamental ways, he cannot see, Pankajam implies, that what she offers—a union of hearts and minds—may free him too. His obdurate refusal to open himself to her, to allow her to know him and to take the trouble to know her costs him too, just as it costs her. At several moments in her writing, Pankajam returns to the theme of Sivaraman's indifferent parenting and his inability to empathise with the suffering of others, even if they were his own children.

Pankajam's writing is marked both by her critique of the stunted version of masculinity embodied in the persona of her husband and her fulsome praise of an alternative version that she witnessed. I allude to Pankajam's adoration of her uncle, her maternal aunt Kanagam's husband. When writing of the early years of her childhood, Pankajam describes the uncle who had a 'special knack' for nursing and curing people's pain when illness visited the house, 'a character in anyone that [she] simply loves'. She recalls with affection and gratitude, a young man 'full of laughter and songs', who cracked jokes, told wonderful stories and often played with her and her little brother 'like a child'. He was an adult who appreciated young Pankajam and talked to her 'as if to an equal'. Pankajam was aware of how unusual her uncle was in a social universe in which 'men are not interested in their children at all', as she writes elsewhere. Pankajam knew that Sivaraman's disinterest in his children during their childhood and adolescent years was not (only) an individual defect, but reflected a way of organising life that alienated men from the world of children and the joys and heartbreaks of raising them.

In *Vidhiyum Madhiyum*, the protagonist Kamala and her younger cousin Saro are married off at the same time. When Kamala has a ritual ceremony to celebrate the arrival of the first child, Saro and her husband Sridharan attend the function. Kamala notices how unlike her own husband Sridharan is—how attentive he is to his wife's condition and needs (Saro is also pregnant) and how effusive, gregarious and full of good humour he is, unlike her own withdrawn and taciturn husband. Constructing Sridharan as the literary 'other' of her own husband Sivaraman, Pankajam makes us see that if men remained aloof from the worlds of women, children and child care, it impoverished them. As Pankajam realised (and without reading either Woolf or Russ), women knew *other* than what men knew and men were the poorer for it.

And yet, Sivaraman did grow mellow over the years and lavish this granddaughter with affection. I can certainly testify to this. I was also pleasantly surprised to read the letters that he wrote to Mythily during her year of stay in Delhi. The letters, in which father and daughter exchange ideas, wit and banter, reveal that the two shared a close, warm and trusting relationship. As Sivaraman aged, 'the man who did not need a companion', as his young bride discovered to her great sorrow some decades ago, wrote his daughter long letters of his fear of sickness, loneliness and death, provoking thoughtful responses from Mythily. It would appear that both Sivaraman and his father-in-law PRG sought from their respective daughters the companionship, solicitude and tender affection that they would not extend to their wives.

# 48

## Can the sociological imagination free you?

Pankajam's interests extended beyond the fictional re-telling of domestic drama. She was also a keen observer of what women were doing in worlds outside the home. We know this from one of Pankajam's papers titled 'The World Women's Progress over a Decade'. Written in Tamil, this was likely to have been the transcript of a Tamil speech that Pankajam gave for Radio Singapore in early 1966, when she visited Singapore for a few weeks and stayed with Sivaraman's sister. In a letter to Mythily written from Singapore in January 1966, Pankajam mentions giving a radio interview that she did not hear herself, having gone out sight-seeing. Pankajam's paper is interesting as it gives us a sense of her response to the larger social and economic changes of her times. I reproduce a translated extract from Pankajam's Tamil paper written in early 1966.

Women have made remarkable strides in the past ten years across the world in several fields. Some years ago, it was enough for girls to study up to the SSLC [end of school] ... But, for several years now, young men have insisted on only marrying girls with a college degree. For this reason, parents have sent their daughters to college in order to secure a good groom for them. In present times, this education-for-marriage scenario (*kalyana padippu* in Tamil) has changed and girls have begun to study for the sake of education and for paid employment.

Globally, women are studying and working and earning a living ... This has removed fear, self-doubt and ignorance from women, replacing it with courage, self-confidence and the capacity to reason (*pagutharivu*). They have become independent women ... This change has taken place in India and Asia only over the last ten years, with old ways of thinking giving way and women now moulding their lives according to their wishes and desires ...

In Malaya, I hear that many women have studied law and become well-known lawyers and advocates ... Women have begun to achieve much in sports too in the last ten years. For instance, in the recent South East Asian Peninsular games held in Kuala Lumpur [December 1965], Mary Rajamani created new records in the 200-, 400-, 800-metre races and won three gold medals. She has beaten the record of the Japanese sprinter K. Ogawa. In the Olympics games held in Japan two years ago, many women won medals from all over the world. Until about ten years ago, even if girls went to college, they did not participate in sports. It was seen as a man's activity ...

Women have made a mark in Science and Technology research too. A few years ago, women were only studying history and languages in college ... Valentina Tereshkova is well known in this field, having travelled by rocket alone to the stratosphere. There are many women like her learning science in Russia ...

While the title of the paper refers to the 'World's Women', it appears that Pankajam saw the decade that had just ended (1955-65) as significant from the point of view of Asian women claiming their place in the sun. Pankajam's location in Singapore may have been the impetus for her to emphasise developments in the Asian region more broadly, rather than limit her focus to India. Provided with an opportunity to reflect on the 'women's question' for the radio talk, Pankajam may have felt that a great deal had changed since 1927 when sixteen-year-old 'Drama Pankajam' was pulled out of class nine in the middle of the school year and not even allowed to add the title 'SSLC' to her name. In 1966, Pankajam believed that she inhabited a world where young women had taken over limited, reformist agendas (such as education for marriage) and subverted their instrumental intent by infusing them with new meanings and aspirations.

Interestingly, Pankajam does not echo the platitudinous sentiment that education makes better mothers of women and enhances the quality of (future) citizenship in the country. She had self-consciously crafted herself as an enlightened mother who proactively sought out books on child-rearing. Yet, she did not see the value of education for girls in terms of fostering a better quality of mothering. In her paper, she unequivocally asserts that girls' education is a worthy agenda in its own right and to be welcomed for building women's sense of autonomous personhood, their capacity to reason and their 'ability to mould their lives according to their wishes and desires'. Besides, the ambit of education for women was expanding to include the masculine domains of science and technology, where at least Soviet women seemed to be blazing ahead. It is not surprising either that Pankajam had kept herself abreast of the world of sports over the years. As a schoolgirl, she had loved games and 'played them all', besides organising a tournament in Marakkanam in 1928 and staying connected to sport events through the tournaments that her father organised in Kakinada during the 1930s.

Pankajam's paper was an earnest and joyful appreciation of women forging ahead in diverse spheres of public and professional life. Her sense of bearing witness to historical change ever remaking individual and, in particular, women's lives may have been rendered more acute by seeing from close quarters the life of her younger daughter Mythily. Whenever she received news of Mythily's work life in the US, Pankajam responded with a sense of wonder at what was possible for a young woman to do and to be in a changing world. In a letter to Mythily (November 1966), she writes,

> It is interesting to hear of the GS sessions and the luncheon and cocktail parties. Yes, the experiences are valuable. Is it not great to be in the Assembly and watch and take part in the Sessions? I always knew you were meant for something better than I could offer you at home, dear. I am equally glad to hear that you are not overwhelmed by them all. Sure, you must do great work when you return to India, putting to use all your experience and knowledge.

As part of her job in the UN, Mythily participated in the committee responsible for decolonisation, carried out research related to non-self-governing territories and their problems and prepared statements to be made by the Indian delegation to the UN on issues related to colonialism and the birth of new nation-states. In a letter to Mythily, Pankajam writes,

> Your name was in *The Hindu* of 1 September. Column says you supported the transfer of power demanded by the people of Nauru. Imagine your name coming up for India! You are becoming great dear, because of your noble and brave ideals. We are all proud and we have bought several copies of the paper ... (5 September 1967)

Besides her cheerful disposition, it was Pankajam's ability to see herself as a subject of history that allowed her to remain intellectually curious and open-minded about a changing world, without rancour or bitterness that these changes had passed her by. I propose that we may see Pankajam's way of being in the world as an outcome of the 'sociological imagination' that she possessed in abundance. 'Neither the life of an individual nor the history of a society can be understood without understanding both', wrote the sociologist C. Wright Mills in his seminal book,

*The Sociological Imagination* (1959). Mills defines the sociological imagination as a 'quality of mind' that enables one to perceive the intricate connection between the patterns of human lives and the course of world history, and thus 'grasp the interplay of … biography and history, of self and the world'. However, Mills points out that, 'ordinary men do not usually know what this connection means for the kinds of men they are becoming and for the kinds of history-making in which they might take part'. Unable to make sense of the troubles they endure in terms of historical change or comprehend 'the meaning of their epoch for their own lives', people often felt that their private lives were a series of traps.

Pankajam did not experience her own life in terms of the trap that Mills describes as the lot of 'ordinary men'. The extraordinary woman that she was, she had no difficulty in understanding a broad historical canvas in terms of its meaning for the 'inner life' and the 'external career' of a variety of individuals, others and herself. The world was not a vindictive, vengeful place for Pankajam who (without reading Mills) intuitively grasped his central thesis—that an individual could gauge her own fate, understand her own experience and know her chances in life only by locating herself within her period and becoming aware of the chances of all individuals in her circumstances. If this was a terrible lesson, it was, equally, a magnificent one, Mills observed.

As Pankajam wrote in her autobiography, it was 'Only after seventy [years] and when my husband died and I disbanded my house and started to live with Mythily, did my life see a few changes—not much even then'. Even if her own life changed very little in substantive terms, Pankajam welcomed the 'remote and impersonal transformations' (Mills, 1959) of her times as she saw it reflected in the lives of those close to her or a large collective of women striving for independence and autonomy. At the same time, a touch of sadness occasionally marked the way Pankajam made sense of her life in the light of other lives and possibilities. In a letter to Mythily, Pankajam broke the news of the death of a female relative whose poor health and subsequent demise she attributed to overwork in the kitchen.

> Poor woman. She never was free or happy married to this man, only one step worse than your father in his barbarity of living and thinking ... She confided that her husband will not have a cook as they will not work according to him!!! I feel very dejected since her death ... I may be the next and what worthwhile thing have I achieved? I would like to have achieved something for the suffering humanity ... Here I take off my hat for you—for you are much more mature and sensible and realistic in your outlook of life ... (22 September 1967)

If, by possessing the sociological imagination, Pankajam was able to see the intersections between the biographies of individuals and the histories of their times, her letter makes us see the idiosyncrasies and quirks of personality that allowed for differences between the lives of women in very similar situations. The difference between a husband willing to employ a cook (such as hers) and another who was not, could mean the difference between life and death. To know one's chances in life, one must become aware of the chances of all others in similar situations. If this was a magnificent lesson, it was, equally, a terrible one.

# 49

## An intimate beloved

While I may attribute Pankajam's freedom from a 'sense of the trap' to the sociological imagination, she saw her capacity to find joy and meaning in everyday life as a 'great gift from God' that she had been blessed with. In many instances woven through her autobiographical narratives, Pankajam identifies her faith as a source of strength, succour and solace.

When I was twenty-three, my husband and I took Ram and Lalitha, four and two years old, to the Tirupathi temple for the customary tonsure. In those days, the ghat road had not been built. We climbed the hill on foot. The children were assigned to a *dholi* (cradle). I must state that those were crowdless days. There was no queue and no payment. I sat right in front of the shrine, leaning on a pillar, with my eyes on the Lord, praying and admiring Him ... We returned the same evening to Madras ...

After some time, I found out that I was pregnant. Since I used to suffer from severe morning sickness, I was laid up for two months. One night, feeling very weak, I dozed off and saw before me the Tirupathi temple and the shrine just as it was some weeks ago. Suddenly, I saw the figure of

Lord Venkatachalapathi move and speak, 'Do not worry, for it is I who will be born to you and I will look after you.' Then the voice died away and everything was as before. But I knew what He meant. For just then in my sleep and my weak condition, I was asking God, 'Oh, why a child again—so soon? My health is giving way.' And immediately, this happened in the dream as if in answer ... To this day I remember what the Lord said and how His love stood firmly by me.

Pankajam's dream and the lesson she drew from it is a telling instance of how she experienced her faith—as a personalised relationship with beloved male and female deities, who readily reciprocated the ardent love she harboured for them. In an interesting reversal of conventional gender roles, it was her father who introduced her to religion very early in her life, whereas her mother gave her a love of literature, history, the arts and an active interest in the world outside the home.

In my early years, my father fed me love of music and of God very naturally. From my very early childhood, my ears were filled with musical tunes of the devotional songs he sang during his puja rituals. Father had a rich and melodious voice, unusual in a man. I have heard him sing the *arulpa*, *thevaram* and *thiru pugazh* ... He drew my attention to the beauty of the lines and explained their meanings to me ...

In an essay on her conception of God and what religion meant to her, Pankajam wrote of how Hinduism's pantheon of deities conceived in human form appealed to her emotions (the 'heart'), while the idea of 'godhood as the total energy manifested in the universe' appealed to her reason and intellect (the 'head'). While she had accepted that there was no anthropomorphic god in the sense of a person with a human form, her devotion to 'Siva whose mythological image was engraved in every cell of [her] body' allowed her to personify the noble qualities of 'love, compassion and non-violence' that she hoped to cultivate through her *bhakti*. Two of Pankajam's Tamil poems, titled 'Siva Rathiri' and 'Badri Narayana' are closely modelled on the style of Bhakti poetry in the sense of professing devotion to a personal God, conceived both as all-powerful and an intimate beloved. Pankajam saw her deep sense of kinship with all creation and the pleasure she took in mothering as a natural extension of her 'God-intoxication'. In a short piece titled 'The Daily Contact and Meeting', she writes,

I have been trying His patience by clamouring to see Him only in the form I would have Him ... As I grew older, I continued to meet Him in the joy of my youth and health. I heard Him in the coos and caws of my infants. When my babies threw their little arms over me, I would hug them and crush them but could never capture Him from them, nor free Him from them. He was there in their lovely innocence, tantalising me ...

Her diary entry for 26 March 1992 records a similar emotion:

I saw a male *kuyil* [cuckoo] outside my window. Jet black. It was pecking at the branches, twigs and leaves of the creeper. How graceful it was! Made me think of my Meenakshi [Goddess Parvati]. She gave me darshan today in that form.

Pankajam saw herself as a person on a spiritual quest, awakened and thirsting to know more. Therefore, her faith was more than a source of emotional fulfilment; theology fed her appetite for intellectual stimulation. She took the study of all religions seriously and approached it with rigour and passion, as did her mother Subbalakshmi. For instance, her diary entry of 5 November 1989 reads: 'I was reading the *Tasawwuf* again all over and find it so very enthralling. The Sufis are great mystics and superior philosophers.' If she had occasion to visit a church,

Pankajam found it natural to offer worship. During a visit to the USSR in 1985, Pankajam toured the Kolomenskoye Complex, a former country residence of the Tsars and its famous Church of the Ascension. Moved by the sight of women praying in the church, she writes in her travel diary, 'I too prayed, my heart filled with gratitude to Lord Jesus for having brought me there and made me stand before this grandeur of His. Glory be to Him.' In her diary entry of 25 December 1989, Pankajam writes, 'The first time in my life when a Xmas passed without my reading the Bible and celebrating Xmas. A worst thing.'

Pankajam's sense of herself as a Hindu was not shaped by notions of threat or harm from other religions ostensibly inimical to Hindu identities or interests. We see this, for instance, in her letter to Mythily (of October 1966) in which she describes her visits to charity institutions managed by Christian missionaries that care for abandoned children. She writes that most of the children were Hindu and a few Christian. She adds, 'I did not care, as all are Indians and destitute.' There is no word of suspicion regarding the purported evangelical motives of Christian organisations that shelter and feed the destitute poor of other religions. Nowhere in her writings does she express a sense of beleaguerment as a Hindu who feared that her faith or identity was under threat from belligerent 'others'.

# 50

## The story of the lost child (late 1960s–early 1970s)

Pankajam's indomitable energies and ebullient spirits had shaped her efforts to raise a family and build a home, mirroring a spirit of hope and optimism in an India on the verge of Independence (the 1940s) and the idealism and fresh energies of nation-building in newly-independent India (1950s). The egalitarian promise of post-Independence India had begun to disintegrate by the mid-1960s. In an era of economic stagnation, soaring prices, the inequities of the Green Revolution and growing landlessness in the countryside, a wave of discontent had begun to gain momentum. The rising unrest and disquiet that seized the nation in the late 1960s set the stage for the more or less organised social movements of women, students, the urban poor, factory workers, Adivasis and peasants of the 1970s, that held the nation-state to account for the distributive justice that it had failed to deliver. If the world around her was being transformed, could Pankajam's home remain untouched?

By the late 1960s, it appeared that Pankajam's children had made their life choices in a manner that gave their parents no cause for worry. Ram was in a steady job with Air India. Lalitha was raising her children in Madras. Sundaram was living in Canada and married to a French-Canadian girl, whom Pankajam had come to know and love. Living and working in Bombay, Srini was to be married in December 1968. Somewhat surprisingly, Mythily was the only black sheep in the family's fold. The hope and pride of her family, Mythily had decided to quit her job in the United Nations and return to India. Sivaraman was sorely disappointed that his daughter had not obtained the PhD for which, as he reminded her in his letters, he had sent her abroad. His letters to Mythily during her US years begin with the fond address 'My dear last child'. When Mythily decided not to embark on a PhD in the London School of Economics after initiating a move in this direction, her bewildered father addressed a letter to his 'dear lost child'. In his letter of June 1966, he writes, 'Your plans are inscrutable and ways are mystic and I am puzzled.' The 'loving father of the lost child', as Sivaraman signed off his letter, had hoped that his daughter might at least prepare to join the civil services. But Mythily showed no inclination for the bureaucracy either when she returned in August 1968.

No one in Mythily's family, not even Mythily herself, was quite prepared for the course that her life took. The last child, who had lived six years in the US, had been radicalised by the America of the 1960s. The civil rights movement, the Vietnam War protests, the formation of the Black Panthers and her own experience of working in the decolonisation committee of the United Nations had made Mythily a committed Marxist and fervent anti-imperialist. A clandestine visit to Cuba in 1968 (from the United States) had further convinced Mythily of the justice of the socialist cause. On 25 December 1968, when Mythily was attending her brother Srini's wedding in Pune, forty-four Dalit landless agricultural workers, mostly women and children, were set afire in a little hut and burnt alive in the village of Keezhvenmani of Thanjavur district. Mythily's visit to Keezhvenmani within a week of the massacre was followed by frequent visits to East Thanjavur—a hotbed of agrarian tension between caste-oppressed landless agricultural labourers and dominant caste landlords. Drawn to the communist movement that represented the kisans in Thanjavur, Mythily became a full-time member of the Communist Party of India (Marxist).

*Pankajam and Lalitha at an Anti-Vietnam War Photo Exhibition organized in Madras by Mythily and her comrades sometime in the 1970s*

With a group of like-minded friends, Mythily published a journal *Radical Review* that offered a Left perspective on contemporary social and political events, both Indian and international. In the years of its existence (1969–1973), the *Radical Review's* publishing address was 45 Spurtank Road, the residence of its editor Mythily. Pankajam and Sivaraman's house had willy-nilly become a hub and meeting place for young Left-leaning thinkers, students and activists, a group whose only female member was Mythily. By the early 1970s, Mythily had become a prominent leader of the Centre for Indian Trade Unions (CITU) in the city. Her name and face came to be associated with some of the big and sometimes violent industrial strikes that shook up Madras city. A well-known editor of a popular Tamil daily, whose name was 'Sivaraman', was often misidentified as the father of Mythily. He allegedly publicly clarified that he and his wife had likely committed many mistakes in their lives, but not the cardinal sin of begetting Mythily. Surely, such an infamous daughter could only bring disgrace upon her respectable parents!

How did Pankajam and Sivaraman react to these sudden developments in the life of their last child? Pankajam adapted better than her husband did. Sivaraman would order his wife to lock Mythily out of the house or refuse her dinner if she came home late from political meetings. Pankajam stealthily gave Mythily her dinner and sent her to her room upstairs. Mythily's comrades would look for her signal that the coast was clear before taking the stairs to her room in order to avoid being interrogated by her father, usually seated on the large swing in the living room. Close friends and associates of Mythily from this period recall that Pankajam welcomed and entertained her daughter's comrades, eager to hear their life stories and happy to share her own.

But Mythily was soon reconciled with her father too. Her family was vastly relieved when Mythily announced that she had found a partner and would soon be wed. No matter that he was non-Brahmin. When meeting Mythily's young man for the first time, Sivaraman's reaction captures the tumultuous events that Mythily's politics had exposed her family to. He said to Mythily's fiancée, 'Look here, Mr K. You must know that my daughter will not cook or keep house for you. She often gets back home late at night. Men call on the phone and ask to speak to her at odd hours. The police come here enquiring about her whereabouts. I'm telling you this so that you do not complain later that she is not a good wife to you.'

Sivaraman and Pankajam hosted the wedding in the living room of Panchavati House in January 1972. Ram, who was then posted in Hyderabad, recalls that his mother called him and asked him to come quickly as his sister was to be married in a no-fuss ceremony the next day. He rushed to take a train and arrived on the morning of the wedding with his video camera. There was no puja or priest, no ritual or mangalsutra. Her hair bedecked with flowers, the bride was clad in a cotton sari and wore no jewellery. The couple exchanged garlands and Communist party leaders delivered speeches, one of them exhorting Mythily and her groom to produce 'an army of socialist children'! In all probability, Mythily's family was nonplussed and perhaps not quite sure what they were witnessing. The sense of strangeness may have been compounded by the fact that Pankajam and Sivaraman met their son-in-law's parents and siblings on the day of the wedding. Mythily's in-laws initially mistook her college friend Vasanthi Devi, more dressed for the occasion, to be the bride.

Disoriented or not, Pankajam struck up a firm friendship with her son-in-law, as she did with her daughters-in-law. In a handwritten wedding anniversary card that she gave Mythily and her husband a year later, Pankajam expressed admiration for the idealism and shared values that bound them to each other, while gently hinting that it would be nice if they had a third person to share their love with. When the person did appear, Mythily and her husband moved next door to her parents so that Pankajam could look after the baby. When Mythily went underground often during the Emergency years (1975–1977) and even stayed in Zambia with her brother for two months in order to avoid arrest, it was Pankajam who took charge of Mythily's baby. If Mythily became a celebrated and respected activist in the trade union and the women's movements in Tamil Nadu, it was (also) because Pankajam was fully involved in raising Mythily's daughter. It was Pankajam's care labour that allowed Mythily to throw herself into political activism and public life fulltime, knowing that her young child was in good hands.

The lost child, who had found her own way in the world, may have been fascinated by her grandmother Subbalakshmi in her later years, but recalled with gratitude what she owed her mother. In a birthday greeting card that she gave Pankajam in 1995, Mythily wrote the following lines:

Amma, I dread to think what I would have been like had you not been my mother! Thank you for raising me with so much care, love and above all, the freedom to grow up and live the way I wished. You let me free to find myself, my own way, without crippling me with prejudice and petty-mindedness.

# 51

## See the world and write a diary
## (1970s–1980s)

Kamala, the protagonist of Pankajam's *Vidhiyum Madhiyum*, resolves that she will taste freedom as an adult, travel everywhere, 'see the world and write a diary', and should she have children, show them her diary. And that is precisely what Pankajam did in the 1970s and the 1980s, even if this granddaughter was reading her travel diaries long after her demise. Pankajam travelled more frequently in the later years of her life, taking advantage of Ram's free air tickets and his job-related transfers to Zambia and the USSR to visit and stay with him. In 1971, after visiting Sundaram in Canada, she flew back to India through Rome and spent a few days touring Italy and subsequently Beirut. Pankajam travelled unaccompanied through Rome and other parts of Italy, as she had done in the UK in 1967. Although seventy-five years of age and older when she visited Moscow twice, Pankajam walked about and toured places with enthusiasm. Ram recalls his mother in her sari trudging outdoors in the Russian winter, the snow getting into her shoes. On her travels abroad and in India, Pankajam was not a grandmother on baby-sitting duty—an all-too familiar figure in recent times. She was a keen observer and diligent chronicler of everything that caught her eye—people, customs, lifestyles, landscapes, flora, fauna, local histories and architecture, as her travel diaries indicate.

Beirut (1971): We were walking in the narrow, crooked and crowded streets in the old-fashioned Lebanese part of the town. We had to jostle amidst the crowd and I observed many things. People are light-skinned with dark hair and dark eyes. Only now I know that the Lebanese and Arabs were all descendants of a Mediterranean race, come from Europe or Central Asia. The streets and alleys were thronging with men and women in Arabic national dress. Donkeys and mules were going about naturally as our cows do. The medley in the streets was very fascinating ...

Lusaka (January 1976): When I went out in the car with my son, he would slow down for me to observe all that happened on the roads and sidewalks. Whenever two friends met, they would stop and dance for joy. They would tap their feet in a rhythm and tap-tap a few steps as greeting. The spontaneous dance showed joy and verve of life. It was beautiful to watch ...

Drive to Zavidova from Moscow (1985): The car drive was highly interesting as I had not left Moscow before. On both sides of the road, there were cottages, very crude and primitive. Built with wood and tin. Small pieces of garden are fenced by wood and the owners grow vegetables and flowers. These they sell by displaying them in buckets on both sides of the highway. The village people look thinner than those in Moscow and are very poorly dressed ... Maybe the farmers have a commune and work the fields together as there were no bunds to divide the fields ... I hear those who are poor and unable to work are given fifteen roubles a month ...

Moscow (17 August 1985): We left for Rynek, a market in a huge hall-like building, high-vaulted. There were all sorts of vegetables and fruits of every kind from other

Russian states. But I was more attracted by the faces of the sellers, mostly old ladies. They belonged to every race. So many ethnic races. I wish I could talk with them. The language barrier is there ...

When visiting the Gorki–Leninskiye Estate Museum, where the Russian revolutionary Lenin spent the last years of his life as a convalescent, Pankajam appears to have learnt something about him.

It was Lenin's greatness of mind that prevented the soldiers from plundering the palaces and great houses after the revolution. He ordered hands off all art treasures and that every painting should be preserved. I really admire Lenin for his appreciation of the things beautiful and not wanting to destroy them out of spite.

Pankajam used her travel diaries to take note of gaps in her understanding and knowledge of the world and of what she must further learn.

Church of the Ascension, Kolomenskoye Complex (Moscow): In the sanctum sanctorum, stands a *mandapam* with fluted pillars, the canopy carved intricately ... The priest recites from the Bible in a tune very much like the mantras. It sounded to me like, 'Oh hreem, shreem!!' ... At the end, he uttered some words in a raised voice like a benediction. All in Russian, I heard. Though I doubt it. Could be Latin too. I must find out from books—but where to go for them?? ... In the museum [near the church] there were huge metal bells ... I noticed on one bell Indian designs – the lion-like *yali*[38] and the scroll-like design

---

38   A mythical creature portrayed with a lion's body and carved into temple pillars in South Asia.

we use in our *kolams*[39] ... Made me think of our Eastern influence. How did it come and from where? Who were those who carved? Alas! I am in ignorance ... At least now I know from sight what is a Russian Orthodox Church.

She wonders immediately whether the 'eastern influence' may also be seen in the architectural style and modes of worship of Greek Orthodox Churches.

I have never been inside a Greek Church ... what is it and does it resemble the Russian Church? Or does it have eastern rituals like those of the ancient Asians? These are queries, the answers to which I would give my life to know ...

The opportunity to see other parts of the world meant that Pankajam could indulge her love of all creatures and of nature. Ram arranged for his mother to visit wild animal sanctuaries and national parks when she visited him in Zambia. Pankajam was especially delighted when she experienced the thrill of recognition, chancing upon something that her wide reading had already exposed her to. In the Kafue National Park, Pankajam saw 'a tree full of thorns, bearing fig-like fruits, red outside and inside, with pulpy seeds'. Informed that the fruit was eaten by elephants, Pankajam recognised at once that these were the fruits that 'make elephants groggy, giddy, sway and nod, as if they had consumed hard drinks'. She wrote, 'I remember my joy at finding this fruit.' The sighting of birds, known and unknown, never failed to move her either.

Amboseli Game Park (Kenya, 1976): The Amboseli plain was once a lake ... In the place where we dined, there were birds at our feet. Water was sprouting in the lawns and

---

39  Decorative designs drawn with rice flour on floors and thresholds in courtyard spaces in South India.

birds were drinking, bathing and insect-hunting close by our seats. Starlings, weaver birds, fire birds, blue birds. Flitting in the lawn near a cess pool, they met my eyes as I walked into the huts. Angels sent by God to receive me. I sat near the water hole at night, hearing a jackal howl ...

Pankajam used her travel-inspired learning to supplement her knowledge of the natural world. After visiting a conservatory in Montreal, she filled her travel journal with sketches and description, of 'huge ferns with new leaves unfurling, Spanish moss, Desert stone plants, Staghorn fern and Epiphytes that have leaves with holes in them'. On a holiday visit to the Andamans with her family in 1984, Pankajam writes of wading in the sea and gathering stones, shells and huge conches from the island Jolly Boy.

The tide had receded and we saw hundreds of sea cucumbers alive and many unknown sea creatures and crabs moving about, swarming the shore. I identified the primitive mud fish, which were the first ones in the evolution of life on earth outside the sea. They have both lungs and gills. I am so happy to have seen it alive. The others were snorkelling and reporting wonderful things under the sea. They tried to teach me to use the tube to breathe. But I could not learn it. So I just took the head glasses and held my breath and went into the water and lo what a sight. Multi-coloured fish and huge coral rocks. I could stay a minute or so under the water. All praised me for going in the water without the breathing tube and holding my breath voluntarily at my age. They made such a fuss about it!

Pankajam's travels in India were not always in the company of family, and some took place under less-than-ideal circumstances. She writes with wry humour of these circumstances when traveling to the Ajanta Caves.

*Pankajam in the Andamans, 1984*

More than sixty delegates from all parts of India met at Hyderabad at the annual conference of the Sarada Sangh. Some of us wanted to visit the Ajanta and Ellora Caves, while most returned home. So I packed happily, looking forward to a pleasant journey. But at the railway station, I found that none of my companion ladies could speak English—they were all Bengalis. We tried to communicate through signs and got along as best as we could. Some of my friends discouraged me from undertaking such a trip with people I could not communicate with. But nothing could deter me from my purpose of visiting the caves.

So off I went with them in the small rickety train that left for Aurangabad. I knew a smattering of Hindi and I exhibited it to my companions throughout my journey without, however, making any impression on them. They kept talking to me in Bengali, taking my silence for appreciation. At the hotel, the food was a problem for me. Three times a day, they gave me potatoes and chapatis! To get what I wanted, I tried to talk to the hotel proprietor in Telugu, Hindi and English in succession. But he remained unperturbed and talked to me in a mixture of all the three (a sort of Esperanto), which was intelligible only to him.

Finally we reached Ajanta after five hours of tedious journey. The fierce sun was beating mercilessly when the taxi stopped at the foot of the hill. I did not have my breakfast or lunch because I was fatigued and ill and did not like the food. So, as I climbed the steep steps of the hill, I began to think my friends were right after all when they called me foolhardy ... When I entered the first cave, I felt a sudden transport of joy. I knew I was right to have taken all the trouble. For turn where one wills, lustrous eyes full of meaning glance at one ...

... Another appealing figure with fine expressions on the face is Yashodhara, gently urging her son Rahula to demand from his father, the Buddha, his inheritance. The sad and beseeching eyes of Yasodhara, the wondering eyes of Rahula, the serene eyes of the Lord are depicted so eloquently ... The eyes of the figures are akin to the eyes of oxen we meet on the road, of a dark night. Since the caves are nearly dark, the eyes shine and you feel that all eyes in the hall are focused on you. This is a strange experience ...

Pankajam's travel diaries also capture her capacity for complete immersion in transcendent moments of quiet and beauty.

Victoria Falls on Zambezi River (1976): I stood gazing down while clinging to a gnarled tree perched on the steep side of the bank above. I was a bit dizzy. White mist and

frothy water against black rocks—a sight for the gods ... I
sat dangling my feet in the river just a few yards from
where it plunges into the gorge. Rocks were strewn about.
Cormorants by my side. Hornbills on tree tops. Baboons
scampering here and there. I sat on a rock, greedily
enjoying the scene ...

Travel meant the possibility of meeting new people and making
friends—an opportunity that Pankajam never passed up. In her
Andaman diary, Pankajam writes:

I met Paula an Anglo-Indian woman married to a Malayalee
man. Her father was a walking encyclopaedia—a fund of
information on his experiences with the tribals over thirty-
five years. Made friends with Paula's mother—a very kind
lady ... We met many others as well, even a hippie. It was
interesting meeting all kinds of people who come to this
island drawn by a spirit of adventuresome ...

Pankajam's spontaneity, her effervescent persona and trusting
nature enabled her to easily forge connections with anyone she
ever met. A letter written (to Mythily) by a young student from
Botswana S.T. Ketlogetswe in 1965 affirms this. Ketlogetswe, who
was studying economics at the Madras Christian College (MCC),
Tambaram, is likely to have met Mythily between 1961 and 1963
when she was teaching Tamil to foreign students residing in
Madras. When Mythily left for the US, Ketlogetswe continued
to visit Panchavati House in order to meet and spend time with
Pankajam. In a letter (14 March 1965), he writes to Mythily, 'I
like your mother very much and her sincere frankness. Whenever
I go to 45 Spurtank Road, I always come back the richer on some
aspect of Indian culture.' However, the most enduring friendship
that Pankajam made was when she visited the USSR.

# 52

# From Russia, with love (late 1980s–1990s)

When visiting Ram's home in Moscow in 1987, Pankajam met and befriended Alexander Dubiansky who had made her son's acquaintance when booking his air tickets to India. A professor of tamil studies at the Moscow State University and a reputed scholar of Tamil language and literature, Dubiansky's scholarship lay in the field of Sangam literature—the earliest corpus of Tamil writings, compiled between the first and third centuries CE. Dubiansky's work may be located in a post-Independence history of cross-cultural exchanges between India and the Soviet Union, which had promoted the study of Indian languages. After the fall of the Soviet Union and the waning of state patronage in Russia, individual scholars such as Dubiansky had taken upon themselves the mantle of preserving and reviving ties forged between two nations and their literary cultures.

When Dubiansky met Pankajam, he must have recognised that her familiarity with Tamil Saiva Bhakti poetry as well as the works of Tolstoy, Pushkin and Chekhov made her a rare conversationalist. She, in turn, must have been charmed by the impeccable classical Tamil that Dubiansky spoke, as were most Tamil speakers who met him. She re-christened him 'Alex Chandran', a Tamil–Russian friend who became as dear to her as her son Ramachandran. He kept up a lively letter correspondence with Pankajam and stayed with her on his visits to Madras. When I first met Dubiansky, I was a teenager devoted to L.M. Montgomery's cult classic *Anne of Green Gables*. Like Anne, I sought 'kindred spirits' with whom to share my love of everything that made life worth living. I was not sure I had found any. But, from their animated conversations—often poring over books together—I sensed that my grandmother and Dubiansky, although thirty years apart in age, were kindred spirits.

On 19 November 2020, the Indian Embassy in Russia announced that Dubiansky had passed away from Covid. News of his demise led to an outpouring of tweets and social media posts from writers, scholars and prominent leaders across the political spectrum, including the chief minister of Tamil Nadu and the leader of the opposition. Many rued the loss of 'the adopted son of Mother Tamil' whose passion for the Dravidian language had 'linked the Volga and the Vaigai Rivers' (*The New Indian Express*, 2020). Beset with a sense of great loss on hearing of Dubiansky's death, I immediately looked for and found six of his letters from 1988 to 1994—sent from Moscow, written in Tamil and signed as 'Alex Chandran'. With disarming candour, Dubiansky's letters reveal his deep affection and regard for Pankajam. They give us a sense of his joy and fulfilment in his chosen vocation, his eager anticipation of the new projects he planned to take on and the setbacks and frustrations that complicated his work.

In a letter dated 1 January 1988, Dubiansky graciously thanks Pankajam for the 'lovely books' she has sent him. While he has the entire collection of the Sangam literature, the separately-published books she has sent him are nevertheless convenient and valuable. He writes,[40] 'Such an old and beautiful publication is not to be found anywhere in the Soviet Union ... I want to translate

---

40   All extracts from the letters have been translated from the original Tamil.

*Nalavenba*[41] into Russian. But I know this is a hard future task that I have set myself. I want to make the Kamba Ramayanam[42] popular in Russia. It is not well known in my country. Am I ready to shoulder such a heavy burden, I wonder … Thank you for offering to send me more books.' On 6 April 1992, he writes that persistent headaches in the past months have left him exhausted in the evenings, unable to do any work and therefore low in spirits. 'Your two letters gave me much joy,' he writes.

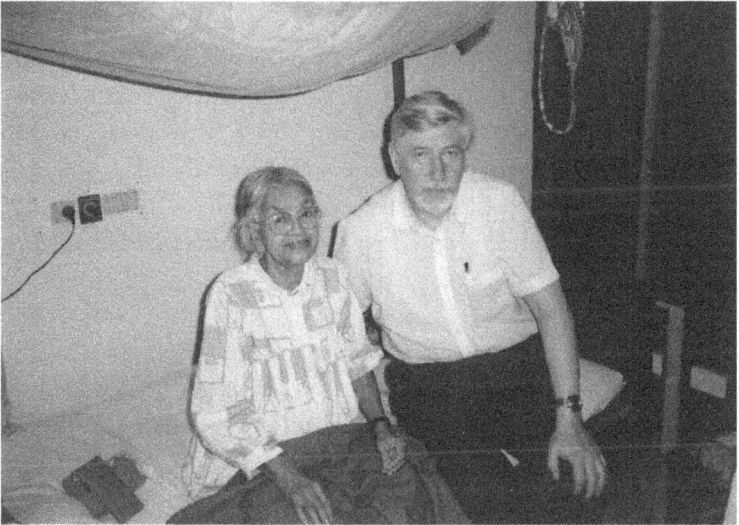

*With Alexander Dubiansky, 1995/96*

In October 1995, Dubiansky describes with excitement the rich intellectual exchange he enjoyed with fellow scholars at a conference in Sweden on the celebrated Tamil epic *Manimekalai* and its association with Buddhism. He writes, 'When leaving

---

41  The story of King Nala and Princess Damayanti from the Mahabharata, the Nalavenba in Tamil was composed by the poet Puhalendi possibly sometime in the thirteenth century CE.

42  Based on Valmiki's Ramayana, the Tamil epic Kamba Ramayanam was composed by the Tamil poet Kambar during the twelfth century CE.

Madras airport after my last visit, I saw the city through the plane window. Wonder of wonders! We were flying over the Chetpet area and I looked carefully and clearly saw your house. In my heart, I sent you affectionate greetings.' He writes of meeting Pankajam's granddaughter (Sundaram's daughter) who was then studying Russian literature in Moscow. 'When Chantal came here, we spoke of you extensively … We got along very well, I felt. I was sad when it was time for her to leave. More than anything else, there was a reason for my sadness. I saw you in her eyes and her face in a way.'

In the early 1990s, Dubiansky's letters reflect the sombre mood of the chaos, the civil strife and the bloody conflicts that followed the dissolution of the Soviet Union. How does one find meaning and pleasure in daily life and work when the world is falling apart, he wonders. In his letter of 15 June 1993, he notes with regret that a letter and card sent by Pankajam had failed to reach him.

> All government institutions in our country are in disarray. There is no stability in social life … We hear of bloodshed in the country's borders every day. Prices soar like missiles. One cannot remain unheeding of these troubles. But one must not focus all attention on them. It is possible to find satisfaction in the life of the spirit. Besides, there is family. There are friends. There is the work I like to do … In this ever-changing world, I believe we must look for permanent things … I think of you often, of our friendship based on true and permanent things. You must know that I value this friendship always. I read your essays and poems often. The ones I like best are your essays rich with philosophical insight.

A Soviet and Indian citizen whose lives intersected serendipitously in the twilight years of the era of Indo–Soviet friendship, Dubiansky and Pankajam opened their hearts and minds to each other and conversed about the world with a sense of wonderment.

Enchanted by the beauty of the world, they sought to know it with humility. All that was different or unfamiliar did not scare them or make them feel vulnerable or seek an armour. They listened to stories and perspectives with empathy and without prejudice, always aware of how much there was to know and of the privilege of bearing witness to other lives and histories. A few days after Dubiansky's death, I spoke to his daughter Tatiana. She told me that her father had been working hard until Covid struck. He had nearly completed translating the classical Tamil poetic work *Natrinai* and was full of plans for the future. She offered to look among his papers for my grandmother's letters to him. Dubiansky, she assured me, never threw anything away. I await those letters. If they are found, they will be sent to me. From Russia, with love.

# 53

## The world that was her head

As Pankajam aged and her children grew older and left home, she had more time for reading and writing. In February 1980, Sivaraman, who had just taken a midday walk in the garden, died within minutes of a sudden cardiac arrest. In a letter written a few months later, Pankajam's decades-old friend Paxye Thornhill commented on the unmissable implications of her widowhood. 'My dear little Indian mother, … Sivaraman can renew his journey through time and once more grow and evolve. Trapped in an old body and with entrenched ideas due to a restricted environment, people become embedded in a rut and it is beyond their means to get out and evolve. You Pankajam have also got a chance to escape your particular rut. Now you are free to do what you really want with life. How marvelous! Don't let your family be your all …' In the years that followed, Pankajam did have more leisure and freedom to pursue her literary and scholarly interests, especially after she moved in with Mythily's family and no longer had a household to manage.

*Pankajam in the garden at Kodaikanal*

Rummaging through her material when working on this book, I found that my grandmother had filled up several notebooks with her longhand notes that she had painstakingly copied from multiple sources. These notes were undated. They were written in the long-ruled essay notebooks of her children and grandchildren. A child's schoolbook label on the cover page was the only clue as to whether she had worked on something in the 1960s, 1970s or the 1980s. In the short autobiography that Pankajam wrote after she had had a stroke, she recalled the *Book of Knowledge* that her father had gifted her when she was sixteen years old and what they had done for her. 'My head became a world from which I know everything,' she wrote in 1995. Determined to learn more of this world, I ploughed through her notebooks filled with passages and quotations from scholars and thinkers whose work spanned science, religion, philosophy, metaphysics, natural theology, literature and psychology.

*Pankajam holding Cosmos, Carl Sagan (mid-1980s)*

Reading Pankajam's notes, I was conscious that I was straying into domains that I had no familiarity with and would never have dared to pronounce an opinion on. But she had dared and I had to follow where she led. In this venture, I was ably assisted by the masterful summaries she had made of her readings, capturing the crux of an author's argument and identifying differences of thought or emphasis from other scholars' positions. It was as if a well-trained PhD scholar were making the notes that would help her formulate her own arguments. Her notes included (among numerous others) extracts from the German physicist Werner Heisenberg's uncertainty principle; Surendranath Banerjee on the *History of Indian Philosophy*; Sigmund Freud on dreams, neurosis, paranoia and trauma; Carl Jung on the *Transformation of Libido*; Julian Huxley on *'Religion without Revelation'* or how religion without the notion of a supernatural being could be made compatible with modern science; Gerald Heard on the significance of the biological sciences for developing a natural theology; a dialogue between the historian Arnold Toynbee and the Buddhist thinker Daisaku Ikeda on the enduring questions that confronted humanity and Pankajam's thoughts on how Herman Hesse's novel *Steppenwolf* compared with his celebrated and better-known work *Sidhartha*.

*Pankajam, early 1990s*

Wide-ranging as her readings were, I realised that she had paid close attention to specific themes. If the Advaita philosophy of non-dualism rejected the dualistic view of a realistic world, real souls and a real god creator, how then did the 'world appearance' manifest itself? Through her notes, Pankajam had traced debates on the idea of the 'world appearance' (the semblance of an outer world of objects that exists apart from an inner world of thoughts, ideas, emotions) in Buddhist philosophy as well. Pankajam's history notebooks were a different universe of scholarship. They contained extensive longhand notes tracing the beginnings of Egyptian history, the ancient Mesopotamian civilisations, Greco–Roman Culture, ancient China, Arabic civilizations, early Indian history, ancient Mexican culture and history, the Byzantine empire and a calendar of events in Iraq from 6000 BC to current times. It appeared that she had updated her notes over the years. An entry in her daily diary (of 22 April 1989) read:

Copying historical notes about Zarathustra and the Indo-Aryans and Indo-Iranians comparison. In the history note book.

In 1989, Pankajam had suffered recurring bouts of fever and diarrhoea, later diagnosed as typhoid. She had put the enforced bed rest to good use and read feverishly, as her diary suggests.

January 12, 1989: In bed and reading National Geographic (NG) about 'the peopling of the earth'. Also about the Afrikaner, blacks, whites and the coloured people.

Jan 14: Read *Peony* by Pearl Buck from which I learnt about the Jews who settled in China and how they got integrated. Interesting.

Jan 21: Reading NG about Spain and the Moors.

Jan 25: Finished reading about the Moors. It is wonderful. Still the Europeans do not respect the Muslims or their art which is unique and greater than the westerners' art, past, present or future.

Jan 28: Finished reading all about Australia and the aboriginal people. Their history, myth, beliefs. They appear to have been living with nature, identifying themselves with animals, birds, reptiles, rocks, rivers, mountains. A

very correct way of thinking—true philosophy and religion
...

Pankajam's folders containing clippings from newspapers and journal articles were grouped and categorised as 'Science' and 'General Topics'. It is hardly surprising that she should have devoted a separate folder to science. In 1928, sixteen-year-old Pankajam, living in the coastal town of Marakkanam with her parents, had informed her father that she wanted to know physics and chemistry, unlike her mother Subbalakshmi, whose wide readings did not include the sciences. Pankajam's science folder shows us that she had closely followed new theories, findings and speculations on the fundamental constituents of matter and energy, the nature of quarks or elementary particles, scholarly reflections on Einstein's contribution and body of work, and scientific deliberations on where to draw the dividing line between inanimate matter and living beings. Her special interest in astronomy was reflected in her extensive reading on binary stars, the birth of black holes, the collision of galaxies, the death of

*Her collections*

stars and phenomena such as cosmic rays and showers. Questions relating to the emergence of life on earth, the origins of *Homo sapiens*, new theories of evolution and the birth of mountain ranges such as the Himalayas had evidently fascinated her.

Drawing from her extensive readings, Pankajam wrote essays in which she attempted to bring together her readings, juxtapose diverse perspectives and worldviews and seek a coherence of meaning and underlying thought patterns that she delighted in tracing. Her introduction to an essay (titled 'Science and Religion') shows us how she aspired to grasp complex ideas, simultaneously conscious of and yet undaunted by her lack of formal training.

Whenever I read science or philosophy, the connection and oneness between them always strikes me. I shall give a few simple examples of the truths I have gathered from the great 'savants' of these subjects ... Of course, everyone is entitled to their opinions and I would be glad to hear any discussion on this subject. But I have no contact with the great ones, the scene of my life having unfolded in an orthodox Brahmin family which believes in trampling upon a woman's independence of spirit and which thinks a woman's existence is only to feed the main appetites of the master of the house. This exists even in the twentieth century!

... I have never been inside the portals of a college and not seen a lab and I must be disqualified to even utter the name of science. But the daring spirit in me says I should write about what I have gleaned from books ... that the eminent scientists in their great mercy and upsurge of desire have put forth theories and deduction in simple language understandable to the layman. It is thus that I have gathered these great fruits of knowledge ...

Why did Pankajam write these essays and fill up notebooks with extended extracts from various texts? As I see it, the essays she wrote and the notes she made were an important part of her lifelong striving to know the world better and broaden the horizons of her mind. If her formal education had not even culminated in a school degree and had been left incomplete, how could her informal education ever end either? If she had been fortunate enough to learn and understand 'profound truths' about the universe from scientists who had mercifully shared their insights with a wider public, she too must share her knowledge with others. In her case, it was her family who were to be her only audience. In a book in which she had laboriously copied passages and poetry from 'the great souls of the world' that included Romain Rolland, Rabindranath Tagore, J. Krishnamurthi, Sri Aurobindo, Alexander Pushkin, Afanasy Fet, Sarojini Naidu, T.S. Eliot, W.H. Auden and Walt Whitman, Pankajam wrote on the first page, 'These are my treasures that I bequeath to my children and grandchildren.' In every book that she ever owned, Pankajam would write the name of the grandchild, who she believed would appreciate it and to whom it must pass after her death.

# 54

# The tyranny of love

Reading Pankajam's notes and essays, I was reminded of the question that the feminist historian Gerda Lerner (1986) eloquently poses in *The Creation of Patriarchy* regarding the historically conflicted relationship that women have had with intellectual labour. What does it take for women (or men) to generate abstract thought and new conceptual models? How might one contribute to theory formation by making a creative leap into a new ordering? Lerner writes that this activity depends on the individual thinker's education in the best existing traditions and her acceptance by a group of educated persons who, by criticism and interaction, provide 'cultural prodding'. It is this 'cultural prodding' that Pankajam alludes to in a fashion, when she writes (in the introduction to her essay) of having no contact with the 'great ones'.

Lerner writes of how, historically, educated women have had to choose between living a woman's life with its joys, dailiness, immediacy and its immersion in the 'irredeemably particular', and living a man's life in order to think in abstractions, make symbols, advance conceptual models and explain the world. Can one generalise while the particular tugs at one's sleeve, asks Lerner? A wife, caregiver and mother of five children, Pankajam knew intimately well the 'joys, dailiness and immediacy' of a woman's life and all that it entailed including the constantly fragmented attention and the daily submergence in the 'service function' expected of a woman. And yet, she was not to be dissuaded from attempting abstract thought or longing to converse with the 'savants' of science and philosophy.

In her book, Lerner probes with acuity the unacknowledged restraints that are buried deep in women's psyche and continue to hold back thinking women. She argues that the loss of communication with or the withdrawal of love and approval by the men in their lives was historically the means of discouraging women's exercise of their mind and intellect. Pankajam herself had little to lose in this respect. Having severed all emotional ties with her husband early in her marriage, she cared not for his approval and could not be tyrannised by any effort on his part to starve her of affection. Had the emotional life of the marriage lasted, he may have disapproved of her reading, writing and inhabiting a 'kingdom of the mind' in ways that might have wounded her, eventually inhibiting her intellectual growth. The absence of conjugal love and a companionate marriage had likely intensified Pankajam's quest for self-actualisation through books and reading. She could expand the vistas of her mind without fear or shame as she did not have to be a subordinate companion-wife, but was free to mould herself as a tutor-mother who must grow so that her children could follow her lead.

On this question, I must allow Pankajam to have the last word. Her diary entry for 9 August 1992, when she was eighty-two years old, records the visit of Sivaraman's niece who had reminisced about the early years of Pankajam's marriage.

R called on us. She was telling Lalitha how dedicated I was towards my children. How they were all the world to me. She has understood my past days and has watched me. She thinks her uncle [Sivaraman] was suffering from an inferiority complex and hence he disliked me. I do not know. All I know is that God had thought it fit to put me in that place where, after floundering, I began to clamber up and managed to live for the children, while thinking of science, books, spiritual yearning, music, painting and bird-watching.

# 55

## Look for me in a tiny bird

When leafing through Pankajam's diaries of the early 1990s, I realised that she had been reading many of my books during this period—Mrinal Pande (*Daughter's Daughter*), Shashi Deshpande's stories, Arlene K. Zide's anthology of contemporary Indian women poets, Githa Hariharan's *The Thousand Faces of Night*. I was then a college student with a grandmother who would ask if any among the friends who came home to visit was a boyfriend and if so, I must tell her which one, what sort of chap he was and what it was like to have a boyfriend! We would giggle together over my imitation of the awkward, stilted Tamil voiceover of the popular Doordarshan series *Junoon* that was aired in 1993 and that she had taken to watching, as many Tamil households did. On 31 July 1994, I left home to begin a master's degree in Jawaharlal Nehru University. Pankajam's diary entry of the day reads thus,

> A very important day in my life and that of Kalpana's. She left with her father to Delhi. My life is changing. I must learn the lesson not to get myself attached to any person. Learn to feel happy and secure in His and His love alone.

A week later, I received the news that she had had a stroke and was hospitalised. After the stroke, Pankajam practised memory and writing exercises for a year or so. The short autobiography that she wrote during this period was part of her effort to retrieve her cognitive skills. Despite her impressive efforts in the immediate aftermath of the stroke, we witnessed the slow decline of her capacities over the next thirteen years. In the last years, the only books under her pillow were the much-thumbed and tattered copies of *Jane Eyre* and *Pride and Prejudice* that had to be periodically replaced. It was not clear if she was reading them, but they seemed to be a talisman, an amulet that signalled a time past and offered a protection of sorts. But she had not lost her capacity for humour. For several years when she was bedridden, she continued to ask that I sing a particular *gaana* (song) that I had introduced her to. In the song, an older woman serenades a young man—a prospective son-in-law and asks if she should serve him whisky or brandy; he replies that the local arrack (*sarayam)* is quite enough. She asks if she should cook him chicken curry or mutton curry and he replies that plain rice will do just fine. Will he have her older daughter or the younger one, she asks? Why, you are more than enough for me, he declares! Pankajam loved this song and would burst into raucous laughter each time I sang the last line.

Inspired by Walt Whitman's *Song of Myself* (Part 52) in *Leaves of Grass*, Pankajam wrote an epitaph in which she told us where to find her, should we think to look for her.

*My epitaph (November 1991)*

I bequeath my flesh to the fire
I bequeath my bones to the dust and earth
I bequeath my spirit to the eternal spirit
If you want me, look for me in a tiny bird
If you want me, look for me in the splendour of sunsets
Look for me in the distant stars
That stand sentinel and witness to passing time

And wink at human frivolities
If you want me, look for me
In the love I left behind.

Looking for Pankajam in the love she left behind gives us reason to reflect on the conundrum that Pankajam's life poses for us. In the foreword to her autobiography, she writes, 'Heroes of mighty deeds and sacrifices are known and honoured, while humble souls struggle in obscure silence and make sacrifices as great as those of the known heroes.' How may we read and situate the life story of a nameless, faceless, inconsequential woman such as her, who, when she was writing her foreword in 1949, knew that she was raising a family and building a home for a new nation and that her labour and efforts, dedicated, thoughtful and loving must count for something too, in some manner of reckoning?

# 56

## Life is everything

In her book *Fragments of a Life*, Mythily Sivaraman raises the question of what the structures of family and caste, in their entanglement with the colonial state, allow a woman like Subbalakshmi to be and to do. Subbalakshmi's life points to how women—in late colonial India—were resolutely not allowed to inhabit the public sphere, or indeed the world of ideas, and were asked to remain content with being partially modern, to the extent of being companionable helpmeets to their spouses. Pankajam's life shows us how these limits notwithstanding, a vivacity of spirit and a curious mind can create a world in which a woman might be able to experience a measure of happiness and self-worth, even if her life was lived out largely within the web of family and kin. But no one was more conscious of this than Pankajam herself. If she was quick to seize the joyous possibilities of the present moment, she also knew that social structural forces had circumscribed her life and her choices. As they had with her mother Subbalakshmi.

Pankajam knew that her mother's many illnesses stemmed from the stultifying life that she had been forced to lead. In a biographical essay on her mother that she wrote in 1989, she describes Subbalakshmi's frustrations and thwarted desires that had made her 'turn against life'. Describing her mother's death, Pankajam writes, 'a great proud, independent, idealistic, uncompromising spirit left the fetters of the body.' Vividly seeing the links between her mother's ailments and the shackles that were placed on her, it was only natural that Pankajam should have looked within and tried to understand how she had dealt with her own heartbreaks and the denial of opportunities that she too had experienced. In her characteristic forthright fashion, Pankajam asked herself this question and reviewed her life through retrospective essays that she occasionally wrote on her birthdays as she grew older. In an essay titled 'Thanksgiving and Retrospect Thinking' that she wrote in 1990, she grapples with the question of how to read her life, the way she had lived it and the choices she had made. She begins the essay by situating herself as a witness both to momentous historical change and the unfolding of her own life.

At seventy-nine, standing perhaps at the last milestone of my life journey, and the threshold of the new one, I turn back to review my life. The rumour is in the air, the transfer. It is imminent. However, before I assume my new journey and take up my new assignment, I would like to look back ... Through these long years of my life, the changes I have seen are astounding, if one could only afford time and inclination to think about them. I have lived through a world war and a non-violent revolution by the people of India for independence ... But I shall confine myself to the changes that affected my life—my inner life ...

God or Nature has endowed me with two qualities for which I cannot be grateful enough.

One is that I can easily give up things I cannot get and the other one is that I came to like whatever I was asked to do in life. Even when I did not choose to do some hard job and when circumstances made me do it, I began to like it when I started on it. Cooking, child-rearing, nursing, housekeeping, etc., became interesting and I developed a flair for them when they came my way … If one door was shut, I looked to other channels as an outlet for my feelings. I began to explore other avenues that needed not the world's or society's permission. In the narrow confines of my house and circumstances, I invented or wrested out of dame nature pleasures galore …

Only these qualities and a singular lack of ambition helped me lead a peaceful, uneventful and ordinary housewife's life. I never rebelled against my situation or position … (any person of my intellect and my talents would have rebelled). I did not struggle against my elders or teachers or people who came into my life later, my husband, chiefly, for I am blessed with a temperament that likes everything and accepts everything …

I often used to wonder if my life is a total failure. Immediately comes the thought that it is not entirely a failure … It may not have the glamour or fame of a worldly, successful life. And yet, in certain other respects, it may be called a successful one, I think. That is, it may be a success in the sense that I have passed through all the tests that fate had set me and deserve a promotion. May it be so.

Reading Pankajam's comments on her mother and her retrospective essay together, we see the lessons that a daughter may imbibe from a mother's life. An 'idealistic' and 'uncompromising' woman, as her daughter described her, Subbalakshmi had suffered from her idealism and her uncompromising ways alike. While Pankajam admired her mother greatly, she had witnessed from close quarters her illnesses and the bitter unhappiness and depression her mother had endured. Pankajam had also suffered from her mother's detachment from family life and social relationships. On the other hand, Pankajam's natural resilience and buoyant good cheer had made a world of difference to her five children, blessed with a 'mother, tutor, teacher, playmate and friend' who embraced with zeal the challenges that life threw her way.

While Pankajam often describes herself as an 'ordinary woman' in her autobiographical writing, she nevertheless knew herself to be a woman of formidable capacities who was placed by the weight of history and society in an 'uneventful, ordinary housewife's life'. And yet, if she had not rebelled against her domestic situation, it was not because she did not think that she was cut out for more, as she writes with resounding clarity. At the same time, she did not fetishise the pathways to happiness that she had chosen, nor did she advocate them as a way of life for others. Indeed, there was little that Pankajam would prescribe for anyone, no matter how close they were to her. In a note titled 'My Last Instructions', she strictly forbids her family to perform any funeral rites or annual death day ceremony for her after her time. Since no one understands the Sanskrit chants anymore ('not even the priests who recite them'), why perform an exercise without meaning, she asks. In this note, she extends her point further to assert that she does not offer lessons for others to emulate, nor does she seek to make a virtue out of the way she lived her life.

> I may believe in many things that others close to me may not. I have no right to force or expect anything from anyone … This world is too wide and its people have diverse beliefs and understand things differently. So, no one can prescribe one way for all to follow … There is no absolute sense or nonsense in any act except what one attaches to it. If I set a *Golu*,[43] arrange flowers in a vase, decorate my room, paint or write, it is neither a virtue nor a sin. We do it because we like it or because our temperament is like that, artistic. An act derives its meaning from the intellectual, aesthetic, emotional or spiritual interpretation of each individual who acts …

---

43 A display of figurines and dolls on a festive occasion such as the Navaratri festival.

Through the many everyday acts that infused her life with meaning and purpose, Pankajam explored to the fullest the potential for transcendence of her circumstances. She constructed her 'kingdom of the mind' through books and reading, an unceasing project of self-education, a love of nature and the natural world, a boundless curiosity to learn all that was worth knowing about the universe and intense friendships across countries and cultures that allowed her to see the world from others' eyes. She did, however, long for engagement with a wider universe and more expansive social responsibilities through the pathways that she was most familiar with—teaching young minds, raising children and caring for people. In her Thanksgiving essay (1990), Pankajam pondered the question of what she may have been and the lives she may have led, had her circumstances been otherwise.

Five children, their children, cows in the shed, nursing and looking after my old and ailing parents, kept my nose tied to everyday mundane things. If I had not had these obstacles, perhaps I would have aspired to achieve and accomplish certain things dear to my heart … Perhaps given a chance, I would have done the same things that I did for my children, to other children of the world. Run a school and an institution completely dedicating myself to their needs and aiding them to understand and appreciate nature and develop a love of humanity. I have been trying to instil in my children and their children a sense of wonder and teach them to appreciate everything and take an interest in everything—for life is everything.

# Bibliography

Allen, Matthew Harp. 'Rewriting the Script for South Indian Dance'. *The Drama Review 41*, 3 (T155), Fall, 1997.

Chakravarti, Uma. *Rewriting History: The Life and Times of Pandita Ramabai.* Kali for Women, 1998.

Das, Santanu. *India, Empire and First World War Culture: Writings, Images and Songs.* Cambridge University Press, 2018.

Fuller, C.J., and H. Narasimhan. *Tamil Brahmans: The Making of a Middle-Class Caste.* The University of Chicago Press, 2014.

Geetha, V., and S.V. Rajadurai. *Towards a Non-Brahmin Millenium: From Iyothee Thass to Periyar.* Samya. 1998.

Karlekar, Malavika. 'Kadambini and the Bhadralok: Early Debates over Women's Education in Bengal'. *Economic and Political Weekly*, Vol. 21, No. 17, 1986.

Lerner, Gerda. *The Creation of Patriarchy.* Oxford University Press, 1986.

Mills, C. Wright. *The Sociological Imagination.* 1959.

O'Shea, Janet. *At Home in the World: Bharata Natyam on the Global Stage.* Wesleyan University Press. 2007.

Pillai, Nrithya. 'Cycles of cultural violence within performance and scholarship of Bharatanatyam'. *The News Minute*, June 2022, https://www.thenewsminute.com/voices/cycles-cultural-violence-within-performance-and-scholarship-bharatanatyam-165159.

Raman, Sita Anantha. *Getting Girls to School: Social Reform in the Tamil Districts (1870–1930)*. Stree, 1996.

Rioux, Anne Boyd. *Meg, Jo, Beth, Amy: The Story of Little Women and Why It Still Matters*. Norton & Co, 2018.

Russ, Joanna. *How to Suppress Women's Writing*. University of Texas Press, 1983

Sinha, Mrinalini. *Specters of Mother India: The Global Restructuring of an Empire*. Duke University Press. 2006.

Sreenivas, Mytheli. *Wives, Widows and Concubines: The Conjugal Family Ideal in Colonial India*. Indiana University Press. 2008.

Woolf, Virginia. *A Room of One's Own*.

## Additional References

Agnihotri, Indu. "'Women's oppression is integrally linked to capitalism': Mythily Sivaraman", *Frontline*, 16 July 2021, https://frontline.thehindu.com/the-nation/mythily-sivaraman-interview-women-rights-left-movement-india/article34996314.ece.

Ali, Subhashini. 'Mythily Sivaraman, An Untiring Worker for the Cause of Marginalized Communities'. *The Wire*, 3 June 2021, https://thewire.in/rights/mythili-sivaraman-obituary.

Geetha, V. 'Obituary: Mythily Sivaraman (1939–2021)'. Indian Journal of Gender Studies, December 2021, https://journals.sagepub.com/doi/full/10.1177/09715215211056993.

Kalpana, K. 'My Mother, Comrade Mythily'. *Newsclick*, 2 June 2021, https://www.newsclick.in/my-mother-comrade-mythily.

Menon, Parvathi. 'Mythily Sivaraman 1939–2021: Life and Legacy'. Review of Agrarian Studies, Vol. 11, No. 2, July–December 2021, http://ras.org.in/f1b499e8db3046ebec712209e22f830d.

'Russian scholar Alexander Dubiansky, who taught Tamil for nearly 50 years, passes away'. *The New Indian Express*, November 2020, https://www.newindianexpress.com/states/tamil-nadu/2020/nov/19/russian-scholar-alexander-dubiansky-who-taught-tamil-for-nearly-50-years-passes-away-2225421.html.